THANK YOU for buying this book! My name is Chris Green and this is the first book that I wrote about selling products online and sourcing them at retail stores.

I first published this book in September 2011. The story behind this book was that I wanted to write a long PDF about Amazon and FBA that answered all of the most common questions that were being asked. After I started writing, it ended up being a lot like a book so I looked into self-publishing options. It ended up being really easy and this book was released. I later stopped printing the book because I felt that the book was too long and basically covered two topics. The fist being the business model of arbitrage (along with Amazon and Fulfillment By Amazon (FBA)) and the second being process of sourcing products at retail stores. Not everyone who wanted to learn about arbitrage, Amazon, and FBA also wanted to learn more about sourcing products at retail stores. For them, the book was unnecessarily long and that also added to the production cost of the book.

So I rewrote the book, took out the retail sourcing stuff, and just called it Arbitrage. It was published in September of 2013. It was shorter and priced at just $9.95.

It's on Amazon here:

http://www.amazon.com/dp/1478251891

You can read the reviews here:

http://www.amazon.com/dp/1478251891/reviews#customerReviews

It's an updated version of this original book. It's only $9.95 and you get the Kindle copy for free with paperback purchase. Kindle copy is only $2.99 by itself, or you can read the Kindle copy for free if you are an Amazon Prime member.

After I pulled the original Retail Arbitrage, existing copies kept being sold on Amazon on the third-party marketplace. Price routinely went over $100 even though I updated the Amazon product page to tell people about the new version for only $9.95. I tracked the sales and was surprised that it kept selling for over $100 several times a week. I'm flattered, but this book is not currently worth over $100. For that reason, I am re-releasing it as kind of a throwback edition of my original book.

Since writing this book and Arbitrage, I've also written a new book called Online Arbitrage. It's more of a course in sourcing product online to resell for a profit. It's about $200 on Amazon and consists of 480 full-color pages, 40 private YouTube videos showing actual Online Arbitrage deals, lifetime product updates, and even a 30-minute coaching call with me!

You can find it on Amazon here:

http://www.amazon.com/dp/1500333824

And read the reviews here:

http://www.amazon.com/dp/1500333824/reviews#customerReviews

I'll soon be writing a completely new and updated version of Retail Arbitrage in the same format as Online Arbitrage. It will be a full course, similar to Online Arbitrage, with examples, private videos, and coaching. Look for soon with updates posted on www.retailarbitrage.com

Want to connect? Find me online at Facebook.com/Chris or email me at chris@scanpower.com

If you're on Facebook, please join our group at www.facebook.com/groups/scanpower

My trilogy of books about Amazon, FBA, and sourcing products consists of Arbitrage, Online Arbitrage, and Retail Arbitrage (coming soon).

You can find them on Amazon:

Arbitrage:

http://www.amazon.com/dp/1478251891

This book retails for $9.95 and explains the arbitrage business model, selling on Amazon, and the Fulfillment By Amazon (FBA) program.

Online Arbitrage:

http://www.amazon.com/dp/1500333824

This is an all-inclusive course in sourcing products online that can be resold for a profit. 480 color page textbook, private videos, and private coaching.

And coming soon, the NEW Retail Arbitrage!

A completely updated re-write of this book in the same format as Online Arbitrage with updated examples, private videos, and much more.

For updates, please visit

www.retailarbitrage.com

This is an outdated book! Some links are no longer active and some Amazon fees, rules, and policies have changed.

Please check current websites for up-to-date information referenced in this book!

THROWBACK EDITION

NOTE: FBAPower and FBAScout are now ScanPower.

For all current content, please visit ScanPower.com

# RetailArbitrage

The Authoritative BLUEPRINT for Buying Retail Products to Sell Online for BIG PROFITS.

HOW it works, WHY it works, and how you can get in on it.

(Don't worry; we'll cover books & media, too ☺)

Chris Green

PBLLC Press, Rehoboth, MA

2011

Retail Arbitrage:

The Authoritative BLUEPRINT for Buying Retail Products to Sell Online for BIG PROFITS

Green, Christopher John

Hi, Mom!

Throwback Edition published January 2015

Edited by Chiara Therisod & Tom Sutton

Published by PBLLC Press, Rehoboth, MA 02769

First Printing, September 2011

ISBN-13: 978-1466303546

ISBN-10: 1466303549

Printed in the United States of America

Dedicated to my loving wife, Jenn.

Without her love and support, none of this would be possible.

This book is the result of a lifetime of learning. I am very thankful for support that I've received from family and friends along the way. The last five years have been one amazing ride. Not everyone gets to work with amazing people and amazing products everyday and it is even more rewarding when those products are able to produce a positive change in so many people's lives.

# When Chris Green talks, FBA sellers listen.

## Opportunity Summary

We live in an amazing time! Entrepreneurs now have access to powerful tools and information that were simply not possible just a few, short years ago. Barriers to entry have been shattered and small entrepreneurs can now compete with the big boys on the biggest stages practically from day one. Information has always been power, but never before in history has information been so powerful and at the same time nearly universally accessible. A smartphone in your pocket gives you access to Wikipedia, your Kindle library, a few thousand apps, and let's not forget this little thing called the Internet. The next wave of successful entrepreneurs will be the ones who use this information to their advantage. When you see the world this way, you see that there are so many opportunities all around you. Since time is limited, you can't do them all; so find your passion, find people who share your passion, and take action!

Setting up an Amazon business that utilizes the Fulfillment By Amazon (FBA) program is much like buying a franchise opportunity. With a franchise, you buy a package, get some knowledge and equipment to get started, and then it's up to you to run with it. One of the big differences is that buying and selling online using FBA really has no 'buy-in'. There are no major upfront costs to get started. All you really need is a little knowledge, some motivation, and some inexpensive tools and services. You probably already have a computer with an Internet connection at home in order to list products for sale and a smartphone like an iPhone or Android phone that you can use to gather pricing information on products. It is common to underestimate the real, legitimate income that can be generated by this business because it is a business that truly does not have a high cost of entry.

Retail Arbitrage is the first book of its kind to provide a complete and exhaustive look at the fascinating world of arbitrage and resale.

This book is intended to be much more than just descriptive information about topics related to Retail Arbitrage and selling online. This book explains the WHY behind everything that you'll be reading. Sure, I could stop by just explaining what FBA is, but the important part is understanding WHY FBA works. I could tell you how to price FBA items, but I want you to understand WHY you can price them that way. I could tell you that you can buy retail products from local retailers to sell online for big profits, but I want you to understand WHY you are able to find the same product at dramatically different prices from two separate places and WHY some buyers are willing to pay much more for that same product from a different sales channel.

It's the difference between giving you a fish, and teaching you to fish.

In this book, you learn about the primary market (retailers, both brick & mortar and online) and the secondary market (Amazon third-party sellers and eBay). You'll also learn to understand SUPPLY and DEMAND and how they affect PRICE, as well as how TIME affects all three.

In this book, I will give you the keys to the Retail Arbitrage kingdom with the mindset of unlimited opportunities and abundance rather than one of scarcity. The techniques described in this book can be used by anyone, anywhere to build a small side business or large empire. The only limit is your imagination.

Arbitrage is the practice of taking advantage of a price difference between two or more markets, striking a combination of matching deals that capitalize upon the imbalance. The difference between these two market prices is the profit realized by whoever brings the deal together.

Think of it this way; you want to be able to 'SEE' items that are selling locally for much less than what they are selling for online. These items represent the potential for arbitrage opportunities (and profit).

At the same time, you want to avoid items that cost more locally than what they sell for online.

When you have the right information, it's like you have special goggles that allow you to see all of the opportunities around you (while those without the information simply cannot).

Remember this: the markets are terribly inefficient and buyers do not make all buying decisions based solely on price. Identical items sell for different amounts in different places all day, every day. Sometimes items are less expensive at local retailers; sometimes they are less expensive online. When you can identify these differences, you can be the one who profits by matching the lower cost supply with the higher priced demand.

Things change over time. At the time of this writing, all links, fees, rules, and laws are represented accurately. It is always best to check the current web pages for any changes that may have occurred between the writing of this book and when you start your business. The fees to sell on Amazon.com and eBay.com can change and will affect prices and payouts. Laws may change regarding paying and collecting sales tax.

I suggest finding a good certified public accountant (CPA) that can help steer you in the right direction. Like any service, they should save you more money than they cost you. If they don't, fire them!

**Earnings Disclaimer**

I can't make any promises as to how much money you'll make in this business. It's up to you to go out and run with this information. I can't promise that you will make a certain amount of money, or any money, or not lose money, as a result of following the information in this book. What I can do is give you as much useful and accurate information that I can and trust you to learn it and use it to the best of your ability.

I'll show you deals that we have done and the profits that we made but there is no guarantee that you will be able to replicate them exactly. With any business, your results will vary and will be based on your personal abilities, knowledge, and level of desire (among other things). Each person's results will vary.

The use of the information provided in this book should be applied and used based on your own due diligence and you agree that we are not liable for your success or failure.

Basically, we can help, but it's up to you to actually run your business. ☺

The good news is that we are here and we are happy to help!

To your success,

*Chris Green*

-Chris Green

Director, ScanPower

For latest updates, new releases, and additional features, always check the websites:

http://Scanpower.com

http://retailarbitrage.com

## Table of Contents

## Introduction

So, who is this Chris Green guy and how does he know so much about Retail Arbitrage? How did FBAPower and FBAScout (now SCANPOWER) get started? I'm glad you asked! Here's the whole story.

When I was in the sixth grade, I had never heard of a thing called Retail Arbitrage. Like many kids my age, I was too busy collecting sports cards. Growing up in Canada, hockey cards were the most popular. I became fascinated that one card could be worth so much more than another. I didn't care who was on the card; I was more interested in the values and how they changed. I would read the price guides every month and track 'values' as they went up and down. I had a paper route that put about $25/week in my pocket and I would buy and sell sports cards at the local weekly card show. It got to the point where I would browse the card show and identify cards that one dealer was selling for a price that was too low, and flipping them to another dealer who was pricing them too high. I would find one dealer would place a value on a card that was too low, and I'd find another dealer who placed a higher value on that same card and I'd have a buyer lined up before I even paid for the card. Little did I realize where all this was heading.

Fast-forward a few years when my family moved to Texas at age 13. My aunt was a jewelry dealer who would have high-end jewelry shows in her home. One summer I was at a garage sale and found a pile of gold necklaces with a gold flower and pearl pendant on them. They appeared to be new and were all individually bagged. The seller had a price of $1.50 a piece on them. They weren't real gold or anything but they looked nice and I was hoping that my aunt could put them in her jewelry shows, even if just as an inexpensive option for her clients. I bought all twenty of them and brought them over to see what she thought. She said that I did well! She said she could easily sell these in her show. She bought them all from me for $10 each. Sweet! Easy money, right? Of course I was still young and naïve, and briefly felt bad, even cheated, when I found out that she sold them in her show for $25 each. For a moment I thought that I should be the one getting $25 but then I started to realize that she did work as well with organizing the show and that she took a risk as well buying them from me. I was acting as a middleman and so was she. Why did I sell for $10? Because I was happy with the price! Just because I found out later that she sold them for more should not change that fact.

This one was a two-step process to get the supply and demand to meet. There was a demand for this item at $25 that would have never found the products at $1.50, but between my aunt and myself, we were able to match supply with demand and both realize a profit along the way.

She also instilled in me the concept of 'value'. Just because someone says it is 'worth' something, doesn't mean that it will sell for that price. I would get caught up with this from the sports cards days where a price guide would say a card is 'worth' a certain value. She would tell me it's only worth something if someone is willing to pay it. On Amazon, this is known as the difference between what an item is 'listed for' and what it is 'selling for'.

Now let's fast forward to my college years. It's now 1996 and this fancy new thing called the Internet is quickly becoming popular. This was the dawn of a new day in terms of matching sellers with buyers. EBay was a magical site where anyone could sell anything to anyone in the world! You could also search for and find anything that you may have been looking for at garage sales for years. Being a child of the 80's, I was into Transformers. With the Internet, so much more information was now available. I learned that when the US television show stopped airing, it continued on in Japan. There was a whole new series of Transformers cartoons that had never been seen or even heard of by most US Transformers fans. This was too cool; I wanted these videos! I originally wanted them just for myself but it quickly became apparent that there were lots of people like me who would pay for these videos. Out of all of these potential buyers, some would pay a little, but some would pay a lot. Knowledge is power and I had the knowledge of where to get them so I bought and sold cartoon videos to pay my way through college. My roommates all thought it was pretty crazy, but it paid the bills. This market unfortunately dried up for two reasons. First, even though I was the first to enter this specific market, when there is money to be made, other sellers will eventually find it, enter the market, and prices will fall. They will fall until the equilibrium price is met. Second, the number of people who grew up in the 80's and still wanted to watch Transformers cartoons is fairly small and once the people in this market have purchased them, the market is pretty much dead. It is not an ongoing, sustainable market in the same sense like the Star Wars brand, which stands the test of time with old fans and new ones alike all across the world.

As fate would have it, I ended up getting a degree in Economics.

So, I finally graduated and found a job in sales with Bosch Power Tools calling on Home Depot and Lowe's (known as the home center channel). I did this for five years and it is what propelled me into a full time Retail Arbitrage business owner. You see, when you are in a Home Depot almost every day for five years, you notice things; things like product cycles where new models replace old models. The old models get clearanced out, sometimes at ridiculous prices. You see seasonal cycles as well as lucrative promotions such as Buy-One-Get-One-Free on top of an already-discounted clearance price.

Here was this enormous pool of inventory that could now be purchased for prices well below the market price. When you pair this with the Internet opportunities on eBay and Amazon, you've just struck a golden balance where you can be as big as you want to be with practically no risk. It means that you can buy your inventory on credit card and just wait for a buyer. And if you can't find a buyer, you can get a full refund!

Purchasing inventory at the retail level meant that you had none of the restrictions of buying from manufacturers. There were no minimum order quantities and no pricing agreements. You buy your inventory and you can do whatever you want with it.

All the pieces were in place to take this thing to the next level. There was demand out there that valued these items at prices higher than what I could get them for. But without the Internet and sites such as eBay and Amazon, that demand would not be able to find that supply. And if I didn't buy the supply and make it available to that demand, then this supply and demand would never meet. Without each piece, the sources, the prices, and the ability to get the supply to the demand through the Internet, this business wouldn't work.

On top of all these pieces falling into place, I was working in Dallas, Texas where there were over sixty Home Depots within a one-hour drive. Let's run some numbers (simplified example): a $300 item goes clearance for $100. I can sell for $200 and make $100 profit. Buyer is getting a $300 item for $200 and is happy with the deal. I find the twenty Home Depots that have the highest inventory levels and go out and pick up an average of ten units from twenty stores. In one day, I am able to get 200 units at $100 profit a piece. $20,000 profit on just one item, one day of the year. I think you can now see where this is going.

Retail Arbitrage on a grand level was starting to take place. I was still limited by my regular full-time job, even though it was great to keep me in the stores to spot the latest trends and price changes. It got to a point where I had to make a choice and the choice was to quit and go full time in Retail Arbitrage. Thankfully we had over 2,000 square feet of storage space to store products and pack and ship orders (this was still the pre-FBA days). It was getting big, it was generating great income, but I was running into the same limitations that plague all online sellers: Space and time restrictions. We can only store so many products in a limited amount of space and we can only manage so much of the business (including packing and shipping orders) with a limited amount of time in each day. My wife was helping a great deal at this time and the business was slowly taking over our lives. If we ever wanted to go out of town to visit family, the whole thing had to be shut down.

Enter Fulfillment By Amazon, or FBA. This is the piece of the puzzle that takes Retail Arbitrage to a whole new level. What FBA is and why it works so well will be explained in greater detail in Chapters 3 & 4, but the basics of FBA are that Amazon will store, sell, pick, pack, and ship your items for you. FBA does all this at a price that allows you to maintain profitable margins. Even the storage fees are so low that it doesn't make sense to store your own products. With one new service, we could now remove both the space and time restrictions that were limiting the growth of our online business.

The additional piece that makes FBA work is understanding the FBA buyer. When a seller uses FBA, all of their items are eligible for the same free shipping programs as Amazon's own inventory such as Free Super Saver Shipping and Amazon Prime. The reason that we were so quick to adopt the FBA program is that we BOUGHT so much from Amazon. We were pretty much Amazon power-buyers and had been Amazon Prime members since the day Prime was announced. We valued the fast shipping and customer service that you get with every Amazon order. We knew that there were tons of other buyers out there just like us who would choose our products over our competitor's products, even at a higher price because they were FBA items (much more on this later in the book).

So we sent everything to FBA warehouses and we are still 100% FBA today. Processing orders and packing boxes is not hard, but we would rather spend our time on the most profitable parts of our business and sourcing new products.

This is when we first got into books and media items. I was browsing online one day and came across the barcode scanners that people were using to tell them the online value of books. This was fascinating. You could scan a barcode and see what the market price was for a book. Compare it to your cost, calculate profit, and make buying decisions. Too cool; I was hooked and I was in. I was buying books and listing them as fast I could. It was great that I had a new product line, but now I was back to shipping my own orders again. At first, I thought that there was no way that FBA could be used on books. After all, books were used, onesie-twosie type items and not new, multiple quantity, commodity-type items like the power tools we were used to sending in. When Amazon said that the FBA program could be applied to used books, a whole new world opened up before me. Right away, all books and media were labeled and sent to FBA.

Now we had a new problem. Time and space restrictions were gone, but now the business had a new bottleneck – speed. We could get products to sell online; that was not hard. And we could sell them with FBA, which was also not hard. The new bottleneck was getting the items prepared for FBA. We couldn't get the items listed fast enough, priced properly (FBA items are priced much differently, more on this later), and labeled in an efficient manner. We were touching every item multiple times so the workflow was not optimal. The final straw was when my wife and I had over 400 books and media items facing spine up on the kitchen table. We each had sheets of FBA labels in our hands and we were scanning items over and over again trying to match up these items with the labels. It took us forever and we only hoped that we didn't make any mistakes.

We needed a new system, so I posted a short job description on the freelance developer website, elance.com. This is where I met Paul Retherford who is currently the CTO of FBAPower. When Paul and I first talked, FBA was still a very new and widely unheard of service. What I was describing in my job description was something that had never been done before. We talked back and forth many times before the job was approved and work started. I still remember the first item that I processed through version 1.0 of this software (it wasn't even called FBAPower at this point). The FBA label printed out individually and instantly as I processed the book. This was powerful stuff. A whole new world of online selling was about to begin. Paul and I talked about making the software available to other FBA sellers. After many discussions, we named it FBAPower and we agreed to be partners. We actually worked on FBAPower for over a year before ever actually meeting in person. FBAPower was released in July 2010 and the rest is history!

Retail Arbitrage was about to take off. Almost all of the pieces were in place to create a powerful, 100% scalable, nearly risk-free business model that literally anyone can do with no prior experience. FBA was there to do all of the storing, selling, picking, packing, shipping, and customer service. FBAPower was there to help sellers process inventory fast and price their FBA items properly. There was still one piece that did not exist.

You see, the scanning tools available were all designed for books and media only and designed for sellers who processed their own orders. This made sense when it was only booksellers who bought and sold only books and shipped all of their own orders (pre FBA days). When you use FBA, you quickly realize that you can buy and sell practically anything! This changed the needs of the scanning programs.

We needed a scouting program that could scan any barcode on any product and provide pricing data for every item on Amazon, not just books. The scouting programs that were available were simply not good enough, so we had to make our own. It was built from the ground up and designed specifically for Retail Arbitrage through FBA. We called it FBAScout. It was first available on Android devices and is now available for iPhone and iPad as well. There is nothing like it in terms of power in your hand to make the best buying decisions at the lowest risk. Profitable items are everywhere! Retail stores, pharmacies, grocery stores, you name it. Book sales are fun and thrift stores are great, but they can be some of the most competitive environments. And some book sales are only once or twice a year, while some retail stores are open 24 hours a day. FBAScout was the last piece of the puzzle that would allow anyone, anywhere, to identify any opportunity around them. Put it all together with FBAPower to get your items to FBA fast and efficiently and you're now leveraging FBA to sell your products to more customers at higher prices. You now have a truly remarkable business model that simply did not exist in this form just a few short years ago. It is an exciting time to be selling online and it will only get bigger and better. Amazon is growing at a remarkable rate and at the same time providing their third party sellers with powerful tools to compete with big, established companies from day one.

Sellers who see the opportunities in front of them and take action will be building an amazing business for themselves; a business that many sellers would describe as too good to be true. As you read through this book, test what I've written and see if it isn't 100% accurate.

You may be thinking that as a seller myself, wouldn't I be inviting competition by not only letting other sellers use the FBAPower and FBAScout software, but also by writing a book and teaching others how Retail Arbitrage works and all the secrets about how to do it? The truth is that I'm not. I know that I am a small fish in the vast ocean that is online selling. There are so many different products that it would be irrational for me to think that I could somehow go out and get ALL of the deals (more on this in Bonus #3 at the end of this book).

Think of it this way; there are over 2,000 Home Depots in the United States. Calculate it out with travel time and it would take an entire year to go to each store once (and of course be away from home all year long). And don't think that Home Depot only has one deal a year; if I only went once a year, I would miss out on all the other deals throughout the year. This says nothing about Target, Wal-Mart, Toys R Us and Big Lots deals that are out there every day.

As for teaching people, we are in a unique position in this industry. We are not just a group of programmers who decided to make something that we think sellers might need. FBAPower and FBAScout have features that I know sellers need because I am a seller. They were designed by me and for me; we just let other people use them because we are super nice guys. I know what pricing information I need in order to make a good buying decision and that's why it is included in FBAScout. I enjoy helping other sellers use our products optimally. Hearing success stories from our users makes it a very rewarding business to be a part of. FBAPower and FBAScout are pretty much the industry standard when it comes to FBA and when sellers know how to use FBA optimally, the utility of our programs becomes very evident. Still, no one has to use our programs. There is a whole bonus chapter later in the book (Bonus #4) explaining how to start a Retail Arbitrage business with zero risk and not use any of our programs.

Well, that's my story. That's where I started and this is where I am today. Arbitrage is just something that I've always been good at, I suppose. I feel very blessed to be part of a team where we all do what we are individually good at and we are able to create something powerful and useful that other people can use to their own success.

There is a lot of information out there and there are a lot of experts popping up. Some are great, some are good, and some simply do not know what they are talking about. As with any business, test the methods and test the author.

**Personal guarantee:**

I've tried to write this book as accurately and concisely as possible. Sometimes it can be difficult to write out details that are better explained in a one-on-one conversation. This is an entirely new type of business and the exact concepts of WHY it works are not always easy to grasp the first time around.

If you have any questions about this business, I invite you to call or email me directly.

214-298-6866 – yes, that is my cell phone number and I invite you to call. I'm Eastern Standard Time so please consider the time when calling. Also, please read the whole book before you call. ☺

If you prefer email: chris@scanpower.com

For general technical support for FBAPower, FBAScout and FBARepricer please visit http://www.scanpower.com as well as the support & help pages at http://help.scanpower.com

Or send an email to support@scanpower.com and someone from the FBAPower support team will be happy to help.

**Conflict of Interest?**

There will be some people who read this book and believe it to be nothing more than a book to get people to sign up for our programs like FBAPower, FBAScout, and FBARepricer. I assure you that it is not. I'll write it right here: you do not need to use any of our programs to run a successful Retail Arbitrage business.

If I wrote a book that was simply designed to get a ton of people to sign up for FBAPower but didn't explain the ins and outs of the Retail Arbitrage business, then most would quit pretty much right away. Getting customers to sign up for FBAPower or FBAScout and then failing at this business and leaving after one month does not make any sense. The only way a seller stays with our programs is if they are successful! Do we want them to stay? Of course! So we want to do everything that we can to help them achieve that success. When they are successful, we are successful!

I promote FBA education. When sellers understand how to use FBA properly and optimally, they will see why we do the things that we do. They will also see where our competitors fall short. Sometimes they simply just don't know what they don't know!

We are in a unique position in this industry. It is rare for a company to not only produce the best programs related to that industry, but to also have the best understanding of the industry and actively promote the education of that industry. There are other companies out there that will teach you to use their programs, but you are on your own to really understand and run your business. Do any of them possess such an in-depth understanding of the actual industry? And if so, are they willing to share so openly?

There may even be critics or distractors who claim that by sharing this information, it will 'destroy the market' or 'kill their business'. This should almost be seen as a good sign as it means that they KNOW there is money to be made and they want to be the ones making it, not you.

I believe that the free market will work itself out and that sellers who can compete will thrive in the good times and survive in the bad times. Those who cannot compete will go out of business.

I encourage all readers to read this book and evaluate what it says. Test what is written and decide for yourself if it is or is not accurate.

## Chapter 1 – What is Retail Arbitrage?

I'll be using the term Retail Arbitrage a lot in this book, so it's important that we give it a definition and understand what it means.

Let's start with the Wikipedia definition of Arbitrage:

http://en.wikipedia.org/wiki/Arbitrage

> In economics and finance, arbitrage is the practice of taking advantage of a price difference between two or more markets: striking a combination of matching deals that capitalize upon the imbalance, the profit being the difference between the market prices. When used by academics, an arbitrage is a transaction that involves no negative cash flow at any probabilistic or temporal state and a positive cash flow in at least one state; in simple terms, it is the possibility of a risk-free profit at zero cost.

> In principle and in academic use, an arbitrage is risk-free; in common use, as in statistical arbitrage, it may refer to expected profit, though losses may occur, and in practice, there are always risks in arbitrage, some minor (such as fluctuation of prices decreasing profit margins), some major (such as devaluation of a currency or derivative). In academic use, an arbitrage involves taking advantage of differences in price of a single asset or identical cash-flows; in common use, it is also used to refer to differences between similar assets (relative value or convergence trades), as in merger arbitrage.

> People who engage in arbitrage are called arbitrageurs—such as a bank or brokerage firm. The term is mainly applied to trading in financial instruments, such as bonds, stocks, derivatives, commodities and currencies.

Phew! That's a lot of fancy words to describe the many different forms of Arbitrage.

It is summarized here for simplicity:

Arbitrage is the practice of taking advantage of a price difference between two or more markets, striking a combination of matching deals that capitalize upon the imbalance. The difference between these two market prices is the profit realized by whoever brings the deal together.

This simply means that you find products that you can buy low and sell high. You're finding items to buy and sell for a profit. You're matching up supply and demand. You're identifying market inefficiencies and capitalizing (profiting) on your knowledge of these inefficiencies. There are many different ways to say the same thing. A recurring theme of this book is that knowledge and information are POWER. Those who have the knowledge, those who have the information, have the power. Without the knowledge and information, could you walk into a store and identify all of the items that have a higher value on the secondary market (Amazon or eBay) that can be purchased at a price that leaves room for profit for you? You can try to get some, but you'd never get them all. And you might bring some home that turn out to be complete duds. One of the most enjoyable parts of this business is when you find those items that you would never expect to have a high value online, yet they are items that you can find locally for so much less. Odds are, that without the proper information, if you didn't know it was a winner, neither did anyone else.

Retail Arbitrage can also be called resale and those who buy products for resale are called resellers. These terms will also be used throughout this book.

Another important distinction to make when discussing Retail Arbitrage is the retail market and price compared to the secondary market and price. Retail stores are the primary market and they are bound by pricing agreements with manufacturers as to what prices they can or cannot charge. When supply and demand change rapidly, the price at retail stores is not affected. What is affected is the ability to purchase those products at the retail price. If demand spikes, then you may not be able to find any at retail stores, or the primary market, because all of the stores sell out.

On the secondary market, price is set by supply and demand exclusively. When demand for a product spikes and the supply available for sale stays the same, then the price on the secondary market goes up. This is all just simple economics and human behavior. When the price on the secondary market exceeds the price at retail stores, entrepreneurs, or resellers, will enter the market by purchasing any available product for the artificially low retail price and bringing that supply to the secondary market when the price set by high demand and low supply is much higher.

From the arbitrage definition: The PROFIT being the difference between the market prices.

When EBay first started, they brought an entirely new concept to the world of Retail Arbitrage. They basically allowed anyone, anywhere to sell anything to anyone. This created an open secondary market where price was set by supply and demand. It was so open that prices would often quickly return to the equilibrium price. It got to the point where it became difficult to find anything for a price lower than the eBay price. Sellers practicing Retail Arbitrage long before you could sell on Amazon were finding products to buy and selling them on eBay. If an item could be purchased for less than the market price on eBay, it ended up on eBay. EBay ended up being the baseline of low prices online.

While eBay still represents some opportunities for Retail Arbitrage, as well as some strategies for selling at higher margins when prices and market conditions on Amazon change, for the most part this book is about Retail Arbitrage using Amazon.com as your primary sales channel.

## Chapter 2 – Amazon vs. eBay

I am frequently asked the question of what are the differences between Amazon and eBay. While they are both places that you can use to sell products online, the similarities pretty much end there.

The simplest way to explain the real differences are to contrast the two methods used to display products to the buyer. Many people are familiar with the eBay way of doing things. Every seller creates listing pages for each of their items. When a buyer searches for an item, say a specific item like a DW959 DeWalt drill, eBay will display all of the item pages that match the search terms DW959, DeWalt, and drill. Some items will be DeWalt drills, some will be drills from another brand, and some won't be drills at all. The buyer has to wade through the jumbled results to find the listing pages that are actually for DW959 DeWalt drills and then click through and compare several different listing pages on eBay to find one that they would like to buy. There may be 50 different sellers selling this drill, and all of their listings, or offers, are mixed together in the search results. Some will be auctions, some will be Buy It Now listings, and some buyers will have better feedback than others or more favorable return policies than others. It is up to the buyer to make sure that what they are looking for is accurately represented in the eBay listing. They may be expecting a DeWalt drill kit with two batteries but the eBay listing mentions that it only comes with one. It is the buyer's responsibility to read the entire listing before making a buying decision. Comparing all of these listings can be an arduous shopping experience for the buyer.

Compare to Amazon where the DW959 DeWalt drill kit has a single product page. This page is where all of the different sellers list their price and description. Sounds pretty simple from a buyer's perspective. There is one place with a consistent product page where the buyer knows what they are buying. Amazon as the marketplace maintains the product page and requires that all sellers who list on the product pages sell items that are exact matches to the details on the product page. This makes it very easy for the buyer to shop and it is one reason why so many buyers continue to go to Amazon as their first choice when purchasing items online.

You may be thinking that if all sellers are listed in one place, and all sellers are required to sell the exact same item, then wouldn't price be the only thing that matters? Wouldn't the lowest-priced seller get all of the sales? It's a valid question, but I can tell you from years of experience that there are many more things that go into a buyer's buying decision other than price. This book will explain why and show you how to differentiate yourself as a seller in order to protect your margins and to allow you to stop competing on price alone.

## Ways That a Seller Can Differentiate Themselves on Amazon

Let's back up a bit. The Amazon marketplace has product pages and all sellers have to list on those pages. This means the customer gets to see all offers in one place. Some sellers see no other way to differentiate themselves other than price, so they lower price in a race to see who can make the least amount of money without going out of business (don't do this).

**Price** – Amazon sorts the seller offers by price. The lower your price, the more visible you are (in theory, not always in practice).

**Feedback** – Buyers check a seller's feedback prior to purchasing. If you have higher feedback than your competition, you can often command a high price by inspiring greater buyer confidence. A seller's feedback rating is displayed as both a percentage and as a total quantity of feedback received. Some buyers prefer to buy from sellers with less feedback because they feel as if they are helping out 'the little guy' instead of buying from a large mega-seller.

**Product Description** – Many sellers use bland, generic product descriptions that do not inspire any buyer confidence. A buyer will often choose an identical item from a seller with an accurate, professional product description. They do this because they have more confidence that the seller takes the time to describe their items in greater detail compared to a seller who used a generic description for all of their items. Buyers can see when sellers put more time and effort into the listing and will have more confidence that the item that they receive will accurately match the seller's description. They may feel as though they are taking a chance when buying from a seller with a generic description.

**Return Policy/Customer Service** – Some sellers offer a more generous return policy that gives the buyer more confidence in choosing them as a seller in the event that something goes wrong with the product or the order. Amazon recently implemented a new seller policy that states that a seller must offer a return policy that is at least as favorable as Amazon's return policy.

Keep in mind that none of these things are absolutes. Buyers buy from different sellers for many reasons and those reasons are not even always rational. All things being equal, a buyer may choose one seller over another because they have a lower feedback rating in order to 'help them out'. Some sellers have store names that some buyers find offensive so they choose not to buy from them even at a lower price. Some buyers will favor a store name that they connect with and pay a higher price. Some sellers may have a witty description that makes the buyer laugh and the buyer buys from them. These things happen all the time.

**FBA** – This is the game changer and the most powerful way to differentiate yourself as a seller on Amazon. When you are an FBA seller, you are now able to offer things that your competition simply cannot offer. Your items are now part of Amazon's fulfillment network meaning that your items are now eligible for the same shipping options and promotions as Amazon's own items. Amazon spent how many millions building the most advanced shipping and distribution systems in history? Now your items can take advantage of this system! This is ridiculously powerful.

Using FBA to differentiate yourself means that you are able to cater to a powerful sub-group of all Amazon customers who put a high value on Amazons' fulfillment process. You may not get the next sale, or every sale, but you'll still get sales. The good news is that your sale is at a price that protects your margins. Amazon even lets buyers sort the offers page by only items that are eligible for Amazon Prime and Free Super Saver Shipping. This makes other sellers, regardless of price, simply disappear from the buyer's view.

**Listing on Each Site**

The listing process is very different between Amazon and eBay. Because Amazon has product pages already defined, all you have to do is tell Amazon that you have the item, how many you have, and what your price is. A few clicks and you are done.

EBay is more work because each product that you sell has its own product page that has to be created. That means typing out titles, taking and uploading pictures, writing descriptions, and setting all of your seller-specific settings on the eBay listing page.

**What Items Sell Best on Each Site**

Amazon and eBay are both great sites for selling stuff, but certain items certainly do better on each site.

Amazon is great for new items, commodity-type items, and items of which you have multiple, identical quantities. You can sell practically anything on Amazon (for a list of restricted items, refer to the Amazon rules in Chapter 15) and if it already has a product page, you can have your items offered for sale in a matter of seconds; just find the product page for the item, enter the quantity that you have for sale, enter your price, and you're done. If it's not on Amazon, you can choose to create a new product page. This is not difficult and normally requires a UPC on the product (UPCs can also be purchased, more information in Bonus #2 at the end of this book). It is more work than listing on an existing product page, but the good news is that you only have to create the product page one time. Creating new product pages can be very rewarding, as you can enjoy being the exclusive seller on Amazon.

EBay is great for items that may not have product pages on Amazon. EBay is also great for one-of-a-kind items as well as collectible items. Many collectors will always check eBay for those specific, hard-to-find items that may not get listed anywhere else.

Many items will sell well on both sites. An eBay buyer's money is not worth less than an Amazon buyer's money so don't turn away buyers or sales for no reason. Some buyers just go to eBay first out of preference or out of habit. They may still believe that Amazon only sells books.

**Other Differences**

**Listing Fees**

Amazon has no listing fees so you can list as many items as you like for free. This is a powerful position to be in. I like to use this fishing analogy: with no listing fees, it's like you are fishing (for sales). You can throw as big of a net (list items) as you want. You don't even have to catch much (get sales) each time you throw your net. With no listing fees, you can keep throwing your net over and over again. The sales that you get are all bonus.

Contrast this with eBay where you pay a fee for every item that you list, whether it sells or not. This prevents you from throwing a large net or even throwing a net at all. Listing fees, even if small, will restrict the size of the nets that sellers are able, or are willing, to throw.

## Payment Processing

When it comes to payment processing, Amazon includes this in the commission that they charge in each category. This is important to remember when comparing the fee structures of selling on Amazon vs. selling on eBay. To process payments on eBay, buyers have to go through PayPal which has its own set of fees. When you compare Amazon commission to eBay fees + PayPal fees, you'll see the fees are pretty close.

One thing that still kills me about eBay is that they remain the only place on the planet where a buyer can buy something but not pay for it. When you sell on Amazon, there is no such thing as a non-paying bidder!

## Better (easier) Buyers

It's nothing personal against eBay, but I place a huge value on simplicity. When you sell on Amazon, especially as an FBA seller, it will be pretty rare for you to get questions from buyers. On Amazon, the price listed is the price of the item. No auctions, no offers, no haggling. You won't get questions after the sale either, because Amazon will handle all of the customer service on FBA items (more on this in the next chapter).

## Higher Prices

As a seller, you will generally enjoy selling items at higher prices on Amazon than on eBay. There are many reasons for this. If you have a background on eBay and you are coming over to Amazon, this is an important facet to consider. Amazon shoppers will generally know what they want and will want to find it, buy it, and get on with their lives. They are not interested in waiting for auctions to close or waiting on Best Offers to be responded to. They put a value on simplicity and this value translates into higher prices.

EBay is often seen as a garage sale while Amazon enjoys a position as more of a premium marketplace. This is nothing personal against eBay; this is just how many buyers and sellers generally view the two sites.

## Feedback

On eBay, feedback is left much more often than it is on Amazon. You can expect to receive feedback on about 5-15% of all of your Amazon orders. Maintaining 100% positive feedback on eBay is doable and is a great source of pride for eBay sellers. On Amazon, it is nearly impossible to maintain 100% positive feedback. I would say that 98% positive on Amazon equates to 100% positive on eBay.

Amazon has a feedback scale of 1 through 5. I know some people who will say that they never give out a 5 out of 5 because that would mean that the seller would have no room for improvement. I do not agree with their reasoning, especially as a seller myself, but there are buyers out there like this. Some buyers will consider a 3 out of 5 to be positive feedback even though it is considered neutral feedback on Amazon. If you sell enough volume on Amazon, you will have this happen to your account. I warn you about this now so that when it inevitably happens to your Amazon seller account, you won't be surprised. Take it all in stride and remember that it is all just par for the course when you sell on Amazon.com. You'll get negatives that are undeserved and even feedback comments that the buyer meant to leave for another Amazon seller.

There are services out there that will help you get a higher percentage of your buyers to leave you feedback, but I don't really recommend them. One reason is that when you are an FBA seller, you have enough things going for you to differentiate yourself as a seller that having a greater quantity of positive feedback will not make a difference in the mind of a buyer. If you use a feedback requesting service, you also run the risk of receiving negative feedback that you would not have received if you had simply left your buyers alone. Some buyers simply do not want to leave feedback and don't want more email asking them to leave it. You may just be asking for a negative.

It is still important to keep your feedback as high as possible. It is more important to have a high feedback percentage than to have a high quantity of feedback. You should periodically check your feedback to see if you've received any neutral or negative feedback scores. If you get too many, you run the risk of having Amazon close your seller account. Amazon takes customer satisfaction very seriously (more on the rules of Amazon in Chapter 15). If you do get a negative feedback, contact the buyer through Amazon's messaging system and ask what you can do to correct the situation. Because buyer and seller interaction is not as common on Amazon as on eBay, there can easily be simple misunderstandings. If you are able to work with the customer to their satisfaction through communication and explanation, refund (partial or full), or some other form of customer service, you can then ask the customer if they would consider removing their negative feedback.

Do not ever make removal of negative feedback contingent upon your customer service. Take care of the customer first; work on removing the negative feedback later.

If you are not able to come to a resolution or if you are not able to reach the customer, then it can help to leave a follow up comment to any negative feedback comments that you may receive. Always stick to the facts and show that you care about customer service and stand behind your items.

Later in this book you'll see why if you sell everything through FBA and sell all new items that it's actually pretty hard to get negative feedback (and what you can do in the event that you do).

## Deciding What To Buy To Sell On Amazon

If you have been selling on eBay, then you probably already know that a great place to help you decide what to sell on eBay (and how to price it) is to view the Completed Listings. You can search for the item that you want to sell and you can see recently listed items that are either identical or similar. You can see if they sold, when they sold, and how much they sold for.

Advanced eBay sellers may be using a service called Terapeak. Terapeak offers additional Completed Listing data from eBay that is not available directly from eBay anymore. This is a subscription based service and the information that they provide can help you make better decisions about what to sell as well as help you decide how to price your eBay listings.

On Amazon, there are no sales histories. This is a policy from Amazon's legal department so don't expect this to change anytime soon. So if you can't see what has sold, when it sold, or for how much it sold, how do you make good decisions when deciding what to sell on Amazon as well as how to price your items?

Fair question, but let's back up a bit.

There are no guarantees when it comes to online sales. Just because an item sold last month for $300 on eBay and last week for $350 on eBay doesn't mean that it will sell this week for $300 or $350. Depending on the item, it may never sell again at any price. What you are deducing from eBay Completed Listings data and Terapeak information is the likelihood that an item will sell again, how quickly it will sell, and how much it will sell for. If an item has many completed listings on eBay and they are all fairly recent and all around the same price point, then it will be more likely that it will still sell in the near future at or near that same price. If an item only has one sale in the past two months as well as several Completed Listings on eBay with no winning bidder or buyer, then it will be <u>less likely</u> that the item will sell again quickly or at a price equal to the last successful eBay listing.

You are playing a guessing game on eBay. You are making educated choices by using all of the available data at your disposal, but you still have no guarantees.

It's the same way on Amazon. On Amazon, you have different data with which to make the same decisions as to which item to list for sale as well as what to set for your price. An Amazon listing will have a Sales Rank and competition. It may not seem like much, but you can extract a lot of information from what you see.

First, let's start with Sales Rank. Without going into extensive detail on Sales Rank, understand that Sales Rank is an indication of a recent sale and nothing more. If an item has sold recently, it will have a better Sales Rank than an item that has not sold recently at all. The item with the better Sales Rank will have a more recent sale or a higher quantity of recent sales than an item with a worse Sales Rank. When you can tell that the Sales Rank reflects a recent sale, then your next step is to decide how to price. Much more on what Sales Rank is as well as what it is not is covered later in Chapter 16.

The Amazon marketplace is an open marketplace. This means that everyone can see all of their competitor's prices. If an item has sold recently, you will not be able to tell exactly which seller made the sale or the exact price at which the last sale was made. What you can see is what all sellers are charging for the item. You'll find that on most items, sellers will be offering similar, competitive prices. There may be sellers that are offering the item at an abnormally high price. This is likely not what the last item sold for, but in rare circumstances such as only one FBA seller and an Amazon buyer needing the item quickly, it could be. You can make an educated guess at the market price by looking at the competition. Amazon sellers can be very competitive. If there are multiple sellers for an item and absolutely no one is making any sales, then the Sales Rank will get worse and worse. You'll find that if this happens, some sellers will look to lower their price to attract sales. Many times other sellers will follow with price drops. As the price lowers and the item attracts buyers, Sales Rank will change.

Another easy factor to consider is the number of sellers for any specific item. This is especially true for FBA sellers who will have more at stake by listing and sending inventory to FBA instead of just listing it as merchant fulfilled. If there are multiple sellers selling the item for a certain price, then you know that each of these sellers consider this an item worth selling and worth selling for the price which they are charging. If lots of sellers deem an item good to sell on Amazon, then it is likely a good item for you to sell as well.

When it's all said and done, only you can decide if the item is good for you to sell because only you know your specific product cost, your risk tolerances, and your available funds for inventory.

There are no guarantees in online sales, so don't fall into analysis paralysis when deciding what to sell. Consider the margins on your items as well as your competition. Gather as much information as you can. There is a lot of information available on both eBay and Amazon; you just have to know where to look and how to read it.

## Chapter 3 – What is FBA?

Can you explain FBA in a few simple sentences? It's pretty much not possible (believe me, I've tried). FBA is simple in and of itself, but truly explaining what it is, why it works the way that it does, and how to leverage its power could take hours to explain and weeks to grasp. I've been 100% FBA for years and I've talked to hundreds of different FBA sellers and I'm still learning new things all the time. With that said, I'll do my best to explain everything that I know about FBA without too much rambling.

If you sell online, then you have likely already heard of Amazon's fulfillment program called Fulfillment By Amazon, or FBA. Sellers have been leveraging the FBA program for several years and the sellers who have embraced this new service and taken advantage of its capabilities have truly transformed their businesses.

Here is an incredible video of the inside of an Amazon FBA warehouse:

http://g-ecx.images-amazon.com/images/G/01/fba-tour/FBA-FC-Tour._V216203492_.html

FBA stands for Fulfillment By Amazon and it is Amazon's version of a fulfillment company. Fulfillment companies have been around for a long time and they are still around today, but there has never been anything like FBA before.

Traditionally, a fulfillment company would be a large warehouse that would store shippable products for many companies. When a company received an order for a product, that company would send the order to the fulfillment company who would then ship the company's product to the customer. The fulfillment company would charge the company for this service, while leveraging their large shipping volume to get good shipping rates. The fulfillment company does what they are good at which is storing inventory, picking, packing, and shipping orders while each company that uses the fulfillment company continues to do what they are good at which is selling their products. The companies also benefit by not having to have their own warehouse and shipping department to process all of their own orders themselves. It was a win-win relationship.

The difference between a traditional fulfillment center and Amazon's FBA program is that Amazon is not just the fulfillment company, they are also the marketplace. They have an active interest in seeing the products sell. Amazon makes money by charging a commission on the products sold on Amazon.com as well as the fees that they charge to use FBA (fees explained a little later).

So you are not just sending your products to a traditional fulfillment center and then left on your own to find customers and make sales. Amazon.com is the website that you are selling on and they are the ones doing the fulfillment for you. They WANT your items to sell just as much as you do; maybe even more so since they get paid whether you are making a profit or not. More on this later to make sure that you are maintaining margins and staying profitable. Additionally, FBA items are eligible for Amazon's shipping promotions including Free Super Saver Shipping and Amazon Prime. This is what makes FBA incredibly powerful. The FBA seller enjoys many advantages over their non-FBA competitors that will be explained in detail in the next chapter.

**FBA can be described as a Triple Win.**

**Win #1. Higher prices, higher margins, higher payouts**

Since items sold through FBA are eligible for Free Super Saver Shipping and Amazon Prime, FBA sellers actually raise their prices to match their competitor's total price (price + shipping). So even with the addition of FBA fees, the FBA seller still receives a higher net payout from their Amazon sale because of the higher sales price. For example, a seller who ships their own orders and sells an item for $20 with $5 shipping will show the same as an FBA seller selling the exact same item priced at $25. Actually, the FBA seller will show first because FBA is the tiebreaker. That additional $5 that the FBA seller charges more than covers the additional FBA fees that they pay. Amazon is basically absorbing the shipping costs for you.

**Win #2. Less work**

FBA sellers sell items 24 hours a day, 7 days a week. Items ship all hours of the day or night including weekends. They ship whether the seller is at home or on vacation. Once an FBA seller prepares their items for the FBA warehouse and sends them to Amazon, they don't have to do anything else. They can monitor inventory levels and adjust prices as needed from anywhere with an Internet connection. They don't have to stock boxes, envelopes, packing materials, or shipping labels anymore. They also don't wait around for their UPS driver or go to the post office every day. You are outsourcing your entire shipping department.

**Win #3. Happier Customers**

It is estimated that 50% of Amazon buyers have never bought from a third party merchant. Amazon customers want to buy from FBA sellers. They trust Amazon and they know that their items will ship quickly and if there is ever a problem, Amazon will help (including an extended return policy). When your items are shipped through FBA (either for Amazon orders or Multi-Channel Fulfillment orders) they will attract these types of Amazon buyers who are willing to pay more to get their items shipped by Amazon. This is an important point to grasp: Amazon customers are willing to pay more for the exact same item if it comes from Amazon or an FBA seller. They do this because they know they will get their item fast and that customer service will be top notch.

Through FBA and third party sellers, Amazon has been able to expand the depth of the catalog of items that they can offer to their best customers.

**Scalability Helps Small Sellers**

The competitive advantages that the big sellers have enjoyed for years have vanished overnight with the introduction of FBA. A new seller on Amazon may have made some good money by selling items out of their garage in their spare time, but if they wanted to make a real income they would have had to scale up and get more space to handle more inventory and hire employees to help with all of the orders. Now they may make more money but they have additional overhead. There are two things that have kept small sellers small and those are space and time limitations.

As a small seller, you only have so much space in which to store products and you only have so much time to list, sell, and ship your orders. Ten orders a day can be fun. Twenty may get you excited. But can you fulfill 300 orders in a day? Can you do this day after day? And shut down your entire business if you ever wanted to go on vacation?

With FBA, you can grow your business as much as you want. FBA removes the space and time limitations and allows you to compete on the same playing field as the big, established sellers on day one. There are no scalability restrictions with FBA. If you have access to products, you could sign up with FBA and ship them fifty thousand products in one day and be selling 500 items a day within the week. Manage your inventory properly and you could run an FBA empire from a studio apartment.

**Here is how FBA works for Amazon sellers.**

You open up an Amazon account and you sign up for the FBA Program. Before you send items to an Amazon FBA warehouse, they have to be labeled. You'll print special barcoded labels that you'll affix to each product that you send in. They'll have to cover up any existing UPCs because when Amazon receives your items, they will scan the barcodes to identify the product as your specific inventory. Once your inventory has been received at FBA, it will be made available for sale on the Amazon website.

**Amazon describes FBA this way:**

> With this innovative service, you send inventory directly to Amazon where it is stored and managed in a secure, climate-controlled facility. When orders are received, Amazon will professionally pick, pack and ship the product directly to your customer.
>
> Amazon.com processes millions of orders a year while consistently ranking as one of the most trusted and highest customer satisfaction rated e-commerce companies. To maintain this unique combination, we have developed one of the most advanced online order processing and fulfillment operations in the world. From the advanced web-to-warehouse, high-speed picking and sorting system to our complete shipping carrier integration, Amazon's technology results in your customers getting what they ordered, when they ordered it.
>
> Whether you're considering just a few items and shipments a week or millions of products and orders per year, you can put

Amazon's expertise and experience to work for your business with Fulfillment by Amazon.

**Put Amazon's Fulfillment Technology to Work for You.**

You sell it, we ship it. Amazon has created one of the most advanced fulfillment networks in the world, and your business can now benefit from our expertise. With Fulfillment by Amazon (FBA) you store your products in Amazon's fulfillment centers, and we directly pack, ship, and provide customer service for these products.

**Enjoy these benefits when you use Fulfillment by Amazon.**

**Eligible for FREE Super Saver Shipping & Amazon Prime**

Customers love FREE Super Saver Shipping and Amazon Prime. FBA Listings on Amazon.com feature these delivery messages increasing awareness of product eligibility for free shipping.

**Competitive Pricing:**

Your FBA listings on Amazon.com are sorted by the item price without a shipping cost. Amazon assumes they will ship for free with FREE Super Saver Shipping or Prime, which gives you an edge when competing!

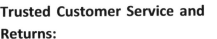

**Trusted Customer Service and Returns:**

FBA listings are displayed with the "Fulfillment by Amazon" logo, so customers know that packing, delivery, customer service and returns are all handled by Amazon.

**Fulfill Orders from other Channels:**

FBA can fulfill your orders from other sales channels from your inventory stored at an Amazon fulfillment center. You manage your inventory through a simple online user interface, and can direct us to return the inventory in our fulfillment centers at any time.

## FBA Fees

There are fees that are associated with FBA. The good thing is that they are all known ahead of time and most of them are fixed. The only one that differs is the commission, as it is category specific, and it only changes if you change your price. If you sell an item for a certain price, you'll know all fees ahead of time and you'll be able to calculate your payout and determine the product's profitability (or not).

Amazon even provides a handy FBA calculator here:

https://sellercentral.amazon.com/gp/fbacalc/fba-calculator.html

You can use the FBA calculator not only to calculate expected payouts on your FBA inventory, but also to compare total fulfillment costs when deciding between using FBA for your items or keeping them for self-fulfillment.

## Inbound Shipping Fee

This is the cost of getting your items to the FBA warehouse. Amazon lets you use UPS partnered shipping so you get Amazon UPS rates, which you can probably imagine are the best in the world. This is a tremendously advantageous feature of FBA that is oftentimes overlooked or taken for granted. This discounted rate can turn items that were at one point not profitable for you to sell into items that are now profitable. A 50 pound box typically ships for around $9-$15 depending on how close you are to your nearest fulfillment center. You can also arrange to ship pallets by LTL shipments (Less Than Truckload) or choose your own shipper.

Your inbound shipping fees can change if Amazon decides to change which fulfillment center your items are going to. While this can affect the profitability of your items, changes in these fees should not make or break an item in terms of overall profitability. If they do, then I suggest selling different items with higher margins.

## Amazon Commission

This varies depending on the categories that you sell in.

## Pick & Pack Fee

Amazon charges a fixed fee for picking and packing your orders.

## Weight Based Fee

Amazon charges a weight-based fee on the outbound shipping fees. Heavier items will incur higher weight-based fees when they ship so price your items appropriately.

## Storage Fee

Storage fees are very low and the first 30 days are free. You can manage your FBA inventory levels and replenish your inventory as needed to keep 30 days worth of sales in stock to prevent paying any FBA storage fees. Even if you do end up paying storage fees, you'll find that they are very reasonable.

## Long Term Storage Fee

FBA Long-Term Storage

The Long Term Storage Fee is $45/cubic foot that is charged on items stored in FBA warehouses for more than one year. This does not mean that every item that you send to FBA has to sell within 12 months. There is an exemption for single units of any specific product. This means that Amazon still wants your Long Tail items (items that sell, they simply don't sell very often), they just don't want three copies of a book that sells once every three years. This would be nine years supply of inventory and it is not how Amazon envisioned the FBA program.

Here are some examples of the Long Term Storage Fee on a book and a toy:

| Item | Dimensions | 1 unit | 2nd unit | 10 units |
|------|-----------|--------|----------|----------|
| Book | 8" X 6" X 1" | $0.00 | $1.10 | $9.90 |
| Toy | 11" X 8" X 2" | $0.00 | $4.58 | $41.22 |

Believe me, Amazon does NOT want to charge you the Long Term Storage Fee. This is not a profit center for them. They want FBA warehouses humming with inventory coming in and orders going out. This is what they are good at. They do not want to be in the storage business.

**Avoiding the Long Term Storage Fee by Analyzing Your Aging Inventory**

Log into your Amazon Seller Account:

https://sellercentral.amazon.com/gp/homepage.html (seller account required)

Look under Reports, and then click on Fulfillment.

Under Inventory, you'll see two reports. One called Inventory Health, and the other called Recommended Removal.

Request both of these reports to be downloaded. Save, and open in Excel. Familiarize yourself with these reports; they are very helpful. Right now you want to look at the columns that relate to Inventory Age (270-365 days & 365+ days) as this will show you the items on which Amazon will charge you the Long Term Storage Fee.

**Creating a Removal Order**

FBA Manual 6.4 Create Removal Orders

Amazon has actually made this process fairly easy. Here's how I did it on my accounts:

Go to your Seller Account, Reports, Fulfillment, choose Recommended Removal, View Online, click on Generate Report.

You'll now see the first 150 items from your Recommended Removal Report. These are all items that will be charged the Long Term Removal

Fee or that have single quantities of inventory that have been in stock for 365+ days. Click on Begin Removal Process.

Most of these items you will want to remove or destroy. The ones to double check are the ones that have a Fulfillable Quantity of one and Available Quantity of one (even if at FBA for 365+ days). These may be Long Tail items that you want to keep in inventory. Remember, single inventory units per ASIN are exempt from the Long Term Storage Fee. I copied and pasted the ASIN into Amazon to check the prices and Sales Rank for these items to decide if I wanted to keep the items at FBA or remove/destroy them. If you want to keep them, check the box in the Delete column to remove the item from the removal order. Once you have reviewed the items, click the Continue button at the bottom of the screen and complete the process. If you have more than 150 items to review, repeat the process for the additional items.

**Creating a Disposal Order**

Follow the same steps as above for creating a Removal Order, but instead of clicking Ship To Address and entering an address, you'll click on Destroy. Trust me; when Amazon says they will destroy the items, they will be destroyed.

**What's Really Going On?**

This fee is designed to encourage FBA sellers to manage their FBA inventory better and to not simply use FBA warehouses as a cheap storage unit for their entire inventory. The FBA storage fees were so low that many sellers (myself included) simply sent Amazon everything because it was so cheap to store it at FBA that it made sense to do so.

In the fourth quarter of 2010, Amazon halted inbound FBA shipments because FBA warehouses were full. This fee will prevent this from happening again. Amazon wanted nothing but to receive inbound shipments and get stuff listed and sold, but too many sellers filled up the warehouses with slow moving inventory. The new Long Term Storage Fee will discourage this practice and keep FBA warehouses able to receive products without any delays.

## Which Fulfillment Center Will My Items Go To?

This is an important question because depending on where you live geographically and the type of products that you sell, this will affect your Inbound Shipping Fees. Books & Media will go to one place and toys will go to another. Oversize items will go to another and clothing items will go to yet another. Amazon assigns the fulfillment center based on many factors. These factors include (in order):

1. Item Size (regular or oversize)
2. Amazon Category (books, tools, toys, clothes, etc.)
3. The Popularity of the Item
4. Regional Demand/Order Patterns (Amazon wants to get inventory into fulfillment centers closest to the demand to lower shipping times in transit as well as costs.
5. Current Inventory Levels
6. Seller Proximity to Fulfillment Center

So unfortunately, seller proximity to the fulfillment center is only a minor consideration. Always remember to compare the cost of paying regular UPS rates for your inbound shipping. The Amazon partnered UPS rates should be seen as an extra bonus

As a business strategy note, I would strongly suggest that if the inbound shipping rates are causing an item to not be a profitable match for FBA that you simply stop selling the product and source other, more profitable items. Cutting margins razor thin where an item is profitable if inbound shipping is $0.25/pound but not when it is $0.70/pound is not the types of margins that I recommend people play with.

**Summary:**

Think of it this way: only send Amazon a maximum of ONE YEAR SUPPLY of any product and you will never be charged the Long Term Storage Fee. Single quantity items are excluded so you can still send in Long Tail items without worry. Periodically check the Inventory Health Report and the Recommended Removal Report. Most FBA sellers who sell books and media items with a quantity of one will be largely unaffected by this new fee. If you need any help having your inventory returned to you or disposed of, please contact Amazon's Seller Support team using the Contact Us link in your Seller Account.

To be sure you are reviewing the most current FBA fees, always check the Amazon FBA website:

http://www.amazon.com/gp/help/customer/display.html/?nodeId=200 242950

**Pricing Your FBA Items**

There are additional fees associated with FBA, but you will also sell your items for a higher price so in most cases you will actually receive a higher net payout per transaction even though you have additional transaction fees. This would seem impossible considering the fact that by using FBA you are also doing less work and you are keeping your customers happier by providing faster shipping services than you could provide yourself. Much more on how to price FBA items later in the book.

**Return Policy**

Amazon handles customer service for all FBA orders. Amazon is very conscientious about keeping their customers happy. They will allow a customer to return an item for pretty much any reason. This opens the door for abuse sometimes and there are instances where a customer can take advantage of this policy at the expense of your inventory.

If you find that you are receiving a higher return rate on an item that is affecting your target margins, you will have to evaluate the item's compatibility with FBA. You can raise your price to compensate or you can try to sell the item on other channels and ship your orders from your FBA inventory using Multi-Channel Fulfillment (more in Chapter 33). You may even decide that the product is no longer a good match for FBA and you can request that Amazon return the products to you.

## International Orders

Currently, Amazon will ship your books and media items internationally for you at no extra charge (customer pays shipping). To sell your books and media items internationally, you need to add this service to your Amazon seller account (free) and then upload a digital copy of your signature that Amazon will use on export documents and customs forms. If you sell items from other categories on Amazon, they will not be eligible for international shipping (through Amazon direct sales or Multi-Channel Fulfillment). I would expect that Amazon would offer this service in the future.

## Amazon as a Competitor

When selling on Amazon using FBA, you may enjoy a time of being the only FBA seller for an item. This is an ideal situation but it doesn't always last. Other sellers can convert their inventory to FBA and start to drive the price down. Sometimes you may be selling an item that Amazon does not currently carry and have a type of exclusivity. In the event that Amazon starts to carry these products directly, they may be able to sell them at lower margins than you are comfortable with. In cases like this, you can try to sell your items on other channels and fulfill any orders using Multi-Channel Fulfillment. You can do this until you are sold out of inventory, or you can even request to have your inventory removed and returned to you. Then re-evaluate the item considering your costs and profit margin goals and decide if it is still a good match to sell online. There is a bonus section at the end of this book with strategies for competing with Amazon as a seller.

## Unfulfillable Inventory

If a customer returns an item, Amazon will determine if the item can be resold or not. If it can be resold, it will be added to your existing FBA inventory. If not, it will be marked as 'unfulfillable' and you will have to request that it be returned to you or destroyed. Best Practice is to remove your entire unfulfillable inventory once a month or so. You may find that items were damaged or that there was nothing wrong with your items. Just reprocess them to your FBA account if they are still in sellable condition. Amazon can also automate this process for you and send your unfulfillable inventory back to you on a regular schedule.

## Downsides of FBA

Even with all the positive things that FBA allows sellers to do, there are some things to keep in mind when deciding if you are going to send all or some of your inventory to an FBA warehouse. FBA has the power to transform your business overnight, but it is important to know how it all works and the potential risks involved when handing over a significant portion of your business process to another company.

## You Lose Control Over Your Order Processing

You are handing over all aspects of order processing to Amazon. You are trusting them to store, pick, pack, and ship your items. This can be a scary thought for some sellers who take great pride in providing their customers with a high quality shipping process. You may decide to only send certain items to FBA and keep higher valued items or items that would require special packaging at your location to ship yourself.

## You Hand Over Customer Service to Amazon

Amazon will handle all customer service issues on your FBA orders. This means that you lose control of the returns process (a customer can return an item without approval from you, the seller). It is possible (although unlikely) that a buyer abuses this liberal return policy at the expense of your inventory. If you suspect anything like this, report it to Amazon. They monitor excessive customer returns as well as A-Z Guarantee claims.

## Possibility of Loss or Damage to Your Products

It is possible that your items are lost or damaged either by UPS on the way to Amazon or by Amazon themselves, but that same risk is there for every item dropped off at the post office. Amazon will reimburse sellers for lost or damaged items automatically. It is important to monitor your inbound items as they are received. Amazon will send an email if there are any problems receiving your items.

## Items not good for FBA

Unfortunately, FBA is not perfect for every type of item. Here are some items that I would be cautious to send to FBA as well as the reasons why.

## Low Margin Items

If you have low margins, then one or two returns can wipe out all profitability on the entire product. Returns are inevitable and the cost of returns should be factored into your expected margin on every item that you sell.

## High Fraud Categories

Categories that can be more susceptible to fraud and abuse are computers and electronics. Because Amazon handles the customer service, fraudulent buyers may try to take advantage of the generous return policy. Consider this when deciding what to send to FBA. FBA still works in these categories, but a buyer looking to take advantage of Amazon is more likely going to do so over an iPad than over a shower curtain. Amazon monitors buyers just like they monitor sellers. Buyers can also be kicked off of Amazon.

**Expensive Items**

Use your own discretion when considering sending high-dollar items to FBA. While they do enjoy the same boost that you will get for all FBA items by attracting Amazon's best customers, they will also be open to fraud and return policy abuse. This just makes more work for you to do if you have to track extra returns and inspect the items more carefully. An expensive return can hurt a lot more than an inexpensive one.

**Collectible Items**

Amazon is not currently the optimal sales channel for one-of-a-kind collectibles. EBay is still the best place for these types of items. I know exactly how Amazon could add this category through FBA, but that's the subject of another book.

When considering these types of items, consider the overall impact of the item on your sales. If you receive additional returns on an item, do those returns negatively impact the OVERALL profitability of that product over a period of time? Run the numbers for a few months to get a good sample of sales. If you sell ten of an item a month when you fulfill your own orders, but twenty per month through FBA, are the overall additional sales worth any increase in returns? If yes, send to FBA. If not, don't send to FBA.

FBA is a very powerful program and if used correctly, will greatly improve your margins, profits, and efficiency. It can give you back your time to focus on other parts of your business such as sourcing products or just spending more time with your family.

## Types of Amazon Seller Accounts

There are primarily two types of seller accounts on Amazon.

### Individual Account

You can start selling on Amazon with absolutely no fees. There is no fee to have an Individual Account to list items for sale. You pay fees when your items sell. These fees will include a Per Transaction Fee of $0.99/item. You cannot create new product pages if you only have an Individual Account.

### Pro Merchant Account

If you are running a Retail Arbitrage business, then you will most likely be a Pro Merchant. The cost is $39.95/month. You get access to many additional reports as well as the ability to feed data and files directly to your seller account. A Pro Merchant account is required to use FBAPower for this reason.

Pro Merchants do not pay the $0.99 Per Transaction Fee that Individual Account sellers pay on every item. So as long as you sell 40 items a month, a Pro Merchant account is basically free. If you sell hundreds of items per month, then being a Pro Merchant will actually save you a ton of money.

Pro Merchants are able to create new listings on Amazon.com.

If you are just starting out and you don't know which account to sign up for, remember the tipping point of selling 40 items per month means a Pro Merchant account is basically free. Follow the principles laid out in this book and selling 40 items per month will not be an issue.

A lot of this book will focus on FBA, but you do not need to use FBA to fulfill your Amazon orders. You can sell on Amazon and ship yourself, although once you use FBA, even one order a day can seem like a huge inconvenience. The same economic principles of supply, demand, price, and margin will apply; you'll just be shipping your own orders.

So now that you know what FBA is, let's explain <u>WHY</u> FBA works so well.

## Chapter 4 – Why Does FBA Work?

So why does FBA work? There are many reasons that FBA works and works well, but the thing to consider is that FBA works all around; it works for sellers as well as for buyers. It also works for Amazon.

### FBA for Sellers

For starters, FBA sellers enjoy many competitive advantages over their non-FBA competitors known as merchant fulfilled sellers. Many of these advantages are listed below:

FBA sellers have a greater probability of winning the Buy Box, even without being the lowest price.

FBA sellers can win the New and Used Buy Boxes in the Books, Music, Videos, and DVD categories.

FBA sellers are listed first on the offers pages, even if selling for the same net price (price + shipping).

FBA sellers get their items marketed on the Amazon.com website with guaranteed delivery dates.

FBA works because it puts your inventory on the same level as Amazon's own inventory and markets it to Amazon's best customers. Amazon's customers are smart; they know what they want and they trust Amazon. Amazon buyers pay more for the exact same item in order to get it from Amazon rather than from a third party seller. Why? Isn't it the same item? The same item, yes, but buyers are buying more than just the item. They are buying the customer service, they are buying the return policy, and they are buying the order fulfillment process. For these reasons, buyers will pay more to get their items from Amazon or an FBA seller than they will to get their items from a third party seller who ships their own orders. Consider Amazon Prime members (explained in more detail below) who get free 2-Day Air shipping on everything that they buy as long as it ships from Amazon or an FBA seller. Buyers choose FBA sellers over merchant fulfilled sellers over and over again, willingly, very willingly.

Consider an item that ships fast and free by UPS 2-Day Air for Amazon Prime members compared to the same item for the same price from a merchant fulfilled seller who ships by USPS Parcel Post or Media Mail for books. At the same price, it's a no-brainer. Even at a higher price, the fast shipping is such a value that many buyers are happy to pay a little more (sometimes a lot more) to get the same item faster.

We'll talk more about understanding the Amazon customer in the next chapter, but first we need to talk about a huge piece of the FBA success puzzle and that is Amazon's free shipping programs. They are called Amazon Prime and Free Super Saver Shipping (FSSS).

**Amazon Prime**

Amazon Prime is brilliant. Amazon Prime members pay $79/year and in return receive free 2-Day Air shipping on everything that they buy on Amazon. This applies to all items sold by Amazon and through FBA sellers. There are rare exceptions for items that do not qualify for Amazon Prime, but they are so rare that I have not even seen one recently enough to put in here as an example. Amazon Prime members can also choose to pay $3.99 for Overnight shipping on any item.

Think about that. This is powerful stuff! Even if you, personally, don't find this service useful, you can bet that a ton of Amazon buyers do. I know I'm one of them! We buy practically everything we can from Amazon, and often at the best price. Getting it delivered free in two days (sometimes next day) is just an extra bonus.

**Amazon Prime Program Details; Amazon.com/prime**

**Unlimited FREE 2-day shipping on all eligible orders** – You don't have to order that much from Amazon to get a lot of value out of this program. Even one package a month would cost you more to request 2-Day shipping than the $7/month for Amazon Prime.

**No minimum purchase required for free shipping** – Even a $5 pair of scissors will be at your door in two days for free if you're an Amazon Prime member. Are you really going to drive to the store just for scissors?

**Send gifts across the continental US at no additional cost** – You don't just have to ship to your house. You can have Amazon ship birthday gifts, wedding gifts, or Christmas gifts right up to the last minute, all free.

**Add up to four accounts in your household to your account** – Just about anyone in your house can use Amazon Prime and get things delivered free in two days.

**Get overnight shipping for only $3.99 per item**

Seriously? $3.99 to send just about anything overnight? Order today, at your house tomorrow for under $4. I'm not driving halfway across town over $4 unless I absolutely have to have the item tonight (which is pretty rare). You can get DVDs, toothpaste, cereal, and diapers, all at your door the next day for under $4. Can you see how a buyer could get used to this? Did The Weather Channel just forecast a hurricane in your area next week? Just order your generator from Amazon and get it delivered TOMORROW for $3.99. Yes, even some heavy generators ship overnight from Amazon for $3.99.

**Amazon actively promotes and markets their shipping capabilities (and items that qualify)**

Amazon will even tell you on the product page how much time you have left if you want the item delivered tomorrow or the next day using two day shipping. Depending on where the Amazon fulfillment center is located, 2-Day Air shipments can often arrive overnight.

Here's how this works in practice: say I want to order the Kindle. I can order it as late as 6:30 CST and for $3.99 it will be at my door tomorrow at about 10:30. If I can wait an extra day, it's free. This is powerful stuff. Forgot your anniversary is tomorrow? Order in the afternoon and it's delivered the next morning.

(Shipping and delivery times will vary by individual, but we get our UPS shipments around 10:30 AM)

More and more Amazon customers are becoming Amazon Prime members. This will mean more and more customers who begin to value the fast, free shipping services that Amazon Prime members enjoy on every order. Amazon has several programs that introduce Amazon buyers to Amazon Prime with free trials such as Amazon Moms and Amazon Students.

As an extra bonus, Amazon Prime members get access to the entire Amazon Prime Instant Videos catalog. Not really related to selling on Amazon, but I mention it here to show you that Amazon is pushing Amazon Prime to more and more of their customers. The more Amazon Prime members there are, the more attractive items listed by FBA sellers will become versus items listed by merchant fulfilled sellers. The demand for the products will stay the same, but the number of purchases will continue to shift towards the FBA sellers and away from the merchant fulfilled sellers. Whose side do you want to be on?

**Free Super Saver Shipping**

This is another genius Amazon business model. As long as you buy $25 worth of items or more, you get free shipping! Partner this with no tax and the delivered price often beats the local price on many items. Free Super Saver Shipping is not as fast as Amazon Prime and orders don't always ship right away, but they do ship for free and this is all that matters for many cost conscious buyers. It also encourages buyers to add additional items to their shopping carts prior to checkout to get over that magical $25 mark and get the free shipping. Now consider this: a buyer has $21 in their shopping cart and wants to get FSSS so they start looking for something that they need for around $4. They find an item that should work and they look at the offers. If you are the only FBA offer at $4, then they have to choose you because the item has to be from Amazon or from an FBA seller. It's actually less expensive for them to add your $4 FBA item and get FSSS than to checkout at $21 and pay for shipping. As for your merchant fulfilled competition on that $4 item, they are not even being considered because their inventory is not eligible for FSSS at all!

Earlier we briefly talked about how FBA sellers are able to make more money on each item by using FBA than if they fulfilled their online orders themselves. They can do this despite the additional FBA fees that they pay. You may be thinking that this doesn't make sense; how can a seller pay more fees, yet make more per sale? That's what I'll explain here with some examples. Understanding this part of FBA is very important. FBA items are priced much differently than regular merchant fulfilled items. Pricing your FBA inventory optimally is an art form itself because you are not limited to simply competing on price.

## How Sellers Should Price FBA Items

Learning how to price FBA items is one of the most important things that you need to master. This is important for two reasons. First, you don't want to price too low and leave a ton of margin and profit on the table for no reason. Second, you don't want to price too high and miss out on sales. In the next chapter, we'll talk about Understanding The Amazon Customer and why they will often pay more for items sold by FBA sellers. For now, let's stick to the basics of pricing FBA items against merchant fulfilled items.

So if you aren't supposed to be the lowest price and you're not supposed to be the highest price, then how should I price? Good question! Unfortunately there is no perfect answer for how to price FBA items. I'll give you some guidelines as to when to price aggressively as well as when to command a premium price over your merchant fulfilled competition.

The first thing to remember is that your FBA inventory is eligible for Amazon's free shipping programs. This is very important. This means that your listing on a product's offers page will be sorted by the total 'net price', meaning price plus shipping. If you are selling a book and the lowest price from a merchant fulfilled seller is $5 + $3.99 shipping and you price your book at $5 as an FBA seller, then sure, your offer will show first as the lowest price, but you just priced yourself $3.99 LOWER than the already lowest net price. By default, if you want to be the lowest price as an FBA seller against merchant fulfilled offers, then you should be matching their net price. In this case it would be $8.99. So even though your price is $8.99 and their price is $5, you would show first on the offers page because FBA is the tiebreaker. Amazon buyers are smart and they will compare apples to apples and see the total 'shipped' price in their shopping carts. Unless you have a really good reason, such as all merchant fulfilled sellers being listed at artificially high prices, you should not be pricing any of your items below the lowest merchant fulfilled 'net price'.

This comes back to Win #1 discussed earlier in this book where sellers will get higher total payouts on the exact same item when using FBA instead of processing orders themselves. They are able to sell at a higher price so even though they have additional fees associated with using FBA, these additional fees are covered by the increase in sales price. Of course, this is all in addition to not actually having to ship all of your own orders!

Here are two strategies that you can take when pricing your items: The Fast Nickel vs. The Slow Dime.

The Fast Nickel is when you price aggressively in order to get a fast sale. There is a value in getting paid fast. You are able to get in, get paid, and get out. The risk that you took by purchasing the item for resale is gone. Sometimes you may sell for a price lower than what the buyer was willing to pay, but you accept that price for the fast sale and lower risk compared to holding onto the item and trying to get a higher price.

The Slow Dime means that you price yourself a little higher than your competition and you market yourself as a premium seller to the buyer. Higher prices, higher margins, higher profits. You may simply be pricing higher as an FBA seller just waiting for a buyer who puts a higher value on fast, free shipping. If you are holding your items for longer periods of time, you do expose yourself to risks such as price erosion or market price drops. It could be a weaker future demand for the product, which would lower price, or increased competition that would increase supply and bring down price. When this happens, suddenly that quick sale, or Fast Nickel, even at a lower price, starts to look attractive.

Different products will deserve different strategies. You may have to experiment with different strategies on different items. One thing to always remember: if an item sells too fast, it's priced too low. If it takes too long to sell, then it's priced too high (these rules do not apply to Long Tail items that are not as price sensitive). A Long Tail book that only sells twice a year is going to sell twice a year regardless of price (within reason). Long Tail items do not sell on price so lowering price on Long Tail items is not a strategy that I recommend. The item will sell twice a year at $100 or at $20. Lowering your price to $20 to try to attract the sale is only going to cut into your margins. The buyer is more than happy to pay you only $20, but they would also be happy to pay $100.

## Pricing Against Your Competition

Depending on what you sell, there will be different market dynamics that you have to consider when pricing your items. Amazon has New, Used, and Collectible conditions. They also have the dynamic of Amazon as a seller and third party sellers. Third party sellers have the added dynamic of some using FBA and some being merchant fulfilled. Deciding exactly how to price means that you have to consider your competition as well as the products that you are selling.

If you sell toys and you only sell toys in New condition, then you need to look at the Amazon price (if Amazon sells the item), your competition in New condition, and then if there are any FBA sellers.

If you sell books, you need to look at the Amazon price (if Amazon sells the book), the listed prices in New and Used condition, as well as if there are any FBA sellers. Even if you are selling Used books, you have to look at the New prices because sometimes you're going to see a Used book going for $30, the same book in New condition for $20, and to make it even worse, Amazon selling it for $14.95. How does this happen? Sellers who are not paying attention! They are pricing their Used books against their Used competition and not considering the entire competitive marketplace.

As an FBA seller, you can't just look at the FBA competition, either. You'll see items where merchant fulfilled sellers are all charging $25 for an item and an FBA seller at a price of $250. I know we talked about how Amazon buyers will pay a premium for FBA items, but there is a limit. I want to teach you to be more realistic when commanding a premium for your FBA items. Who knows, maybe that seller will find someone who puts a huge value on FBA, and if they do, good for them! It may also be a simple typo of an extra zero on the end of their price.

When you are the only FBA seller on an item, you are able to command a premium price, especially if Amazon does not sell the item. You will be the only seller who is able to offer the item with free 2-Day Air shipping to Amazon Prime members. There is a whole chapter later in this book about not chasing the next sale. What this means in a nutshell is that not all buyers are the same. Some will buy on price and some want fast, free shipping. Relax on price and let the buyers make their buying decisions. Will the next buyer for this item put a high value on FBA? Maybe, but maybe not. Maybe they are buying on price. That's OK; you sit and wait for the FBA buyers. Your margins will thank you ☺

Being the only FBA offer leads me into this next phenomenon, The FBA Land Grab.

**The FBA Land Grab**

A land grab is generally defined as the acquisition of valuable or strategic territory for much less than its actual worth.

**So what is the FBA land grab?**

Amazon sellers are actively seeking out and targeting items that Amazon does not offer directly and where there are no competing FBA offers. They know that they will be able to capture sales easily and often at a higher price than the current competition. They can reach sellers whose needs are currently not met by the current list of third party sellers. Customers like Amazon Prime members, and customers who are looking for items to qualify for Free Super Saver Shipping on orders over $25. Also, customers who just don't trust third party sellers yet and prefer to have Amazon's customer service and A-to-Z Guarantee backing their purchases.

These sellers know that there is a group of Amazon buyers who are not always interested in the lowest price offer. They have other factors that influence their buying decision other than price. Things like shipping speed and customer service.

I heard from Amazon that over half of all Amazon customers have never purchased from a third party merchant who doesn't use FBA. Why not? There are several reasons including slower shipping times and unknown customer service. Using FBA can effectively double your customer base overnight.

Amazon customers want the safety, security, and speedy shipping that they know they will get from items processed by Amazon. They know they'll get great customer service should they need it and they are willing to pay more for that.

**But Don't All Customers Shop Based on Price? No Way.**

Will the lowest priced seller get all the sales? Nope. They'll still get some sales, but remember, price says something. There are plenty of people who simply will not buy from the lowest priced seller for the sole reason that they are the lowest price. Someone has to be the lowest priced brain surgeon, and they'll get some customers, but do you think everyone is choosing their brain surgeon based on price? Not a chance, and it's the same way with every transaction on Amazon. The low price sellers will get some sales and that's OK. It's not about volume; it's about margin (whole chapter on margin later). The FBA seller won't get all the sales either, but their sales will be more profitable and allow them to stop playing the losing game of 'Let's Lower Price To See Who Can Make The Least Amount Of Money'.

FBA sellers are able to cater to these specific smart and savvy customers who know what they want and are willing to pay for it. It's about working smart, not hard.

That's a lot of information about Why FBA Works for Amazon sellers, but while this is a book for sellers, it is important to consider why FBA works for the Amazon buyer as well.

## FBA for Buyers

FBA for buyers works very well. Amazon buyers, especially Amazon Prime members, get very used to free 2-Day Air shipping on every item that they order from Amazon, including even small, inexpensive items. Until FBA came along, buyers who wanted to take advantage of the Amazon Prime shipping program were limited to only purchasing items sold by Amazon directly. If they wanted something that was not sold by Amazon but sold by a third party seller, they were at the mercy of that seller's shipping policies. This would cause some buyers to simply not purchase the item or look for other alternatives.

Now that so many more items are available through the Amazon fulfillment network from sellers utilizing the FBA program, buyers have more confidence to purchase from third party sellers. They get the depth of product selection as well as the confidence that comes from purchasing from Amazon.com. Maybe you have caught yourself looking for FBA items yourself. You find a book that you really want and you really hope that there is an FBA seller at a good price because you want your book in two days for free rather than wait on a Media Mail package to travel across the country. I know I have; I'll happily pay more for an identical item in order to get it from an FBA seller.

## FBA for Amazon

Does FBA work for Amazon? You better believe it!

FBA has been a huge success for Amazon.com. It has allowed them to greatly expand their product selection through third party sellers. At the time of this writing, third party sales were responsible for 36% of Amazon's revenue (2011). That's a big chunk! Much of this growth can be attributed to FBA. It gets the depth of selection available from third party sellers in front of Amazon's best customers who have come to trust Amazon for all of their online shopping needs. I believe FBA to still be in its infancy in terms of the scope of its use and the ways in which it can be leveraged. Game Changer is not a strong enough way to describe FBA.

## Chapter 5 – Understanding the Amazon Customer

When selling on Amazon (whether you are using FBA or not), it is vitally important to understand the Amazon customer. **This one piece of information alone will drastically increase your margins and profits**. It is the key to learning how to price your items on Amazon, and especially when using FBA. Learning to understand the Amazon Customer and knowing what factors they consider when making purchases will change the way that you see Amazon as a marketplace.

To start, remember this: Amazon is crazy about customer service! They have built their business on customer service. They have the best customer service, return policies, and consistently go above and beyond to keep the customer happy and make them customers for life. They have shipping programs that ensure that their customers get their orders quickly and if there are ever any problems, Amazon is there to keep the customer happy.

Amazon has said that almost half of their entire customer base has never bought from a third party merchant who doesn't use FBA. This should immediately show you that Amazon customers prefer to buy from Amazon and FBA sellers, and that price is not always the most important factor in making a buying decision.

Think of it this way; if you put all of Amazon's customers in one group, that group would have different sub-groups. These sub-groups have different characteristics as to what factors they consider most important when making a buying decision. For some, it's price. For others it's a good return policy. **For many, it's if the items are eligible for Free Super Saver Shipping and Amazon Prime.** These groups may not even make sense to you, but don't worry, they don't have to. You don't have to know why a buyer is willing to pay more for an identical item from Amazon or an FBA seller than from a third party merchant at a lower price. You just have to understand that a large portion of Amazon customers put a high value on Amazons' shipping speed and customer service, not price. Just don't think that they don't know what they are doing. They are likely the savviest buyers on Amazon. **They know what they want, they know when they want it, and they are willing to pay for it.** They put a value on shipping speed and will actively seek out and patronize sellers whose products are eligible for the shipping speeds and customer service that they prefer. Amazon even lets buyers sort the offers pages by sellers who use FBA.

The sub-group that you need to understand is the one that seeks out Amazon and FBA offers because they want their items fast and are willing to pay more for the Amazon-backed customer service. **These are the buyers to which you are marketing yourself (and your items).**

Here is another way to look at it. Take 100 Amazon customers. Half, 50, have never bought from a third party merchant who doesn't use FBA. So for a specific item, you could have Amazon selling at $20 and a third party merchant selling for $10 + $5 shipping, or $15. There are 50 people paying $5, or 33%, more for the same item. But are the items the same? Not at all; the physical product may be the same, but the other factors surrounding this product and sale are very different. One order ships and arrives in two days for free. The other order takes 10 days to arrive. One can be returned no questions asked. The other gives the customer a runaround on returns.

To understand this sub-group of Amazon customers, you need to fully understand Amazons' shipping programs that were discussed in the last chapter, Amazon Prime and Free Super Saver Shipping.

When you use FBA, all of your items are eligible for these same shipping promotions and Amazon customers who value the shipping speed will buy from you, even if at a higher price.

Customers do want a good price and often Amazon does have the best price. Buying from Amazon is often a no-brainer because of the best price, no tax (for most), and free shipping. As long as you don't absolutely need the item today, then it often makes more sense to buy the item from Amazon than from a local retailer. This applies to all Amazon orders that ship for free, but more so for Amazon Prime members who will get their items in just two days. Amazon customers will frequently spend more on the same item to get it from Amazon than from another online retailer, even a local store. Why? There are many reasons. You could say, "What's wrong with them? They could go buy it on eBay for less!" Maybe, but some Amazon buyers may absolutely hate eBay and refuse to even look there. They may be very busy and not have time to shop different sites and local stores just to save a few bucks. They may not live near a local store that carries what they need. They may not even have a car to go shopping! **The fact is, they know what they want, they know when they want it, and they are willing to pay for it.** What these buyers want are items that use Amazon's fulfillment network so that they get them fast.

**Examples where price is not the deciding factor**

**Deadlines**

How about birthdays, holidays, anniversaries? These are set on the calendar and if you want to order something online and get it in time, you have to plan ahead. UPS Ground and Media Mail aren't exactly the faster things around in terms of delivery times. When it's two days before Christmas and you're still shopping on Amazon, your options are limited as to which items can still be delivered on time. If you're using FBA, your items can get there in time while your competition simply cannot deliver (at any price).

Or think of it this way; you're going on a cruise in two days and you want to take a specific book with you. That third party merchant offer simply will not arrive in time but that FBA sellers' item will. You are not upset that you had to pay more than the lowest price. You are thankful that the book was available to you at a price you were willing to pay and you're able to take it with you on the cruise!

**They just want the item fast and will pay a few bucks more to get it**

This happens all the time. It's simply a matter of 'time is money'. Most book and media sellers use USPS Media Mail for their shipments. This can take up to two weeks to arrive. Don't you think that Prime member is just going to pay more to get the same item in two days? There is a value in getting the item sooner. Will everyone pay to get it faster? No. Some will wait months to save $0.50, but those aren't the customers you're looking for. You're selling to different customers. **They know what they want, when they want it, and are willing to pay for it.**

## Chapter 6 – Economics of Supply, Demand, & Price

The only thing that sets PRICE in the reseller, or secondary market, is SUPPLY and DEMAND.

You probably remember something about supply and demand from high school economics. Personally, I find the economics of arbitrage and resale to be fascinating. There are some key points of supply, demand, and price that all resellers should know.

First thing to remember is that different buyers place a different value on the exact same item. Different buyers will place a different personal, internal value on any item that they purchase. Think of it like this: when a buyer buys an item, only they know how much they actually value that item. They value that $10 item for AT LEAST $10 (or else they would not buy it), but probably not exactly $10 (meaning that they would not buy it if priced at $10.01). They may be willing to pay up to $12, or even $20. If they had a starving baby at home and it was the last package of baby food, they may put an exceedingly high value on the product!

You don't see this personal, internal value because the prices are set at the store for all customers. They all pay the same price at retail stores even though we know that some buyers place a higher value on each and every purchase. When this is played out online where prices are set by the resellers who have a limited supply of any particular item, it becomes much more evident that some buyers are willing to pay more for a product than the Manufacturer's Suggested Retail Price (MSRP).

Second is that supply, demand, and price are always changing. Each time you look at an item, you are looking at a snapshot in time where price has been set based on supply and demand. As time goes by, the dynamics change. Demand will go up if the product gets increased advertising or demand can go down if it receives poor user reviews. Supply can go up if the manufacturer is able to make more, or supply can go down as buyers buy the items and remove sellable quantity from the marketplace. Price will change accordingly with changes in supply and demand.

I want you to consider one more dynamic at play here. In addition to price, supply, and demand, I want you to add the concept of TIME. We are dealing with the Amazon marketplace at specific moments in time. As time goes by, things will change. When resellers find a deal, and they list their inventory on Amazon.com, this increases the supply on Amazon. The overall supply does not change. That supply used to be for sale at Target and now it is for sale on Amazon.com. So now that the Amazon.com supply has increased, the Amazon.com price will decrease. As time goes by, buyers will buy items and sellers will sell items. How does this affect the overall picture? As sellers sell, their supply goes down. Depending on the product, demand may stay constant, or even increase while supply is dropping. This will of course affect price. Sellers won't have an unlimited supply of their products. As they sell out at whatever price they are charging, they will stop being competitors.

This spike in supply is local to the Amazon marketplace and it is a temporary spike. This means that the decrease in price is a temporary decrease.

I have a great example of how this played out later in this book in Chapter 26 – Online Deals. I also include details on the 'Buy & Hold' strategy that you can utilize when you see this unfold on an item that you are selling. Another strategy to consider is using Multi-Channel Fulfillment (covered in depth in Chapter 33). You can use Multi-Channel Fulfillment to fulfill orders at profitable prices from other sales channels if you find the temporarily lowered Amazon.com price to not be at a profitable level.

## Price Gouging

If you do this long enough, you may run into someone who thinks that resellers are price-gouging consumers and that items should never be sold for more than their original listed price or MSRP. I find this idea to be preposterous. As mentioned earlier in this chapter, price is set by supply and demand, nothing more. This is a free market where buyers and sellers are free to make transactions if both parties agree to the terms. This is how each and every transaction occurs every day. When someone buys a product, they are saying that they value that product for more than they value that amount of cash in their pocket. The store or seller values that amount of cash in their register more than they value that product on their shelf. If neither one of these conditions are met, then the transaction would not take place. It is not as evident at retail stores where prices are fixed for all customers, but certain customers will value different items for more or less than other buyers. This applies to all products, even milk! Say milk is $3/gallon. Some people place a personal value on milk so close to the listed price that they would not buy milk if the price went up by 25 cents. Some buyers would buy milk even if it jumped to $10/gallon! Even though both buyers can buy milk for $3/gallon, one buyer places a higher personal value on the purchase. The store prices milk at the equilibrium price related to supply and demand to maximize their profits through price and quantity sold. If they raised their price to $10/gallon, they would still sell some, but they would not sell as much. So even though they have a higher price and margin per item, they lose out on so many sales that the price is not justified.

Consider when items go into short supply. How about after a hurricane when demand for generators and chainsaws spikes. Stores like Home Depot don't raise their prices, but it creates a shortage because demand outweighs the limited supply. An individual who is not bound by any agreements (the way that Home Depot is) is free to sell their spare generator on the open market for any price that they are able to get.

The generator may have been purchased for $500, but they could put it on Craigslist for $2000. Because of the high demand and low supply, price goes up. What if there had been no hurricane? Would the buyer be able to get $2000? Of course not! Any buyer could just go to Home Depot and purchase one off the shelf. It's a difference of not just price, but availability. Home Depot selling at a price of $500 on a generator is not much use if they are not in stock.

So who is the buyer who pays $2000 for a $500 generator? The buyer who places a personal value of $2000 (or more) on having a generator today rather than in a few weeks when Home Depot gets more in stock. They are paying a premium but they are able to enjoy the utility of the product during a period of time when it was not attainable at the price point of $500. This is not price gouging; this is price being set by supply and demand at any single point in time with all external factors considered. Even at a price of $2000, there may be demand at an even higher price. The seller may sell for $2000 only to get a call with an offer for $2500 or $3000.

Items go into short supply for many reasons. This happens every year with popular toys.

There was a post on an online message board by someone who thought that anyone selling toys on Amazon for more than their MSRP was price gouging. Here was my response:

We live in a world with many dynamics. If someone wants a hot, popular item (any item, not just toys) then they may have to pay a premium if they are sold out everywhere. MSRP doesn't do much good at Toys R Us if they are sold out. Their alternative? Wait until SUPPLY catches up with DEMAND and lowers PRICE.

PRICE, SUPPLY, and DEMAND are all constant at any point in time on any marketplace. They will all change over time. This is the market at work. PRICE too high? Only reasons are either high DEMAND or low SUPPLY. In this case, more SUPPLY will enter the market, and PRICE will come down. As people buy, DEMAND will go down, and so will PRICE. The people who buy when PRICE is high are the ones who value the item the most. People value identical items differently. MSRP is not the value of the item to all people. The only time a buyer buys something is because they value the item MORE than they value the money in their pocket. How much more? That varies by individual. If they did not value the item more than the money in their pocket, then they would not buy the item. This is how all buying decisions are made.

A toy at Toys R Us can be $25 but out of stock. Their price is still $25; you just can't buy it. On Amazon it may be $50, but IN STOCK. That's the difference.

You're forgetting the buyers who are THANKFUL that resellers, through Amazon or another sales channel, are able to get the items available for sale on the open market. They are happy that they are able to get what they want for a price that they are willing to pay. If they were not willing to pay it, they would not purchase the item. Some pay for convenience, some may value the item for even more than the sales price.

Think of someone who spends their time driving around town to track down a hard to find (short supply) toy and they find some. They offer them for sale online. It's the toy that I want and know it's hard to find. I would rather pay a premium for the toy and be done with the purchase and not have to drive all over town shopping (and possibly not even find the toy). Not everyone would put this value on an item, but some will. Some people put an extreme value on their time and will happily spend money in order to save their time. Again, not everyone does, but some do. It's a free market where buyers and sellers are able to make transactions when both sides believe they are attaining the greater value.

Here's an example; my favorite style of sunglasses is not made anymore.

Personally, I will pay more for this style than other people will. I found them on eBay for a fair price, but I would have paid EVEN MORE. If the price were higher, I would still have bought them. I was happy to buy them for the sellers' price. Some people would say that I got ripped off buying old model sunglasses for above MSRP. It's my choice and I am thankful that the seller still had old stock and through the Internet, we are able to make a transaction.

You know that feeling where you got a 'deal'? Where you found something that you wanted and were able to get it for a lot less than you expected to pay? The seller was happy with the price that you paid or else you would not have made a transaction. You were willing to pay more but you got a deal. It may not have been a deal to everyone (and that's OK), but it was a deal to you.

Remember the original Tickle Me Elmo (1996)? People were posting classified ads in the paper since there was no Craigslist, eBay, or Amazon marketplace. Amazon, eBay and other online sites actually bring prices down as close to equilibrium as possible based on supply and demand. The supply is constant at any point in time. Thanks to the Internet, more of that supply can be made available. SUPPLY and DEMAND are the only things that determine PRICE.

I believe most people who complain about this practice are misdirecting their own frustration at themselves for not doing it themselves and making money in the process. Where's the proof? If they really wanted to, they could buy the same hot toys and resell them at cost or MSRP to all the people that they think they are protecting. They will quickly see that the time and effort surrounding a reseller is not 'free'. They'll run into buyers who are willing to pay more, but will happily pay less. They may even sell to a reseller.

## Chapter 7 – The History of Scouting

**A brief history on mobile scouting: How did this all get started?**

When Amazon started to allow booksellers to sell their books on their site, a powerful new sales channel emerged. Anyone, anywhere could start to sell his or her books online. This was something new and powerful. You could see the price at which other sellers were selling an item for and gauge an item's value. Selling books on Amazon became popular because they were easy! They were easy to find cheap (thrift stores, book sales), easy to check (barcodes), easy to store (size), and easy to ship (Media Mail).

The first book scouters would go to book sales and grab as many books as they could that they thought would be valuable. Then go to a corner and call a friend at home and read them the ISBN or UPC. Their friend would then enter the number in Amazon.com and relay back if the book was good or not. This left the library sales with piles of discarded books in the corners of their rooms. If you have ever been to a sale where they say you have to buy 90% of what you pull, this is why. Believe it or not, I still see people doing this and I can only guess they are trying to save the monthly fee associated with a scouting service but it seems terribly inefficient to me.

Technology gradually evolved to allow sellers to come in with Internet connected laptops and use their cell phones to look up items. This was at a time where mobile data speeds were slow; no 3G or 4G back then! Looking up prices live was not efficient and the local database system was born. Companies would compile Amazon pricing data into a database that worked with a PDA and laser scanner. Local database solutions would show you the title, sales rank, and the lowest available prices for an item. You would then make the decision whether you should buy that item. It was the best solution at the time, and still is a viable solution if you often scout where there is no wireless data connection or Wi-Fi (although places like this are becoming fewer and farther between).

Local database services thrived for a few years. When FBA came along, I think they all underestimated the enormous change that was happening on the Amazon marketplace. None of these services were displaying FBA offers (or lack thereof). They were all focused on books and media items only when many FBA sellers quickly realized that they could buy and sell practically anything. The local database services simply did not meet the changing needs of Amazon sellers who were using the FBA platform.

Local database systems are limited to 2 GB of pricing data or less. FBA sellers want the entire Amazon catalog, not a small, little piece of it. And Amazon prices are changing all the time, so when local database services provide sellers downloaded data on a memory card, that data is old the instant that the data download completes. Prices and Sales Ranks change constantly. A book that was good yesterday may not be good today. A dud book yesterday may be popular today because it was mentioned on Oprah; but if you have stale data, you would never know.

I was one of those sellers. I used a local database service, but the limitations became more and more evident. The need for a live service that displayed competitive FBA offers was desperately needed and that need was met with FBAScout. Just as FBA was a Game Changer in respect to selling online, FBAScout was a Game Changer in the world of mobile scanning.

## Chapter 8 – FBAScout – Mobile Scouting App for iPhone and Android

FBAScout was originally created just for me as an Amazon seller who was scouting for inventory at retail stores (we're just super nice guys and let other people use it). When it was first developed, there was nothing available that did what I needed a scouting program to do. As an FBA seller doing Retail Arbitrage, I needed something mobile that could give me the complete competitive pricing picture for any item on Amazon. I knew there were opportunities all around me; I'd been seeing it for years in Home Depot. I wanted to go to all kinds of different stores and pick and choose the most lucrative products for resale. I needed something that does what FBAScout does.

What FBAScout does is it allows you to see the complete competitive pricing picture for any item in any category on Amazon. As an FBA seller, there is no need to limit what categories you scout in such as only books and media items (unless you just want to).

The pricing data that is displayed in FBAScout is the same pricing data that you'll use to price your items as you list in FBAPower (Chapter 9) as well as the prices that we use to reprice your inventory (Chapter 10). The prices include what we call FBA Net prices which means every price that you see in FBAScout, FBAPower, and FBARepricer is displayed as the PRICE + SHIPPING. As we discussed earlier in this book, FBA sellers price their items very differently than merchant fulfilled sellers.

FBAScout shows the actual product image from Amazon. This makes for quick and easy verification that the item that you scanned matches the pricing data that you see. You can also press the product image to go directly to the Amazon offers page to verify any details as needed. Isn't being a LIVE service cool? We think so!

We also show you the specific condition of the competitive offers so that you can compare apples to apples when making buying decisions with FBAScout, initially pricing your items in FBAPower, and repricing your items in FBARepricer.

We show you the quantity that your competitors have in stock so that you can make good decisions all around. When buying, pricing, or repricing, you want to know if your competition has a ton of inventory or just a few and may sell out, which would change the supply dynamic and lead to a higher price.

We show you the Sales Rank and Department because a book with a Sales Rank of 100K is much different than a toy with a Sales Rank of 100K. While Sales Rank won't tell you exactly how fast an item will sell or how popular an item is, it will provide an indication of whether there have been any recent sales and you can use this information when making buying decisions. There is much more information on Sales Rank later in Chapter 16.

FBAScout separates the Amazon price because Amazon cannot be treated as 'just another FBA seller'. Amazon plays by much different rules than other FBA sellers and buyers look at Amazon differently as well. If you are going to purchase an item that Amazon is selling, you need to know ahead of time so that you don't end up in a situation where Amazon forces the price down in order to get sales and leaves you in a no-win position. More on competing with Amazon can be found in Bonus #1 at the end of this book.

FBAScout is a LIVE lookup service. This means that it requires a 3G, 4G, or Wi-Fi connection. If you are getting a new phone in order to use FBAScout, you may want to consider which cell phone company in your particular area has the best service, not necessarily the best price. Saving $20/month to be with AT&T instead of Verizon won't do you any good if you have poor reception. Ask your friends for their honest opinions because the cell phone companies are just going to tell you what you want to hear. There are also sites like http://www.cellreception.com/ that can provide third party information about the service quality in your area.

There are things that can affect the performance of FBAScout since it is a live service. If you have poor reception then speeds will not be as fast. You may find that your phone works great almost everywhere, but that there are places where service is not as good. Don't worry; I have a strategy for that as well. The Toys R Us by my house gets no Sprint service and I use Sprint. Should I be worried because I'll miss out on such an easy and lucrative source of inventory? Nope, because I also have an iPad 2 on Verizon and the Verizon network works well in this store. If you have multiple devices, a good strategy is to diversify your carriers. If you have an iPhone on AT&T, consider the Verizon iPad instead of the AT&T iPad. If you have the Verizon iPad, consider an Android on Sprint.

Another thing that can slow down live lookup services is if an item has a ton of offers. Items with a large number of offers will take longer to compile the data. This is more common in the book category where items can have hundreds or even thousands of offers and getting the FBA offers becomes difficult. When you encounter items like this, remember that you do not have to wait on FBAScout to finish fetching these offers. FBAScout goes to great lengths to display the relevant pricing information such as FBA offers. When you scan an item, you will see the item details (including Sales Rank and the total number of offers) and five lowest used prices immediately. This information is often enough to determine if the item has the potential to be a winner. Items with very high numbers of offers (most often books) typically have too many FBA sellers who have driven the price down to a not-worth-your-time level. Train yourself to recognize these types of items so that you don't waste time scouting items that are not profitable. When you scan one, make the evaluation on the data you see and then decide if you want to wait or just simply scan another item to move on.

I'll admit that there are places where absolutely none of the major cell phone carriers have service AND there are no Wi-Fi connections available, AND there are deals to be found that require a scanner. But these places are few and far between (and becoming more so). I say 'deals that require a scanner' because consider this situation: say you have a Big Lots where you get no service but the other Big Lots in town does have service. You shop at that one and then you know what to buy at the other one. These absolute dead zone places would have to have products unique to that specific dead spot location. There are SO MANY places to scout that you'll only make yourself crazy if you try to have every single base covered for every square foot of retail space in your geographical area.

Another place where FBAScout does not work is on the moon. ☺

If you are buying new hardware to use FBAScout, I highly recommend getting GOOD hardware. There are inexpensive alternatives to everything in life, but there are always reasons that things are inexpensive. Good hardware will pay for itself very quickly and many times over. The iPhone is great because it is high quality and it is consistent, meaning there aren't hundreds of different models of iPhones with varying quality of components.

When it comes to Android, there are literally hundreds of phones to choose from. Each carrier will have a selection of low-end, mid-range, and high-end phones that run Android. High-end Android devices may have 4G data, large, high-resolution (easy to read) screens, and quality camera components. Lower priced Android phones will likely have smaller, lower resolution screens, poorer build quality, and lower quality cameras. Some Android phones will be all touchscreen for data entry and some will have physical keyboards. This comes down to user preference.

When it comes down to iPhone versus Android, it's strictly a user's preference. If you are on a cell carrier that offers both, then my advice would be to go to a store, try them both, and buy the one that you prefer. They are both great devices and the functionality of FBAScout will be the same on both.

We were flattered that we had multiple iPhone users actually drop their iPhones and buy Android phones just to use FBAScout. It's a testament to the power that FBAScout yields in your pocket. Most iPhone users would not be willing to part from their iPhones for anything.

FBAScout for iPhone and Android offer near identical functionality in terms of pricing data displayed. There are some subtle differences that will be explained below.

**FBAScout for iPhone**

To get FBAScout on your iPhone, go to the Apple App Store and search for FBAScout. It can be downloaded to iPhone, iPad, and iPod Touch. It is free to install and will come with 250 free scans. After the free trial scans, FBAScout requires a subscription. Signup details can be found at http://www.scanpower.com

We recommend the iPhone 3GS, iPhone 4, or newer models for Bluetooth scanner compatibility. You don't need a Bluetooth scanner to start as you can use the iPhone's camera to capture barcodes using the integrated RedLaser barcode-scanning app. To use the RedLaser app, just press the little barcode icon at the top right corner of the FBAScout app. This will initiate the camera scanning function.

Here is a screenshot of FBAScout for iPhone. This is in landscape mode so that you can see the fourth column called Net Payout. In portrait mode, you swipe side to side to see the Net Payout column.

Here is a screenshot of FBAScout for iPhone & iPad (in landscape mode):

Here you see the data returned by FBAScout for the Toy Story 3 DVD.

At the top you'll see: Weight: 0.15 lbs., Sales Rank: 163, Department: DVD, AZ (Amazon price): $13.49, Offers: 183

Offers is the total number of DIFFERENT sellers who are offering this product for sale.

**Prices Displayed**

You'll see four columns. The first column is for the lowest merchant fulfilled NET prices in New condition that are color-coded in blue. The second column is the lowest merchant fulfilled NET prices in Used condition (with conditions noted) that are color-coded in red. The third column is the lowest FBA seller offers (with conditions noted) that are color-coded in green. The fourth column is the Net Payout for this item if sold for the listed FBA prices.

The FBA Net payout works like this: if you sold this item for $8.64, you would receive from Amazon in your seller account a payout of $5.88. If you sold it for $9.92, you would receive a payout of $6.97. This may not seem like a lot, but this particular example is an increase in profit of $1.09 on a $5.88 payout. This is almost a 20% higher payout. Consider all of your payouts on every item and if you were able to get 20% more. You use this information to compare to the cost of the items you are scanning to make buying decisions. This is accurate considering all Amazon fees including category specific commissions, weight based fees, and all FBA fees. Net Payout allows you to have confidence when you are buying heavier books or oversize toys.

All of these prices are FBA Net meaning price plus shipping. FBA Net prices are not just for books and media, but also for every item in every category on Amazon. These prices are accurate to the penny. They are not estimated.

You'll also see the quantity that each seller has in stock next to their price. You can use this information strategically. Maybe they have an artificially low price but they only have one in stock. You can wait for that one to sell and then sell yours at a more profitable price. If you see that a seller is pushing the price down too low and they have 500 copies of something, then it may be a good idea to stay away from this item and avoid getting into a pricing war. When you have this information, you can make better buying decisions and reduce your risk.

**Buy Button and Buy List**

FBAScout gives you the option to save, or 'Buy' the items as you scout. Simply press the Buy Button and that item will be saved to a list called your Buy List that can be reviewed, edited, and uploaded directly to your FBAPower account. Using the Buy List feature allows you to eliminate the duplicate work of scanning once at the store and then again at home when you list. Simply upload your list from your phone and it's sitting in your FBAPower account when you get home. You can even send the list ahead of time and have someone at home print the labels and have them sitting there ready for you before you even get home with your items!

To review, edit, and upload your buy list from your iPhone, simply swipe UP on the screen. When you are finished reviewing, editing, or uploading, just swipe DOWN to return to FBAScout.

The bottom row in FBAScout shows Total Bought, Low List Price, and Avg. Rank. These are the totals for the items included in your Buy List.

You can also enter ISBNs and UPCs manually by touching the data entry field at the top and using the iPhone's onscreen keyboard.

**FBAScout for Android**

To get FBAScout on your Android phone, go to the Android Market and search for FBAScout. It can be downloaded to Android phones and tablets that are running Android 2.1+. It is free to install and will come with 250 free scans. After the free trial scans, FBAScout requires a subscription. Signup details can be found at http://www.scanpower.com

FBAScout requires Android 2.1+ both for the app to work as well as for Bluetooth scanner compatibility. You don't need a Bluetooth scanner to start as you can use the phone's camera to capture barcodes using the barcode-scanning app. To use the barcode-scanning app, go back to the Android Market and search for ZXing barcode scanner and download this free app. Once installed, just press the little barcode icon at the top right corner of the FBAScout app. This will initiate the camera scanning function.

Here is a screenshot of FBAScout for Android:

You'll see very similar pricing data that was explained above in the iPhone version details (these screen shots were not taken at the same time so the overall pricing dynamics of the Toy Story 3 DVD have changed).

You'll see in the Android version of FBAScout that the Net Payout is displayed beneath the FBA Price in the FBA-Seller column.

At the top you'll see: Weight: 0.15 lbs., Sales Rank: 163, Department: DVD, AZ (Amazon price): $13.49, Offers: 154

Offers is the total number of DIFFERENT sellers who are offering this product for sale.

Prices Displayed

You'll see three columns. The first column is for the lowest merchant fulfilled Net prices in New condition that are color-coded in blue. The second column is the lowest merchant fulfilled Net prices in Used condition (with conditions noted) that are color-coded in red. The third column is the lowest FBA seller offers (with conditions noted) that are color-coded in green.

The FBA Net payout works like this: if you sold this item for $8.64, you would receive from Amazon in your seller account a payout of $5.88. If you sold it for $11.98, you would receive a payout of $8.72. This lowest price FBA seller at a price of $8.64 is selling at a price that is too low. Sure, he'll get the sale, but he would also get the sale just as fast at $11.98. By being aggressive, or just by simply not pricing smart, they are taking a payout of $5.88 when they would receive a payout of $8.72. A difference of $2.84 may not seem like much, but that's an increase in payout of almost 50% on $5.88. Now imagine increasing every payout on every item 50%. You use this information to compare to the cost of the items you are scanning to make buying decisions. This is accurate considering all Amazon fees include category specific commissions, weight based fees, and all FBA fees. Net Payout allows you to have confidence when you are buying heavier books or oversize toys.

All of these prices are FBA Net meaning price plus shipping. FBA Net prices are not just for books and media, but also for every item in every category on Amazon. These prices are accurate to the penny. They are not estimated.

You'll also see the quantity that each seller has in stock next to their price. You can use this information strategically. Maybe they have an artificially low price but they only have one in stock. You can wait for that one to sell and then sell yours at a more profitable price. If you see that a seller is pushing the price down too low and they have 500 copies of something, then it may be a good idea to stay away from this item and avoid getting into a pricing war. When you have this information, you can make better buying decisions and reduce your risk.

**Buy Button and Buy List**

Just like on the iPhone version, FBAScout gives you the option to save, or 'Buy' the items as you scout. Simply press the Buy Button and that item will be saved to a list called your Buy List that can be reviewed, edited, and uploaded directly to FBAPower. Using the Buy List feature allows you to eliminate the duplicate work of scanning once at the store and then again at home when you list. Simply upload your list from your phone and it's sitting in your FBAPower account when you get home. You can even send the list ahead of time and have someone at home print the labels and have them sitting there ready for you before you even get home with your items!

To review and edit your buy list from your Android device, simply press the MENU button, then press Switch View. When you are finished reviewing and editing, press the MENU button again and press Switch View again.

The bottom row in FBAScout shows Total Bought, Low List Price, and Avg. Rank. These are the total for the items included in your Buy List.

You can also enter ISBNs and UPCs manually by touching the data entry field at the top and using the phone's onscreen keyboard.

## FBAScout for iPad

FBAScout for iPad is an interesting option. You would need a 3G iPad in order to use FBAScout out in the stores. The size does make it more difficult to carry, but other than the upfront cost of the device, it is actually a fairly inexpensive way to use FBAScout. AT&T and Verizon offer inexpensive month-to-month data plans so you can start using FBAScout in the stores without having to sign any type of long-term contract.

Some people actually prefer the iPad because of the larger screen size.

## FBAScout Summary

The pricing data shown in FBAScout is powerful stuff. When you have the most powerful information, you can make better and more informed buying decisions. When you make better buying decisions, you lower your risk. The data provided in FBAScout allows you to lower your risk to practically zero. Feature for feature, there is nothing else like it.

**Recommended Hardware – Scanfob™ 2002 Bluetooth Scanner**

(Scanfob™ is a registered trademark of Serialio.com)

By far the best way to enter data is by using a Bluetooth scanner, both for speed and accuracy.

We recommend the Scanfob™ 2002 scanner. It is small, light, and works with both Android and iPhone operating systems. To use the Scanfob™ 2002 with your Android device, you need to have Android 2.1 or higher. To use the Scanfob™ 2002 on iPhone, you need the iPhone 3GS, or iPhone 4. It also works with iPad and iPad 2 and will surely work with any subsequently newer iPhones and iPads.

Designed for mobility, this pocket memory scanner makes barcode data collection simple for anyone. It can be worn around the neck as a lanyard making data collection fast with the Scanfob™ 2002's 100/scan per second laser.

Only 1.26 x 2.44 x 0.63 inches and weighs just 1 ounce!

The Scanfob™ 2002 is a data entry device. What it does is reads barcodes and transmits the data to your FBAScout app. It does this wirelessly through technology called Bluetooth. This means that there are no wires connecting the Scanfob™ 2002 to your device. It's pretty fancy.

As mentioned earlier, you can get started using the camera function on your iPhone or Android device to captures barcodes. This allows you to start scouting right away without having to purchase any extra equipment. You will find that the Scanfob™ 2002 will pay for itself very quickly in terms of efficiency. Using the camera to scan requires you to press the barcode button, enter the scanner app, hold the phone over the barcode, wait for it to focus, then process the image and send that information back to the FBAScout app. Not hard, but it can be time consuming. When using the Scanfob™ 2002, you just point it at a barcode and press a button. The laser scanner instantly reads the UPC and sends the data to FBAScout. You don't have to touch the screen or leave the FBAScout app the way that you do when you use the camera to scan.

Think about books on a shelf where you can just stick your hand in with your Scanfob™ 2002 and scan each barcode compared to pulling out each book and focusing the camera on every item. Or when you want to scan toys that may be up in the overhead shelves at a retail store. Odds are, if you can see the barcodes, you can shoot them with the Scanfob™ 2002 laser scanner. You can get pricing information for items without even having to touch them, pick them up, or bring them down.

**Multiple Item Search Results**

Not all items on Amazon are a one-to-one match to a UPC. Some UPCs are tied to several Amazon product pages. This is vital information when you are out scouting because if you are looking at pricing data for an item that is completely different from what you are holding in your hand, you will make poor buying decisions and waste your time and money. Worst-case scenario would be that this carries over to your listing of the item and you send the wrong product to Amazon.

If you scan an item that has multiple search results on Amazon, you'll see something like this:

The first screen shows you the potential matches with the product images. You can use this information to make the match to the product in your hand. Press the matching image and FBAScout will return the pricing data specific to that item.

Without seeing the product image, there would be no way to tell the difference. The titles are not specific enough to the items to make good buying decisions. It all comes back to having the BEST data with which to make the BEST buying decisions and lower your risk. Without this feature, you would be crossing your fingers with every purchase. You'd hope that when you got all of your items home that they actually matched the Amazon product pages and that you didn't just waste an entire day out scouting for nothing.

Here is another example where you can see that one UPC has been tied to a series of similar items, differentiated only by color. One color may be a winner while another color may be a dud. Without this data, you would either make a buying mistake or you would miss a deal.

Without this feature, you are left at the mercy of the first search result, which in these cases would be completely different items.

You'll see this feature in FBAPower as well when you are listing items.

## Multiple FBAScout Accounts

FBAScout is designed for one subscription per device. You may find that you want to add a second FBAScout account for a friend or spouse to scout with you. We have a discounted plan of only $20/month for each additional FBAScout account. Email us for a special link to add this to your account.

## FBAScout Registration and Settings

After your free trial period of 250 free scans, FBAScout does need to be registered. Once you sign up at http://www.scanpower.com you will have an email and password. These need to be entered in the FBAScout app settings. The FBAScout settings page is also where you can change the settings of FBAScout. These settings include Show FBA Prices and Show Quantity. Both of these should be turned ON unless you have a specific reason to turn them OFF. You will get the most complete data when they are turned ON.

## Registration for iPhone

Go to the iPhone home screen by pressing the home button. Open the iPhone settings (icon looks like gears). Scroll down until you find the FBAScout app settings. Under Username, enter your email address that you used when you signed up as well as your password. This will identify your FBAScout app to us and unlock unlimited use of FBAScout.

## Registration for Android

Open the FBAScout app and press the MENU button on your phone. Then press SETTINGS. You'll see a screen that looks like this. Under Username, enter your email address that you used when you signed up as well as your password. This will identify your FBAScout app to us and unlock unlimited use of FBAScout.

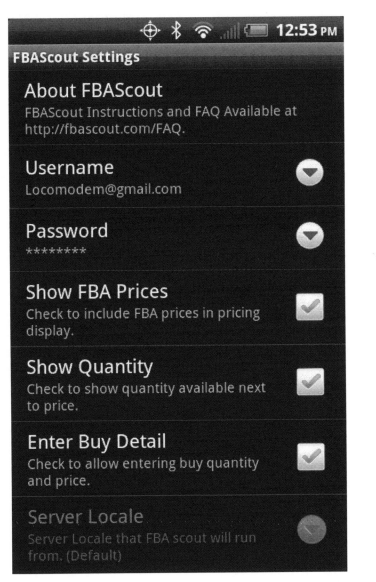

## Things to Watch for in FBAScout

Some items on Amazon will match a UPC but that UPC in your hand is for a single unit while the Amazon product page is for a case-pack or some kind of multi-pack. This is more common in categories like Health & Personal Care (formerly Health & Beauty Accessories) and Grocery & Gourmet Food. If you find an item that looks like a sure-fire winner, do your due diligence and double check the Amazon product page if the item is in one of these two categories. You can do this quickly and easily by pressing the product image in FBAScout to go to the Amazon product page in your phone's mobile browser.

## Catalog Errors and Trigger Systems

FBAScout takes a UPC and returns the data provided by Amazon matching that UPC. With a catalog as large as Amazon's, there are bound to be errors. This is why it is important to always look at the data and look at the product image for verification.

This leads to the question that we get now and again about if we include any kind of audio trigger system so that FBAScout can alert users as to what to buy. The answer is no; FBAScout does not have an audio trigger system. The reason why is because without knowing the cost of the product that you are scanning, a trigger system wouldn't do you any good. Two people could scan the same item but it's full price at one store and clearanced at another. It's a good buy for one, but not the other. FBAScout can't tell this apart. Also, with the errors in the Amazon catalog, if you only rely on data points to make buying decisions, then you will not only get home with junk, you'll also pass over good stuff.

Trigger systems became popular on local database services that were originally designed for only book and media sellers (local database service covered at the end of this book in Bonus #12). A trigger system made more sense then because you could assume a per item cost of about $1 at library sales, book sales, and thrift stores. Even though this was possible, I still would not recommend a trigger system at a book sale because of the catalog errors. Looking at the data is really not that hard, even in a competitive scanning environment like library sales and book sales.

It is very important to learn to read the data and not rely on a device to tell you what to buy and what not to buy. Having access to Sales Rank is great, but it may not always be available from Amazon.

Think of it this way, if you were buying books and you set a trigger system of $10 and 500K Sales Rank, you would miss books priced at $9.50 and ranked at 20K. You'd also miss $100 books with a Sales Rank of 600K. No way I am leaving that much money on the table when all it takes is a quick glance at the screen to verify the item and check prices. Even if you are just starting out, you'll find that you'll get very quick at reading the data and making buying decisions.

PHEW! Explaining FBAScout and the WHY behind every feature was a lot of info!

So, to pick up where we left off in the previous chapter, why do existing scouting services fall short? They simply don't address the needs of the FBA seller, nor do they provide information on competitive FBA offers. Without this information, buyers are in the dark. Sure, they have a little light, a guide of sorts. But why have a candle when you can have a spotlight? Whether you use FBA or not, you have to know your FBA competition. If you just have the lowest Used offers, then you will end up buying items that you thought were profitable only to get home and find out that there are multiple FBA sellers selling at a price that you can not compete with.

As sellers start to use FBA, they soon realize that there is no reason to limit themselves to just books. Sure, books are easy and fun, but they may not provide the highest return on your investment or on your time.

# WEBSCOUT

| 9781565847033 | Show FBA Prices ☑ | Show Quantity Available ☑ |

UNDERSTANDING POWER
THE INDISPENSABLE CHOMSKY

Understanding Power: The Indispensable Chomsky

Weight: 1.20 lbs                          AZ: $15.22

Rank: 49908                              Offers: 178

Dept: Book

| NEW | USED | FBA Seller |
|---|---|---|
| 12.94 (1N) | 6.99 (1A) | $10.65 (1VG) |
| 12.98 (1N) | 6.99 (1A) | $12.25 (1G) |
| 13.57 (1N) | 6.99 (1G) | $12.88 (1VG) |
| 13.57 (1N) | 6.99 (1G) | $13.90 (1N) |
| 13.99 (1N) | 6.83 (1G) | $19.99 (1VG) |
| 39 Offers | 139 Offers | 5 Offers |

We also have a web-based version of FBAScout called WebScout. WebScout will show the same data as FBAScout but is designed to run in a browser window. You can use it on your PC or Mac to evaluate or sort products at your home or business. You can also use it in a mobile browser. This is an option for users who do not have an iPhone or Android device and still want to get started with Retail Arbitrage.

Since WebScout is browser based and is not a dedicated app, it will not perform as fast as the FBAScout app. For fastest scanning, a dedicated app on an iPhone or Android device is recommended.

If you are currently in a cell phone contract and you think that you cannot get a new phone for a couple of years, remember that there is nothing stopping you from purchasing a new phone at any time. Your cell phone company won't give you a new phone for free or at a substantial discount for two years, but you are still free to upgrade at any time. You just have to purchase your own phone. The contract is only because they heavily subsidized the current phone that they gave you when you signed the contract. You can buy a phone new at the store or from eBay as well. Waiting two years to get into this business will cost you many times more money in lost opportunities than the cost of a new phone.

If you are serious about running a Retail Arbitrage business, then the right phone will pay for itself very quickly.

## Chapter 9 – FBAPower – To List, Label, Price, and Ship

FBAPower was the first program developed specifically for efficient FBA listing. It is designed so that you touch the products that you list only one time. The old process was at least twice; once to list, then again to label. Then sometimes a third time to pack into boxes. Touching items once makes your workflow efficient.

FBAPower is a web-based program that runs on PC or Mac. We do recommend Firefox. Because FBAPower is web-based, it means that there is nothing to install or maintain. You can log into your account from anywhere.

The program is dynamic and can be used in many different ways, but the general workflow is to scan an item into FBAPower, assign condition, choose a price, add any specific description notes, change quantity if sending in multiples, and then print the FBA labels. FBA labels print on a label printer such as a Dymo or Zebra printer. Labels for these printers can be purchased online very inexpensively.

The advantage of FBAPower is not just the improved listing workflow, but also in the ability to price your FBA items properly. The pricing data that you see in FBAPower includes the Amazon price (if sold by Amazon), the five lowest New prices, the five lowest Used prices (with conditions noted), and the five lowest FBA prices (with conditions noted). All prices are color-coded and all merchant fulfilled items are displayed as the FBA net price meaning the price plus shipping for every item in every category on Amazon. FBAPower is designed specifically for FBA sellers and the FBA net price is the price that FBA sellers are competing against. This FBA net price is accurate for all items in all categories, including categories where merchants define their own shipping prices.

When you see the pricing popup in FBAPower, you can click any price to match that price. This makes it very quick and easy to match a price as an FBA seller and not start a pricing war by undercutting. You also don't have to do any type of calculations in your head. Remember, matching the FBA net price of a merchant fulfilled seller will still put you as the overall lowest price because FBA is the tiebreaker.

**Importance of Pricing Data**

It is so important to have the complete pricing picture for an item. This is why we show you so much pricing information for each and every item that you list. How many times have you seen an item that sells for $58 Used, $34, New, and $17 from Amazon? What are these sellers thinking? The fact is that they aren't thinking; they are using a poorly designed listing or repricing service that lists or reprices Used items against Used prices only. They ignore the Amazon price entirely and simply don't check to see if it's even priced competitively against offers in New condition or against Amazon. If you price your items using poor data that only shows you the lowest Used offers, then you will not price yourself competitively.

## Instant and Individual FBA Label Printing

Printing your FBA labels instantly and individually is another huge advantage of FBAPower. If you have ever listed a large number of items only to have to print labels in bulk and go back to label all of your items, you'll greatly appreciate seeing that little FBA label print out one at a time as you list.

## Multiple Item Search Results

The Amazon catalog is not perfect and sometimes you'll enter an item by UPC and find out that there are multiple matches on Amazon for that UPC. In cases like this, FBAPower will show you all matches so that you can accurately list on the correct product page. Many listing programs do not catch items like this and you can end up listing on the first Amazon search result that may not be the correct product page. It may be for a similar item, just a different color, or it may be for an entirely different product. FBAPower prevents you from making these mistakes.

## Multiple User Support

Multiple users can log into FBAPower at the same time and submit items to the same Amazon seller account. When doing this we recommend that they use different batch names and MSKU systems to prevent SKU duplication.

## Automatic Shipment Creation

Once you have entered all of your items into FBAPower and you are ready to send the batches to your Shipping Queue in your Amazon seller account, FBAPower will automatically divide your shipment into the correct fulfillment centers.

## Fulfillment Center Identification

Fulfillment centers are identified as you process items so that you can divide your items as you go. By seeing where different items are going to different fulfillment centers while you list instead of at the end of your listing process, you'll pack your shipment properly the first time and avoid fishing items out of the bottoms of boxes.

## FBAPower Workflow

FBAPower is the most efficient and professional way to sell on Amazon using FBA. However, you can sell on Amazon and use FBA without FBAPower and Amazon has an entire team setup to help you get started.

http://www.amazonservices.com/content/sellers-contact-amazon.htm/

Fill out the form and select that you are interested in Fulfillment by Amazon, already sell on Amazon, and want help with starting FBA. It will go straight to the FBA Launch Specialist Team.

This is how FBAPower works: when you send products to FBA, you are creating batches, or shipments. FBAPower helps you build these shipments efficiently. Creating a shipment consists of adding items to the shipment. Typically a user will enter items into FBAPower using a USB scanner. They then choose the condition of the item, set the price, and print the FBA label. They then put the item in a box for shipping. They repeat these steps for each item that they are adding to the box. Once all of the items have been entered, you have to send this shipment to your Shipping Queue in your Amazon seller account. You do this by clicking the Ship button in FBAPower. You'll see a Shipment Preview screen that will show you the breakdown of your items if they are going to multiple fulfillment centers. You can ship each batch one at a time and give each batch a custom name to help you stay organized. This concludes the FBAPower portion of the process.

You'll then log in to your Amazon seller account and navigate your way to your Amazon Shipping Queue. This is where you complete your FBA shipments by entering the number of boxes in the shipment, print the packing slips, enter the specific box weights, and then print UPS shipping labels.

You'll likely be printing your UPS labels on a regular inkjet or laser printer. You can print on plain paper and tape the UPS label to the box, but the easiest, most efficient way would be to order UPS label paper from UPS.com. These labels are free and you can order on their website or just call 1-800-PICK-UPS and ask for UPS WorldShip Peel and Stick Label - 2 per page. The item number is 01774501. You may have to open a free UPS account to place an order.

You can also print your UPS labels on a UPS Zebra label printer on 4"x6" UPS labels. These are also free from UPS and they are called Direct Thermal Label - 4" x 6.25" Rolls. The item number is 01774006. Your Zebra printer may require some configuration to print the labels properly.

One note about packing slips: they are the same for every box. When you send items to FBA, there is not a limit of one box per shipment. When you list products and you fill your first box, just keep on listing and fill up your next box. The contents of each box do not need to match the packing slips; the packing slips are only related to the shipment as a whole. You will get better inbound shipping rates on a per pound basis on larger shipments. While these savings do add up, don't go crazy trying to make super-huge shipments just to save a few dollars. The best strategy is to work with manageable shipments and get your inventory to Amazon as fast as possible so that it can start selling. If it's still sitting in boxes at your house, then your items will not be selling. As time passes, you run the risk of changes in supply and demand, lost sales, and price erosion.

Because FBAPower prints labels individually and instantly, you do need a label printer. We recommend the Dymo 450 and 30252 address labels because of low price and known compatibility. Most of your local office supply stores will carry this printer and you can also purchase it from Amazon.com. Zebra printers also work with 3"x1" labels. Inexpensive generic labels can be found online for both printers.

We also recommend a USB scanner. We use Symbol LS2208 USB scanners but there are also other inexpensive scanners available. The USB scanner serves as a data entry device and will drastically speed up your listing by allowing you to simply pull the trigger to enter a barcode instead of having to enter UPCs manually. Some USB scanners come with an 'always-on' stand so that you don't even have to pull the trigger. You only have to pass the item underneath the scanner.

You may be listing items by UPC and find no match in the Amazon catalog. This happens sometimes and just because a UPC doesn't bring back a match on Amazon, it doesn't necessarily mean that the product does not already have a product page on Amazon. Go to Amazon.com and do a title search for the product that you are trying to list. If you can find the Amazon product page, then you can list the item through FBAPower. Just scroll down to the Product Details and find the ASIN number. Copy and paste this number into FBAPower to list on that specific product page.

## Replenishment

There are two ways to list through FBAPower. The program can create a new SKU for each and every item that you list. This is more common for book and media sellers who have mostly items with only one quantity of inventory. This is not a good system for toy sellers who may be sending in more quantity of an existing item that they have sold previously. FBAPower gives you the option to have Replenishment turned ON or OFF on your account. When replenishment is ON and you enter an item that you have previously listed through FBAPower, the previously used SKU will return. Sending additional inventory to that particular SKU will simply add the quantity that you enter in FBAPower to any existing inventory that you have at FBA. If you have eight of an item at FBA already and you prepare a replenishment order with a quantity of ten, then you will end up with eighteen units for sale at FBA.

## Labeling your Items – Packaging & Presentation

I want to add something here about exactly how to label and prepare your items for shipment to an FBA warehouse. In Chapter 15, we'll talk about the Rules of Amazon and how, if you want to have a long, successful tenure as a seller on Amazon, you should read all of the rules and ask for clarification on anything that you do not understand. This applies double for the specific categories in which you sell. Different items require different methods to prepare for shipment to an FBA warehouse.

For example, you cannot have exposed fabric. This can happen with not just clothing, but also toys where the box has a cutaway and you can feel and touch a stuffed animal. Items like this need to be bagged or boxed. If bagged, the bags need to have child suffocation warning labels. Amazon will keep track of you if you repeatedly send in items improperly.

When it comes to preparing your items, I strongly recommend that you look at your items and think like a buyer. How will this item appear when it reaches its final destination? Keep in mind that it will be being shipped to an Amazon warehouse where it will be processed in a warehouse environment before being shipped again to the buyer. Is it the type of item that benefits from a nice presentation? It is a collectible type of item where the condition of the packaging affects the value to the collector? Think about carded action figures. Sure, some buyers want them to open and play with, but some want them in original, pristine condition for collectible purposes. A bent corner or a dinged up bubble will affect the value to the buyer and lead to possible returns and negative feedback. For items like this, I recommend boxing them up individually and putting the FBA label on the outside. Then tape over the FBA label to be sure that it has no chance of falling off while going through the FBA process. We buy boxes from http://www.uline.com as they have nearly ever size box imaginable. This way you can get boxes that match the size of your items nearly exactly and reduce or even eliminate the need for additional packing materials. This will add to your total item cost, so factor this additional cost into your business model. Compare it to not just the margin on the specific item, but to the cost of processing returns for damaged items that you could have prevented with better item protection.

'Thinking like a buyer' applies to placement of FBA labels as well. On some items, sellers do not care about the FBA label like on commodity-type books. If it is a collectible book where the seller would want to remove any extra labels, then placing an FBA label on the book directly may not be a good idea. You can shrink-wrap your books or wrap them in bubble wrap. Then put the FBA label on the outside of that extra wrapping and cover it with tape to be sure that it stays in place.

Taking this extra care in the preparation of your FBA inventory can also be used to market yourself as a seller. If you sell action figures and you individually box every one of them, you can mention this right at the beginning of your item's description.

"Each action figure is individually boxed to protect your item through the shipping process. We know the condition of your items is important to you and we strive for 100% satisfied customers."

This can be the difference between you getting the sale (and possibly leading to repeat sales) over your competition.

When you are able to exceed your buyer's expectations, you will be a successful Amazon seller.

**Workflow Demonstration Videos**

We have lots of videos showing the workflow, speed, and of FBAPower available on our website.

http://www.scanpower.com

## Chapter 10 – FBARepricer – To Keep Items Priced Competitively

You may have read about Repricers and think that if other sellers are using them that you must need one as well. This is not always the case. Most sellers only need a repricer when their inventory reaches a level that makes it difficult to manage pricing manually. An intelligent repricing program can save a seller tons of time and that is where their value comes from. The value also comes from pricing at levels that maintain margins and not always being the lowest price. Identical items sell at different prices all the time on Amazon, especially when there are merchant fulfilled and FBA offers for the same item. A smart repricer will allow you to be the one selling at the higher prices (and higher margins) while your competition sells at the lower prices (and lower margins). Over time, you can imagine how this pricing will affect the bottom lines of each business.

As an FBA seller, you need to know competitive FBA offers in order to properly reprice your FBA items. FBARepricer provides live, competitive data for all offers, including FBA (and knows if there are no other FBA offers as well). This information allows you to price your items properly to maximize margin and profits.

FBARepricer also calculates prices based on the FBA Net price (price + shipping). FBA Net prices are shown for items in all Amazon categories.

Repricers should be used with a strategy in mind. Do you want to be the lowest price? Do you want to be the lowest FBA price but the fifth highest price? Do you compete with Amazon as a seller or not? There are many things to consider when both initially pricing your items as well as how you want to price them moving forward as the marketplace dynamics change over time. Maybe new sellers will enter the market that were able to acquire the product for a very low price who are forcing the Amazon market price downward. Maybe they only have thirty in stock and you'd rather wait for them to sell out, expecting price to come back up. Maybe they have 600 in stock and the price drop may be more long term.

Repricing services have been around for a while but there has never been anything like FBARepricer. While most repricing services are designed to focus on price, FBARepricer was designed from the ground up specifically for FBA sellers in order to leverage FBA status and maximize margins. When you compete on price alone, you can get into a downward spiral that can make profitable items not profitable anymore. It seems sellers compete to see who can make the LEAST amount of money. This does not sound like a fun game to play if you ask me and I don't recommend that you play it either.

As an FBA seller you have many more ways to differentiate yourself as a seller other than on price. FBARepricer allows you to leverage these things in order to protect your margins. Many times FBARepricer will want to RAISE your price due to the specific market dynamics in place at any specific time on your items. Many repricing programs are all about only lowering price.

## Leverage FBA Status

In Chapter 2 we talked about how FBA sellers are able to differentiate themselves from other sellers on the Amazon marketplace, especially sellers who still fulfill their own orders. When setting your price for your items, it is important to consider all related factors such as your FBA competition (or lack thereof). If you are the only FBA seller for an item, you would want to price very differently than if you had multiple FBA sellers as competition.

## Maximize Margins

Now that you know that you can command a higher price for your items as an FBA seller, the question can then become just how much higher can you go? That is a good question and it's one of the few that I don't have a perfect answer for. On a percentage-of-price basis, can you get a price that is 10% higher than your closest competitor? 20%? Sometimes you can get 100%.

I know several sellers who will price 'penny books' (books that sell for $0.01 from merchant fulfilled sellers) at $9.95 if they are the only FBA sellers. This is a combination of both of these strategies. You are leveraging your status as the only FBA seller for the item and you are waiting for a buyer who wants the item fast. The increase in margins when you compare a merchant fulfilled 'penny book' to a $9.95 FBA book are incredible. If you find it hard to believe that some buyers are willing to pay this much more for an FBA item, you'll just have to try it for yourself.

Like we discussed earlier, buyers and sellers enter into transactions when each side places a higher value on the counterpart of the transaction. The buyer buys that book for $9.95 so you know that they valued it at a price of AT LEAST $9.95. Did they place a value of EXACTLY $9.95 on the item? Not likely. Would they purchase at $10.95? Maybe. $11.95? Possibly. $19.95? Eh, maybe not. How far can you go? You'll never know for sure. If you can figure out a way to sell items to each individual buyer at the exact maximum personal perceived value, I'd love to hear about it and I would applaud you for your success. Until that happens, sellers should set prices that are strategic businesswise as well as prices at which they are happy to sell.

Here is an example of an item that I purchased from an FBA seller at a $10 premium. It was a karaoke game for XBOX 360. My wife's sisters were coming into town and I wanted this game for the weekend. It was Thursday and I wanted it delivered on Friday. It was $40 from an FBA seller or $30 from merchant fulfilled seller. I was happy to pay the additional $10 and get the item delivered in time so that it could be used that weekend. Would I have paid $20 more? Maybe. $30 more? Probably not. There is a limit as to how much of a premium you can charge, but this is not an atypical transaction. This happens all day every day on Amazon.com.

My personal strategy is to be the lowest FBA price (assuming no FBA sellers selling at an artificially low price) and the fifth highest price overall. This way I still get great exposure on the first page of offers and my price (and margins) are significantly higher than my competitors. I may not get the next sale, but I'll still get the sale, and when I get the sale, the transaction will be more profitable.

# Retail Arbitrage

Want to see what happens when you use a repricer that is poorly designed?

## Chapter 11 – An Emerging Business Model

This all represents an emerging business model that has developed recently and it is the most powerful, profitable, low-risk, and completely scalable business model that may have ever existed. Running an FBA business using the strategies in this book for Retail Arbitrage is like nothing that has ever existed before. Without services like FBA to outsource the storage, picking, packing, shipping, and customer service, resellers will quickly run into the physical limitations of the real world that will basically put a cap on how large their business can grow. Without mobile pricing tools like FBAScout to source products and make increasingly risk-free buying decisions, resellers would have to rely on inferior methods for making buying decisions, which would lead to higher risks.

It is only very recently that all of the tools have been put in place to really create this new, emerging business model. It is truly an exciting time to be selling online. I've been selling online since 1999 and I've packed over 100 boxes a day, every day, day after day. That business model was profitable, but it's not ideal and it's not scalable. FBA opens the doors to anyone who wants to take advantage of the Retail Arbitrage opportunities all around them. They can start small and grow as big as they want to get. Don't underestimate how powerful the scalability factor of FBA is. It allows the little guy to start and compete with established sellers on day one and gives them the tools to grow as big as they want as fast as they want.

While FBAScout shows you the complete, current pricing picture for any item on Amazon, it is ultimately up to the user to make buying decisions. A good rule of thumb for doubling your money (100% margin) is the 1/3 – 1/3 – 1/3 rule if scouting for items to sell using FBA. Try to find items that are selling online for three times your cost. If you find a $10 item, you want it to be selling for $30. As rough estimates, you can consider your product cost to be $10, Amazon with all FBA fees will get $10, and your profit will be $10. Use this as a safety guide if you are just starting out. You can also use the FBA Calculator to familiarize yourself with the Amazon fees:

https://sellercentral.amazon.com/gp/fbacalc/fba-calculator.html

Naturally, I encourage all resellers to shoot for the highest profit margins that they can find. Some sellers will be comfortable with margins under 100%. Even an item on which you are making 50% return on your money is a lot better than what you're getting at the bank.

**Efficiency Is The Key**

The key to this business model is efficiency. The technology and tools at the reseller's disposal are incredibly powerful. These tools didn't even exist just a few years ago. These tools allow anyone to make low-risk buying decisions. Without using the best tools, your risks increase and your business will not be running as efficiently as it could be.

Consider these two scenarios. One reseller drives to a store and writes down hundreds of UPCs and product descriptions by hand. Then they drive home and enter them one by one into Amazon.com. They go to many different pages of offers to see the complete competitive pricing picture for the item. They make notes about which items to buy then they drive back to the store. They go pick up the items on their shopping list and find out that two of the best products are now sold out. They check out with their items and drive back home to list them on Amazon.com.

Compare this to driving to a store and using FBAScout on your iPhone to evaluate any product instantly with one simple screen of pricing data. You don't miss a single deal. In fact, you find so many deals that you have to put some of the good deals back so that you can fit all of the great deals in your car. You upload your Buy List from FBAScout to your FBAPower account for listing while you are still standing in line to check out. You print your labels, you pack your boxes, and you're done.

It's easy to see how FBAScout pays for itself very quickly in saved time and improved efficiency.

There are many more efficiency tricks listed in Chapter 25 – Retail Secrets, like how to tie up a whole city's worth of inventory from the comfort of your own home.

Whether you started as a bookseller or not, consider how this business model emerged from the history of scouting you read about in Chapter 7.

Say you started as a bookseller and now you've now made the switch to FBA and life is good. More time to scout and you're finding good books to sell. You meet someone new and they ask what it is that you do and you tell them that you sell online. They ask what you sell, and you tell them books.

**STOP: HERE IS THE CHANGE. HERE IS THE NEW BUSINESS MODEL.**

Stop and ask yourself, "Why am I a bookseller again?" Go back to how it all started. Books: easy to find. Books: easy to scan. Books: easy to list. Books: easy to store. Books: easy to ship. But now you use FBA so the easy to store and easy to ship don't matter. As an FBA seller, you can sell items that may not be easy to store or easy to ship.

Let's look at the others: Easy to find, scan, and list.

Books are easy to find and can be found for prices lower than the market rate. This opens the door for profit to someone who has this information. Users could quickly see that information was power. Having good data was like putting on a special pair of glasses that would make profitable books turn green and non-profitable books turn red. You had super-vision while everyone else just saw a bunch of books.

HERE COMES THE SCOUTING CHANGE: you can now put these glasses on and find green products everywhere that you go. The last piece to this puzzle, the secret weapon, is FBAScout. FBAScout is the next evolution of mobile scouting. Like FBA, it is a true game changer. All limitations of other scouting services are overcome with FBAScout. Can you still scout for books? Of course! I still do because it's fun and profitable, but why box yourself in as a bookseller when you use FBAScout and FBA? Book sales only happen so often each month and if you live in a small town, they don't happen very often at all. Thrift stores only put out so many new books each day. With FBAScout, you have pricing data for every category on Amazon, not just books, so why are you just looking for books?

When people ask me what I do, I tell them I sell online. They ask what I sell and I tell them, "Profitable items." That's really the only criteria I have anymore. Why discriminate? Find a profitable item? Send it to FBA. The categories I generally sell the most in are Books, Media, Toys, and Home Improvement (power tools). This is just because I am most familiar with these categories. If there were more hours in a day I could branch out into as many categories as time would allow.

The thing to understand here is that there is a great change that is taking place. Many booksellers are right on the verge of seeing this incredible opportunity if they can take their 'book blinders' off. If you are using a scanner and using FBA, then you already have 95% of this 'machine' in place.

**Step 1: Find profitable items**
**Step 2: Send to FBA**
**Step 3: Profit**
**Step 4: Repeat**

Stop and ask yourself: why am I just doing this with books? The only real reason is that you have limited data from a book scouting service so you can't scan toys or power tools. Once you get FBAScout, the last piece of the puzzle is in place. 'Books: Easy to find' turns into 'Profitable Items: Easy to find'.

"But I make a lot of money on books! Why would I want to learn another category?"

I'm glad you asked. ☺

Think of it this way: you have your scout, you drive to a thrift store, poke around, scan some items, and find a book that will give you $20 profit. You buy that book. ONE BOOK.

Now, in that same amount of time that it took you to go out and find one book, you could have found one product from any number of retail stores that would yield that same $20 profit. But here's the kicker: you put 16 units in your cart. 16 times more profit for the same amount of work. Live in a big city, go to another store and buy the same item again. If you sell out on Amazon, just go buy more and replenish your stock.

How is this possible? It's actually very easy; the markets are terribly inefficient! Do you think Wal-Mart always has the lowest price? Nope. How about Costco? No way items are cheaper on Amazon than from Costco, right? Wrong. The market is inefficient and it goes both ways. A $10 item on the shelf at Wal-Mart can be selling for $40 on Amazon. A $10 item on Amazon can be selling for $40 at Wal-Mart. FBAScout is like putting on special glasses when you walk into a store that tells you any pricing inefficiencies between Amazon and that store. Think of green and red dollar signs floating over each item. Some of them are bigger than others. Now go find the biggest green ones.

In addition, you'll know if an item is not on Amazon at all. The opportunities that this represents are covered in more detail in Bonus #2 at the end of this book.

On top of this, you can scout at retail stores all day and all night! Many stores open 24/7. You are not limited by thrift store hours or library sale schedules. Even if you have young kids at home all day, you can stay up late and make that extra income in the early morning hours. There is no other business in which you can set your own hours like an FBA business. You choose if you want to schedule your month around library sales, or scout at your leisure for retail products.

Here are the exact steps to take if you are brand new to buying products to sell online.

## 1. You need to find products to sell.

While you don't need a subscription scouting service like FBAScout to start, it will quickly become apparent as to how valuable they are in terms of efficiency. You could go to a store and write down UPCs by hand, then go home and look them all up and make some calculations, and then decide which items to sell online, and then go back to the store and purchase the items. Not a very efficient process, but you get the idea.

So to use FBAScout you do need an iPhone or an Android phone. All major US cell phone companies carry a wide variety of Android devices.

## When to Get The Scanfob™ 2002

You can start on the cheap by using the camera to capture barcodes using a barcode-scanning app like RedLaser on iPhone or ZXing on Android. This requires you to hold the camera above the UPC in order to capture the barcode. This isn't hard, but it is not the most efficient solution. The Scanfob™ 2002 is a data entry device and it dramatically increases the speed at which you can enter data into FBAScout. The

Scanfob™ 2002 is a Bluetooth scanner, meaning that it connects wirelessly to your phone over Bluetooth technology. Once connected, the Scanfob™ 2002 sends the UPC to your phone instantly. You can reach up high and shoot the Scanfob™ 2002 scanner at barcodes on items in the overheads and get the pricing data on your phone. Compare this to having to get the item down from the overhead and having to position your phone over the barcode for each and every item for which you are checking prices.

The right equipment will pay for itself very quickly in the time saved. When you save time in one area of your business, you have more time to spend in other areas. When you have more time, you can scan more items. Scanning more items means that you'll find more profitable items.

The Scanfob™ 2002 is about $300 and is available from http://www.serialio.com. There is a coupon code on the ScanPower.com website that gives FBAScout users a discounted price. I strongly recommend adding the Scanfob™ 2002 to your FBAScout setup.

## 2. Now that you have items to sell, you need to get them listed

This book is all about using FBA for order fulfillment on Amazon but you don't necessarily have to use FBA. Now that you have items to sell, you can list them on Amazon and ship them yourself. To sell using FBA, you follow the listing process outlined on Amazon.com. When you are ready to increase your efficiency, you can start to use FBAPower.

FBAPower is our listing program that will dramatically increase the speed at which you can list, price, and label your FBA inventory. Save time here, and you'll have more time for the other, more profitable parts of your business such as sourcing additional products.

## 3. Now that you have items listed for sale, you need to keep them priced competitively

This is where FBARepricer comes in. FBARepricer not only helps you keep your items priced competitively, it also helps you leverage your status as an FBA seller and maximize the margins on your items.

That's pretty much the evolution of scouting and how it has evolved into the current business model that it is today. It is hard to describe all of the ways that you can use FBA in your business, but throughout this book, I will do my best.

## Chapter 12 – From Toys to Toiletries

I think you are starting to get the idea here that this emerging business model is wide open. There are really no limits as to what you can sell online through FBA (some categories are restricted, so be sure to read the Amazon rules covered in Chapter 15).

You can choose to be a 100% widget seller who pays no attention to what is actually in the boxes that they sell. You can just scan to your heart's content, run the numbers, and send the profitable stuff to FBA. Or you can decide to focus on certain categories.

There are advantages and disadvantages to both types of models. When you consider yourself a widget seller, you don't really have any limits as to where you scout or what you scout for. But if you don't increase your knowledge in any specific area, then you may be leaving a lot of opportunities behind. Scouting in and learning a specific category such as the Health & Personal Care category (formerly Health and Beauty Accessories) can be very rewarding because you learn what to look for. When you have had success with a product line, you can more easily identify opportunities when you see them based on your experience. Your previous experience gives you an advantage over another seller who's only using price and margin to make buying decisions. Your experience can help you take advantage of seasonal swings in supply and demand as well as specific local retailer secrets that can give you a huge advantage.

You also learn what makes a product a good fit for FBA and in turn you are able to more quickly evaluate other potentially good items with more speed and efficiency.

Most FBA sellers will probably end up selling a blend of inventory that includes some pretty random, but profitable items alongside their staple products with which they are more familiar. Personally, I am a widget seller when it comes to books and media. When it comes to power tools and toys, I pay more attention to factors such as the brand, exclusivity, margin, competition, and other factors that affect the item's resale value.

Items can be very lucrative in the Health & Personal Care category (formerly Health & Beauty Accessories). Not only can you find items at retail stores at prices that are much lower than the Amazon.com marketplace prices, but there are also added dynamics at play in this category.

Some people fall in love with a certain brand of shampoo, their favorite eyeliner, or a specific scent of hand lotion. People who put a high personal preference on items such as these will go to greater lengths than other buyers in order to get the specific product that they want. Some will be willing to pay a little more, and some will be willing to pay A LOT MORE. This happens all the time when a manufacturer discontinues certain products that some buyers have a strong, personal connection with. If you are able to identify these types of items, you can bring this limited supply to the demand and keep the profit in between. The buyers of these types of products will thank you that they are able to acquire the limited supply from your part of the country even though they live on the other side of the country. If they didn't value the item that you're selling for your selling price, then they would not have purchased the item.

These same dynamics do exist in other categories so be on the lookout for items that have these same types of characteristics.

Another category in particular that I want to share information with you about is the Toys & Games category. This is one of the easiest and most profitable categories in which to buy and sell using FBAScout and FBA. I want to explain WHY Toys & Games is such a great category and how you can have great success in this category as well.

There are many reasons why toys are so profitable. Toys are heavily marketed to kids and popular toys can be in high demand. High demand can mean high prices, especially if supply is low. When demand outweighs supply, prices rise. They don't rise at the retail level because retail stores have agreements in place with the manufacturers. But on the secondary market, price is set by the forces of supply and demand.

Don't think that toys only sell at Christmas time. Sure, this category sees a huge boost at Christmas time, but kids have birthdays all year long. And don't think that it's only Christmas and birthdays when kids get presents. There are occasions throughout the year. These days kids even by their own toys with their own money.

Toys are also pretty universal in terms of UPCs. Amazon has sold a lot of toys over the years and will already have product pages for most every toy that you can scan. Remember, if you scan a toy and it has no match on Amazon, then you may have just found another opportunity to create a new product page and be the only seller and setting your own price.

Toys are different in the sense that the demand for them can be very specific. It's not like power tools where someone will say to their wife that they would like a new drill for Father's Day and pretty much any drill will do. There will be a demand for a Super Duper Talking Optimus Prime with Bonus Bumblebee Walkie-Talkie Playset. This is a specific demand, not a 'please buy me an Optimus Prime for my birthday' type demand.

Toys come and go at the retail level. This means that items get clearanced and prices drop. This is how you can often buy toys for well below the original MSRP. Just because the demand for these toys is not walking into your local Toys R Us, it doesn't mean that the demand is not still out there looking for these toys. Some of that demand is looking on Amazon, and you can bring that supply to the marketplace and enjoy the profit of the difference in price.

**Retail Exclusives**

Some toys are exclusive to certain retailers. This can create an online demand at a premium price over the local retail price. Why? Because some buyers do not live near each and every retailer. The only way that someone can get an exclusive item is to buy it from someone who lives near the exclusive store and is willing to offer it for sale online. Couldn't they just purchase the item from the retailer's website? Not always. Later in Chapter 21 I'll explain the difference between local retail stores and their online counterparts and why their inventories and even product selection do not always match up.

A reseller is only going to go to this trouble of buying and listing an item if they are able to turn a profit. Two examples of retailers who often have exclusive toys are Toys R Us and Target. They are easy to spot because they have big stickers on the packages that say 'Toys R Us Exclusive' or 'Only At Target'. Stores like to have exclusive products because it can be a draw to get customers into their stores for products that are not available elsewhere. They also do not have to worry about price matching other retailers because no other retailer will have the exact same product.

Consider this as well; toys are collectable. There are collectors out there that want to collect every single Lego set ever made. Maybe they are collecting every single Transformer toy ever. If they want them all and they don't live near every retailer that offers any version of an exclusive, then they will have to find and buy the items online. Like we mentioned before, price set by supply and demand. There may also be collectors who take an interest in a product line long after the toy series was actually current and available on toy shelves. If they want to collect the toys and they are not currently available at all retail stores, then they will have to buy on the secondary market.

**Getting Lucky? Or Being Smart?**

Not all Toys R Us stores are going to carry the exact same items. Some stores will turn over their inventory much faster than other stores and some will be very slow moving. A toy may become popular and sell out at most stores but you can get lucky and find them still sitting at some stores. This may be because it's a store that people normally do not associate with toys. I bought Nintendo Wii controllers from Sears the year that the Wii was released. Everything Wii was sold out everywhere, or so people thought. Where do you go to buy video games? Toys R Us? Target? Wal-Mart? Best Buy? Sure, but Sears? It was not the first place that people think of so people didn't go there. I did and sold a ton of $40 Nintendo Wii controllers for over $100. ☺

Because some stores don't sell the same items at the same rates as other stores, some stores will have products still on the shelves that other stores sold out of a long time ago. Maybe this toy was not even good for resale at the time it was released but has enjoyed some kind of recent surge in popularity (demand). These toys may be nowhere to be found but if you keep your eyes open, you can get lucky and find them sitting lonely on a shelf somewhere, still waiting for a buyer.

Stores may also only appear to be sold out. If there are no products on the shelf, look in the overheads. Ask the store employees to check the computer inventory system. Maybe they have more in the back. Maybe they know when more are due to arrive at the store. Maybe they can check the inventory levels at another store for you. More strategies for tracking down specific items can be found in Chapter 25 – Retail Secrets.

**When Toys Are HOT**

Every year there are tons of new toys that are marketed to kids. Some of these toys end up being THE TOY. This is the toy that every kid has to have. The marketing done by the toy companies created strong demand and when this demand outweighs the supply, prices rise and a strong secondary market emerges. This happens all the time. This is simple economics being played out in real life. It happens a lot around Christmas time, but this phenomenon happens to different toys all year long. Learning the toy market will help you capitalize on this imbalance in supply and demand and leave you with the profit.

There is a bonus chapter at the end of this book called The Pixar Effect (Bonus #5) that goes into greater details about the different dynamics affecting today's retail toys. Supply and demand, even when very small, can now still find each other through the Internet. This is affecting the price of retail toys long after they are pulled from the retail store shelves to make room for the latest and greatest toys.

Remember the chapter about Understanding the Amazon Buyer? That applies here as well. Parents want to buy online and some of those parents want to buy from Amazon.com as their online seller of choice. Price is a factor in the purchasing decision, but it is not always the deciding factor.

## Chapter 13 – THE TIME TO ACT IS NOW!

The pieces that make Retail Arbitrage work on this scale have never before been available in the way that they are today. Without FBA, this type of business would only appeal to entrepreneurs who are willing to fill up their garages with products and commit to processing orders on a daily basis. Without FBAScout, making the best buying decisions would be increasingly risky. Without a guide like *Retail Arbitrage* and the online FBA support communities that have developed, you'd be on your own to make mistakes and try to figure this all out for yourself. This guide will allow you to avoid the learning curve of this business and allow you to start making profits from day one. Now is the perfect time to get in on this emerging business model.

You may be asking yourself, "If other people are already doing Retail Arbitrage, is there still money to be made? Or is it too late?" It's a good question. Always remember, this is a business model of abundance and not one of scarcity. Later in this book under Bonus #3, I'll explain why it's simply not possible for any one person or company to take over all of the Retail Arbitrage opportunities that exist out there today.

This is a cutting-edge business and you'll be using some very high-tech products. It can be a little overwhelming at first, but if you have questions, there are many places online where you can get help. There is a FREE Online Information section at the end of this book with tons of resources and links to online communities that are happy to help new sellers.

The important thing to do is to act; you have to get started. There are deals out there just waiting to be discovered. Consider this like a franchise opportunity but where the cost of entry is practically zero. If you already have an iPhone or Android device, you can download the FBAScout trial and get 250 free scans today. Go to a store like Big Lots or

Toys R Us and see if what is written in this book is true or not. Then the only thing stopping you from starting your own Retail Arbitrage business is putting the items in your cart, checking out, and listing them for sale online.

This type of business will continue to grow and get bigger and better over time. Amazon is moving in the right direction and they are giving third party sellers incredibly powerful tools to help them succeed that were not imaginable just a few short years ago. Amazon is growing at a fantastic pace with too many opportunities to count. If you share this vision and want to participate in this growth, I encourage you to get in now and enjoy the ride.

**The Fourth Quarter**

The fourth quarter, sometimes called Q4, is the common term for the last three months of the year. It includes the Christmas shopping season, which will see a huge surge in retail sales (both in store and online). Don't let the fourth quarter sneak up on you! Be prepared to take advantage of the huge opportunities that the fourth quarter brings every year.

The following pages contain our actual Amazon payouts from Q4 2009 and Q4 2010. You'll see an increase leading up to December 25th and then you'll see a sales decline. This happens every year as the Q4 spike in sales comes back down to normal levels.

You'll also see the returns increase. This will happen to you after Christmas as well, so don't be alarmed. It just comes with the territory of selling in any kind of serious volume. Buyers purchased many of these items for gifts, and some are returned. Many of your returns will go straight back into sellable inventory. Remember, you can only get a lot of returns if you sell a lot of stuff!

# Retail Arbitrage

Here you can see the nice surge in sales that we received in 2009. Note the dates. Sales always taper off right after Christmas.

## November 9, 2009 – November 23, 2009

# Retail Arbitrage

## November 23, 2009 – December 7, 2009

amazon services
seller central

www.amazon.com

HOME | MESSAGES | HELP | LOGOUT

INVENTORY ▼ | ORDERS ▼ | REPORTS ▼ | PERFORMANCE ▼ | SETTINGS ▼

Search   GO

Payments | Amazon Selling Coach | Business Reports | Fulfillment

### Payments

Totals are updated periodically throughout the day. Learn more

**Upload multiple product images**
Check out the new image uploader tool ▸ Learn more

Advertisement

**Summary** | Transactions | Settlement Reports

**Account Summary for** Nov 23, 2009 - Dec 7, 2009

| | |
|---|---|
| **Closing balance:** | $18,239.52 |
| **Previous settlement:** | Nov 23, 2009 |
| **Settlement date:** | Dec 7, 2009 |

**Find a transaction:** Enter Order Number

GO

A payment was made to your bank account ending in 0956 in the amount of $18,239.52. The funds may take 3-5 days to appear in your bank account.

| **Orders** | | |
|---|---|---|
| | Product charges: | $23,755.00 |
| | Promo rebates: | $-1,429.85 |
| | Amazon fees: | $-4,997.17 |
| | Other: | $2,021.66 |
| | **Total:** | **$19,349.64** |

| **Refunds** | | |
|---|---|---|
| | Product charges: | $-339.60 |
| | Amazon fees: | $32.58 |
| | Other: | $26.30 |
| | **Total:** | **$-280.72** |

| **Other Transactions** | | |
|---|---|---|
| (may include amounts from failed disbursements. Learn More.) | Other: | $-829.40 |
| | **Total:** | **$-829.40** |

| **Balance:** | **$18,239.52** |
|---|---|

View Transactions

# Retail Arbitrage

## December 7, 2009 – December 21, 2009

INVENTORY ▾ | ORDERS ▾ | REPORTS ▾ | PERFORMANCE ▾ | SETTINGS ▾ | Search | GO

Payments | Amazon Selling Coach | Business Reports | Fulfillment

## Payments

Amazon Webstore
From zero to Amazon Webstore in just a few clicks.  ▸ Learn more

Totals are updated periodically throughout the day. Learn more

Advertisement

**Summary** | Transactions | Settlement Reports

Account Summary for [ Dec 7, 2009 - Dec 21, 2009 ▾ ]

| | | | | |
|---|---|---|---|---|
| **Closing balance:** | $30,236.33 | **Orders** | Product charges: | $35,899.00 |
| **Previous settlement:** | Dec 7, 2009 | | Promo rebates: | $-1,979.72 |
| **Settlement date:** | Dec 21, 2009 | | Amazon fees: | $-8,553.92 |
| | | | Other: | $3,253.73 |
| **Find a transaction:** | Enter Order Number | | **Total:** | **$28,619.09** |
| | GO | | | |
| | | **Refunds** | Product charges: | $-997.15 |
| | | | Promo rebates: | $9.73 |
| | | | Amazon fees: | $96.85 |
| | | | Other: | $35.71 |
| | | | **Total:** | **$-854.86** |

A payment was made to your bank account ending in 0956 in the amount of $30,236.33. The funds may take 3-5 days to appear in your bank account.

| | | |
|---|---|---|
| **Other Transactions** | Other: | $2,472.10 |
| (may include amounts from failed disbursements. Learn More.) | **Total:** | **$2,472.10** |
| | | |
| **Balance:** | | **$30,236.33** |

View Transactions

# Retail Arbitrage

## December 21, 2009 – January 4, 2010

You'll see the sales already tapering off as this payout period only had a few days of sales prior to December 25th.

# Retail Arbitrage

## January 4, 2010 – January 18, 2010

**amazon** services
seller central

www.amazon.com

HOME | MESSAGES | HELP | LOGOUT

INVENTORY ▾   ORDERS ▾   REPORTS ▾   PERFORMANCE ▾   SETTINGS ▾

Search   GO

Payments | Amazon Selling Coach | Business Reports | Fulfillment

## Payments

Totals are updated periodically throughout the day. Learn more

Summary | Transactions | Settlement Reports

Account Summary for ( Jan 4, 2010 - Jan 18, 2010 )

| | | | | |
|---|---|---|---|---|
| Closing balance: | $3,049.45 | **Orders** | Product charges: | $5,162.65 |
| Previous settlement: | Jan 4, 2010 | | Promo rebates: | $-428.85 |
| Settlement date: | Jan 18, 2010 | | Amazon fees: | $-1,167.57 |
| | | | Other: | $589.91 |
| Find a transaction: | Enter Order Number | | **Total:** | **$4,156.14** |
| | | **Refunds** | Product charges: | $-1,038.30 |
| | GO! | | Promo rebates: | $20.17 |
| | | | Amazon fees: | $105.38 |
| | | | Other: | $42.37 |
| | | | **Total:** | **$-870.38** |

A payment was made to your bank account ending in 0956 in the amount of $3,049.45. The funds may take 3-5 days to appear in your bank account.

| | | |
|---|---|---|
| **Other Transactions** (may include amounts from failed disbursements. Learn More.) | Other: | $-236.31 |
| | **Total:** | **$-236.31** |
| **Balance:** | | **$3,049.45** |

View Transactions

Sales continue to taper off, as buyers are not buying at the same level as before Christmas.

Here you can see a nice surge in sales that we received in 2010. Note the dates. Sales always taper off right after Christmas.

## November 8, 2010 – November 22, 2010

# Retail Arbitrage

## November 22, 2010 – December 6, 2010

**amazon** services
seller central

www.amazon.com

HOME | MESSAGES | HELP | LOGOUT

INVENTORY ▼ | ORDERS ▼ | REPORTS ▼ | PERFORMANCE ▼ | SETTINGS ▼

Search | GO

Payments | Amazon Selling Coach | Business Reports | Fulfillment

## Payments

*Incent Customers with Gift Cards* ▸ Learn more

Totals are updated periodically throughout the day. Learn more

Advertisement

**Summary** | Transactions | Settlement Reports

**Account Summary for** Nov 22, 2010 - Dec 6, 2010

| | | | | |
|---|---|---|---|---|
| **Closing balance:** | $11,682.75 | **Orders** | Product charges: | $17,394.38 |
| **Previous settlement:** | Nov 22, 2010 | | Promo rebates: | $-801.32 |
| **Settlement date:** | Dec 6, 2010 | | Amazon fees: | $-3,594.36 |
| | | | Other: | $1,268.81 |
| **Find a transaction:** | Enter Order Number | | **Total:** | **$14,267.51** |

GO

| | | |
|---|---|---|
| **Refunds** | Product charges: | $-2,788.10 |
| | Promo rebates: | $0.00 |
| | Amazon fees: | $281.38 |
| | Other: | $17.99 |
| | **Total:** | **$-2,488.73** |

A payment was made to your bank account ending in 0956 in the amount of $11,682.75. The funds may take 3-5 days to appear in your bank account.

| | | |
|---|---|---|
| **Other Transactions** (may include amounts from failed disbursements. Learn More.) | Amazon fees: | $-165.98 |
| | Other: | $69.95 |
| | **Total:** | **$-96.03** |

| | |
|---|---|
| **Balance:** | **$11,682.75** |

View Transactions

## December 6, 2010 – December 20, 2010.

amazon services
seller central | www.amazon.com | HOME | MESSAGES | HELP | LOGOUT

INVENTORY ▾ | ORDERS ▾ | REPORTS ▾ | PERFORMANCE ▾ | SETTINGS ▾ | Search | GO

Payments | Amazon Selling Coach | Business Reports | Fulfillment

## Payments

Totals are updated periodically throughout the day. Learn more

**Amazon Webstore**
From zero to Amazon Webstore in just a few clicks. › Learn more

Advertisement

Summary | Transactions | Settlement Reports

**Account Summary for** Dec 6, 2010 - Dec 20, 2010

| | | |
|---|---|---|
| Closing balance: | $27,289.74 | |
| Previous settlement: | Dec 6, 2010 | |
| Settlement date: | Dec 20, 2010 | |

Find a transaction: Enter Order Number

GO!

A payment was made to your bank account ending in 0956 in the amount of $27,289.74. The funds may take 3-5 days to appear in your bank account.

| Orders | | |
|---|---|---|
| Product charges: | | $34,929.47 |
| Promo rebates: | | $-1,231.45 |
| Amazon fees: | | $-7,781.68 |
| Other: | | $2,548.69 |
| **Total:** | | **$28,465.03** |

| Refunds | |
|---|---|
| Product charges: | $-821.86 |
| Promo rebates: | $0.00 |
| Amazon fees: | $81.56 |
| Other: | $19.99 |
| **Total:** | **$-720.31** |

| Other Transactions | |
|---|---|
| (may include amounts from failed disbursements. Learn More.) | |
| Amazon fees: | $-492.24 |
| Other: | $37.26 |
| **Total:** | **$-454.98** |

| Balance: | $27,289.74 |
|---|---|

View Transactions

## December 20, 2010 – January 3, 2011

amazon services
seller central

www.amazon.com

HOME | MESSAGES | HELP | LOGOUT

| INVENTORY ▾ | ORDERS ▾ | REPORTS ▾ | PERFORMANCE ▾ | SETTINGS ▾ |

Search    GO

Payments | Amazon Selling Coach | Business Reports | Fulfillment

## Payments

Reprice faster with the Price Match tool  › Learn more

Totals are updated periodically throughout the day. Learn more

Advertisement

**Summary** | Transactions | Settlement Reports

**Account Summary for** [ Dec 20, 2010 - Jan 3, 2011 ▾ ]

| | | | | |
|---|---|---|---|---|
| **Closing balance:** | $10,967.28 | **Orders** | Product charges: | $14,855.75 |
| **Previous settlement:** | Dec 20, 2010 | | Promo rebates: | $-416.59 |
| **Settlement date:** | Jan 3, 2011 | | Amazon fees: | $-3,365.99 |
| | | | Other: | $1,117.20 |
| **Find a transaction:** | Enter Order Number | | **Total:** | **$12,190.37** |

GO

| | | | |
|---|---|---|---|
| **Refunds** | Product charges: | $-1,233.77 |
| | Promo rebates: | $0.00 |
| | Amazon fees: | $120.55 |
| | Other: | $0.00 |
| | **Total:** | **$-1,113.22** |

A payment was made to your bank account ending in 0956 in the amount of $10,967.28. The funds may take 3-5 days to appear in your bank account.

| | | |
|---|---|---|
| **Other Transactions** | Amazon fees: | $-9.99 |
| (may include amounts from failed disbursements. Learn More.) | Other: | $-99.88 |
| | **Total:** | **$-109.87** |

| | |
|---|---|
| **Balance:** | **$10,967.28** |

View Transactions

Sales stayed stronger this year than last year, but still showed a sharp decline from pre-December 25th levels.

## January 3, 2011 – January 17, 2011

Whoa! Big decline in sales post Q4 and more returns. No surprises here. It happens every year.

You can see for yourself the kinds of numbers that are possible with this business. Don't let another Q4 pass you by without getting in on the action!

IMPORTANT: Don't psych yourself out of this opportunity. Are there other resellers out there doing Retail Arbitrage right now? You bet there are; they are out there and they are making money every day. But as I explain in detail in Bonus #3 at the end of this book, no one can do all of the deals out there. When you are buying and selling items from retail stores or hitting up book sales and thrift stores, do not talk yourself out of being disciplined and evaluating the products for yourself. Just because someone else has scanned an item and deemed it not a good match for their individual business model, it doesn't necessarily mean that the item is not a good match for your business model.

I've seen it so many times and I've even felt that feeling myself. If I get to a book sale late and I see other scanners, I start to think that maybe I should just pack it in. All of the good books are probably gone already, right? Or I see someone walking out of Toys R Us with a ton of stuff and wonder if maybe they are a reseller like me. They probably already got all of the good stuff already, right? WRONG; always wrong. I make myself stay and it always pays off. I've included tons of information in this book as to why this mentality of scarcity is incorrect later in this book in Bonus #7: Your Lazy Competition.

Get your head in the game and remember that this is fun and rewarding work, but it is work nonetheless. Those who put in the work will reap the rewards. Will this be you? Are you willing to test if what is written in this book is true or not?

## Chapter 14 – Anyone Can Do This

I truly believe that anyone can do this business. All it takes is a little motivation and some consistency and you will start to see the opportunities that are all around you. All you have to do is take the first step to making it happen. I have personally trained and mentored many FBA sellers and I truly enjoy doing so. It is rewarding to know that you are really helping someone make that extra income that they need. An FBA business is fairly unique in the sense that you really can work when you want to work and stop working anytime. There are really no commitments. Like I mentioned earlier in this book, this type of business simply did not exist in this form just a few short years ago.

While anyone can do this, this is not a get-rich-quick type of business. This business is work and it can be very rewarding work, especially financially, but you do have to learn this business. Just doing what someone tells you to do or buy what someone tells to you to buy won't do you any good in the long term. I want to see you succeed long term with this business but that involves you making the decision to hit the streets and get yourself familiar with all aspects of this business. Don't be afraid to make mistakes; I know I've made a ton of them! The good thing about making mistakes? You learn from them and you can take steps to not make them again.

So can anyone do this business? Absolutely! But the ones who commit, work, and learn this business through and through will be the ones with long term success. Will this be you?

I've included three testimonials from three different people that I have worked with over the past few years. They all include a link to their Amazon stores as well as their email addresses. I asked them if this was OK and they all said, "Of course!" I get just as skeptical as you probably do when you see all the glowing reviews on a website, they are all fairly vague, and they are all from important sounding people like John H., Amazon seller, or Jane Q., Amazon seller. Who is this Jane Q.? How do I know she is not just some made up person? What if I want to ask her a question about her testimonial? Or see their Amazon store? These testimonials are the real deal from real people and you are welcome to contact them with questions.

In the interest of full disclosure, I will say upfront that one is going to be totally biased because it's from my mom, but her story is an inspiring one. She is our number one scanner in terms of number of products scanned. She can claim this title because she is CONSISTENT. She goes out scanning on a schedule and sticks to it. She almost always finds something, but there are times where she comes home empty handed and that's OK. She was able to retire early and travel often thanks to her FBA business.

Having to teach this business to my mom was actually a huge blessing in disguise. This forced us to make sure the program was 'Grandma-compatible'. If it wasn't easy for her to use, then it wasn't easy enough for other people to use. You could call her the ultimate Grandma beta tester! I set up a blog for her to post about her scouting adventures at http://FBAGrandma.com

## Anyone Can Do This

### Nancy Green

Let me introduce myself - I'm 'Anybody', also known as the FBA Grandma, and I can do it. I will also disclose that Chris is my son and undoubtedly that gave me a big advantage when I was starting out on this adventure. A little background about myself: I've been a treasure hunter most of my life, from furnishing my college apartment, to stocking my booth at Antique Malls, and even filling out my wardrobe. Several years ago when I was still working full time, I was selling some of my 'found treasures' on eBay. While it was worthwhile financially I must admit that I did not enjoy the process of listing the items, taking pictures, monitoring the emails, and then packing, labeling and shipping the treasures that I sold.

While in college, Chris was also selling on eBay and then he continued to use eBay as a source of income after graduation. As the volume of his sales grew to be too much to easily ship daily, he discovered FBA. What a perfect solution! He then became interested in selling books as he researched and realized the profits that could be made. Knowing that I love to treasure hunt in thrift stores and garage sales, he explained the whole process to me. We started out with scanners that we uploaded data into, then set parameters and started scanning books and listening for the bell to ring. Then we had to list, label and pack the books. Well that was okay (I was making money), but my son has always liked to do things the most efficient way possible. The fact that the data wasn't current or complete, and the time consuming process of listing and shipping really bothered him. I'll let him tell you that part of the story…

So - when FBAPower first came out with FBAScout I guess I was one of the first to use it. It's just so easy. I actually have my scanner attached to the back of my phone with Velcro and it goes everywhere with me. I use the EVO on Sprint and I can assure you that I only carry a phone like this because Chris bought it for me (and now for FBAScout).

While I was working, I would head out to a thrift store or two on my lunch hour. I was really lucky because there were several close to the office. Now, you have to remember that this is a treasure hunt, so some days I might only find a couple of books that I felt would be worthwhile buying to resell, but then the next day there would be a whole box of good books. I try to buy most of my books for a dollar or less with a minimum selling price of $8.00, but I will spend up to $3.00 when I see that the value is $11.00 or more. I think everyone will set his or her own parameters as they become familiar with all the information on the screen. I used to not see that Amazon was selling the book, and often for less than anyone else. I only did that a few times! I also check to see how may books are at the lowest price because, sometimes once two or three have been sold you'll see that the market price is now worthwhile. All week long I would fill up my trunk and then one night I would unload them and stack them by size on my worktable. (It just makes it so much easier to pack the boxes.)

FBAPower just makes it so easy and efficient to list, price and label my items. I find that it usually takes me about an hour to complete a box. A portion of that time is removing labels, cleaning any marks, and checking for highlights or underlining on the pages. I usually ship two to three boxes every week.

After I retired I found that I was changing my 'booking' schedules because I could now take advantage of certain sale days at the various stores. Tuesdays are Senior's Day so I have a regular route to take advantage of the 25 - 30% discounts. I can also now go to stores that are further away. I just pick a community that is close, Google for "thrift stores" and then decide if it looks worthwhile to make a trip. I always print out the map and then make notes about the shops before and after I've been there. I keep all these sheets in a binder in the car. Usually one day a week I will head out of town, and it's always an adventure.

Now the best parts - finding books for $.49 to $1.00 that scan for $48.00 or $63.00 or even $89.00 or more! And even better - seeing that they sold and my Amazon payments account is growing. The fact that every two weeks a deposit appears in my bank account has allowed me to travel. Even when I've been away and haven't sent in books, something always sells.

I attended the SCOE 2011 convention this summer and was amazed at how huge the Amazon marketplace really is. With the FBA program the sky really is the limit. Being able to scan the whole catalog is amazing. Sometimes I wish I were 30 years younger because it is a very exciting time to be in ecommerce. However, my empire building days are over and I think I'll stick to my books (and maybe a few toys) where I have a comfort level of what works for the amount of time I want to spend with generous returns for my effort.

Yes, anyone can do it and with the educational materials and customer support that FBAPower offers you should seriously think about trying it yourself. It's fun to be on your own schedule, but it's also easy to scan for a couple of hours while you have a full time job.

I ran my numbers for 2010 for my accountant and came out with some pretty round numbers.

Total spent on inventory (mostly books): ~$8,000

Total Amazon payouts (not sales, payouts to my bank): ~$32,000

So ~$24,000 profit. I like to think of it as turning $1 into $4 about eight thousand times in a year.

This doesn't even account for all the books that are still at FBA that had not sold prior to December 31, 2010.

So, not a million dollars, but enough to make me feel confident enough to retire a little early.

Nancy Green, Irving, TX

http://www.amazon.com/shops/smoxie

nancyjgreen@gmail.com

I met Phyllis Anderson when I was selling scanner hardware (pre-FBAScout days) on eBay with a mentoring package. My favorite story about Phyllis (and I tell it all the time) is how she called me one day and had a new problem; she was making too much money to stay on Social Security! I told her that this is a great problem to have! My advice was to go find a good CPA who can help. She has managed to successfully branch out from just selling books and now sells practically anything that is profitable. She has also since trained several family members who are now also running successful FBA businesses. Here is her story:

## Anyone Can Do This

## By Phyllis Anderson

I am 64 years in age and sort of in the sandwich generation. I retired two years ago and became the caregiver for my mother. My youngest child (age 30) also needed some assistance in completing his education and raising his children. It wasn't long after I retired that I realized Social Security and my pension combined only allowed minimal survival. So to earn extra income I began throwing stuff on eBay and trying to earn extra cash by selling family heirlooms and estate sale items. I ran out of those pretty quickly and needed to do something that would create a steadier part-time stream of income. However, I could not re-enter the workplace due to my mother's health. I needed a way to make money that would fit my lifestyle.

While surfing eBay late one night I noticed Chris Green's eBay listing. It was for a book scanner, but his auction went on to say that he would personally train anyone purchasing one of the scanners on how to make money using Amazon's FBA program. He added that it was easy; Amazon shipped all of your products for you and that eliminated the part that was so time consuming with other online sales (the packing, shipping and ongoing customer service). I was skeptical, but desperate. He included his phone number in the auction so I contacted Chris to find out more. He promised that my online purchase of a scanner from him would guarantee me the opportunity to learn FBA and that all questions would be welcome. He has more than lived up to his promise.

I purchased my scanner in March 2010 from Chris and began scanning barcodes and ISBNs at estate sales, library book sales, flea markets, and just about every retail store that I frequented. I have had lots of questions along the way and Chris has always answered them in a very positive upbeat way. I can't say enough about his honesty and integrity. Had I not been able to rely on his knowledge and expertise, it is quite likely that I never would have tried, or succeeded, with FBA.

With Chris's guidance, I was successful enough in my first year of FBA to have to worry about exceeding my Social Security earnings ceiling! Wow! Earning too much money to stay on Social Security was a problem I hadn't figured on! Believe me, following Chris's FBA program will make you successful whether you want a part-time or full-time income. When he introduced FBAScout last fall I ditched my old scanner and purchased an Android phone and the Scanfob™ 2002. Now I do online sales of everything that I can find including books, grocery items, health and beauty products, and toys. It has opened up a whole new world of online selling for me.

There are so many things about this program that I love:

- Knowing that Chris and the other staff at FBA are there to support you whenever needed
- Allowing me the flexibility to work when and where I want (FBA online sales really do allow you to earn money while you sleep)
- Leaving the customer service and shipping to Amazon (providing me the time I need to scout for more products for resale)
- Best thing of all? Anyone can do this!

Phyllis Anderson, Des Moines, IA

http://www.amazon.com/shops/littlephilly

phphuber@hotmail.com

I also met Cynthia Stine through our eBay listing. She was completely new to selling on Amazon and this whole scanning books business. She had never heard of FBA. At the time, we were in Massachusetts and

Cynthia said that she lived in Dallas/Fort Worth. We would be returning to Dallas/Fort Worth in a few months so we planned to meet up in order to get all of her questions answered. She was a quick and eager learner and she has really run with the FBA program. She came with me on a trip to Big Lots to see first-hand how to scout for items to resell. It can be such a huge help to see someone really doing this business. When you see someone scan an item, then put all forty-two of them in their cart with confidence, you see that finding good deals on items to sell online really are just as easy as people say that they are. It can give you the confidence to make that first big purchase. Here is her story:

## Anyone Can Do This

## By Cynthia Stine

### How I pay for my son's private school...

My life changed dramatically in 2010. My husband and I adopted our teenage son, Eric. The clients for my consulting business went away — some of them owing me large sums of money — or greatly reduced their retainers, and we were overwhelmed with new expenses for our special needs son. I wanted to take advantage of my business slow-down to spend as much time as possible with him, but I also needed to bring in enough extra money to pay for his private school and other monthly expenses — about $1500 to $2000 more a month.

Selling on eBay bewildered me and it was so time-consuming just to get something photographed and listed. Amazon also seemed complicated and time-consuming until I discovered Amazon's FBA program through an online e-book. Once I grasped that I could sell penny books for $4 (or $5 or $7!), I never looked back.

Since I needed a streamlined operation where I could be productive on only a few hours a week, I signed up for FBAPower. It was well worth the money compared to the incredibly confusing spreadsheet that Amazon wanted me to fill out and upload. When FBAScout became available, I turned in my PDA scanner and doubled my income in a month thanks to real-time intelligence on Amazon listings and better thinking about my business.

The week I got my FBAScout scanner, I met with Chris Green and went on a Big Lots shopping trip with him. In one afternoon, my business was turbo-charged. I realized that I was no longer an online bookseller, but an Amazon seller. I bought toys, baby items, Nintendo Wii accessories, calendars – anything with a barcode was now part of my business. For the first time I exceeded $2,000 a month from my Amazon business.

Besides understanding that I could sell in nearly every category, I also learned from Chris that I could often sell for MORE than a merchant seller could because my customer was really the Amazon Prime buyer and they are an impatient breed who will pay more to get it NOW. I signed up for Prime myself so I could understand – and I understand all too well now. Having to wait three to five days for something now seems like agony.

In addition, I learned that just because I would never pay high prices for some of these items (like a plastic baby spoon or a pacifier), it doesn't mean that someone else wouldn't. There are people who don't like to shop, people who live far away from shops, people who are very busy and people who are willing to pay extra for the convenience and speed. This is the nature of arbitrage and while I was initially doubtful of some of the things Chris told me that afternoon, I've learned he is right and I've adjusted my thinking.

For example, I have one product that I sell where I am the ONLY seller – not just the only FBA seller. As an experiment, I keep raising the price every time I send in new inventory. I can't believe how much people are willing to pay for this piece of plastic foam. I net about $30 on every sale. There are similar products on Amazon that are cheaper and that surely come up when my customers search, but they want this one. I will be so sad when I can't find any more because I sell about one a day when I have stock.

Before I had FBAScout, I would sometimes make mistakes because until I got home and listed with FBAPower, I could not see how many FBA sellers there were and their prices for the item. Now I always know ahead of time and can avoid the items with too many FBA sellers.

Chris taught me to scan everything and I take my scanner with me everywhere. One day at the Blockbuster Video, I noticed they were clearing out some weird items like "As Seen on TV!" sweepers, wall stickers for kids' rooms, Silly Bandz, Star Wars toys, and a bunch of other stuff that shouldn't have been there in the first place. They were on sale 75% to 90% off and I nearly squealed when I saw the rankings and prices on Amazon. I like to get at least a 3X return on an item I buy for resale. In this case, I was getting as much as 25X.

A friend introduced me to a thrift store that sells paperback books for 10 cents and hardbacks for 20 cents on Saturdays. They also sell video games for 15 cents and VHS tapes for 25 cents. I've taken $20 and turned it into hundreds of dollars on those Saturdays. We've never seen another scanner there. While we sell many of the books for $5-$7, we've found some for $40 and up that have really made us happy. At this same hole-in-the-wall store, we've found brand new medical supplies, adult diapers and other brand new items on which we've made huge profits. I bought a couple of cans of medical drink powder for $3 that sold for $50 online. You just never know what you will find if you look – and have the means to capitalize on it.

With FBA, I pay very little for warehousing. My last payment was $44 for over 2000 items. I used to have a 10'X10' storage unit for my primary business that cost me $80 a month. It still amazes me that I am able to leverage all the shipping, warehouse, logistics, and sales tools of the largest online retailer on earth for myself. I have a presence on Amazon and it costs me so little.

I live in one of the largest metropolitan areas in the country and yet I rarely see another scanner except at library book sales (and most of them are clearly not FBA and certainly not using FBAScout). When I go to a book sale full of scanners, I am still usually by myself wondering why the other people are wasting their time on penny books instead of grabbing the DVDs, textbooks and other non-fiction books that will sell for high-dollar amounts.

I went to Half-Price Books' 20% off sale over Labor Day and bought around $1000 worth of textbooks and Spanish language programs that I listed for over $5000. Selling through Amazon's FBA program is like turning straw into gold.

If you can't tell, I love my Amazon FBA business. The thrill of finding something with that right mix of rank and price is hard to describe – getting the check two weeks later is even better. I couldn't do it without my tools. I'm a huge fan of FBAPower and FBAScout because they give me competitive information that makes me a much more productive and profitable seller. I'm a small fry compared to others and only have about 30 hours a month I can put in (many of them after Eric's bedtime), but I'm very happy with the results. By leveraging the smarts and tools of FBAPower and FBAScout and Amazon's FBA program, I can achieve my personal and financial goals in a short amount of time each month.

Cynthia Stine, Dallas, TX

http://amzn.to/mypromotebooks

cynthia@promotesuccesspr.com

## Chapter 15 – The Rules of the Amazon Marketplace

This is a short chapter but if you don't read this one, your tenure as an Amazon.com seller may be even shorter.

Whenever you wonder why Amazon does something, ask yourself this question: **does it provide a great experience for the Amazon buyer?** This is the key behind all Amazon programs and policies. Want proof? Amazon puts NEGATIVE product reviews on their site. Why? So that the buyer can make an informed decision and have a great buying experience on Amazon. Sure, Amazon could put all positive reviews on everything and see a short-term boost in sales, but it would affect their long-term goals of providing a great experience to the buyer. If a product fails for 90% of the buyers after two months of use but Amazon only showed the positive reviews from the 10% of the satisfied customers, then 9 out of 10 customers are going to have a poor buying experience and may not choose Amazon as their online retailer of choice for their next purchase.

If you are curious as to how this has worked out for Amazon, just take a look at their success and growth!

This policy should be seen as optimal for not just Amazon and the Amazon buyer, but also for anyone selling on Amazon! When you have a marketplace that has the best, most loyal customers who choose the Amazon marketplace FIRST and REPEATEDLY for their online purchases, you have a great place to sell your products! This environment is conducive to sellers who provide the best experience to the buyer. Good sellers, good buyers, good relationships, good business.

Amazon has spent many years and many dollars building this culture of trust and loyalty and they will protect it. There are policies in place to weed out sellers who do not meet the high standards that Amazon expects out of all of their sellers.

**THIS IS VERY IMPORTANT SO I AM TYPING IN ALL CAPITAL LETTERS**

You have to know and understand the rules of selling on Amazon, and especially FBA. Amazon is much different from eBay where you can mess up and eBay pretty much isn't going to do anything about it. Amazon is extremely customer focused and they have many rules in place that ensure that third party sellers provide Amazon customers with a high level of service. If these rules are not followed, then the customer may have a poor buying experience and that is the last thing that Amazon wants. If you're caught breaking Amazon's rules or provide a poor customer experience, Amazon will ban your account. I'm not talking about ban as in 'just go open another account with a different email address and they'll never know', I'm talking block all new accounts from your IP address, and anything tied to your credit cards or bank accounts. Ignorance of the rules is not an excuse with Amazon. The rules are there for you to read and when you create a seller account on Amazon, you are agreeing to follow those rules.

Compare this policy to eBay where providing a poor buying experience to the buyer simply means that you will likely get lower sales prices or fewer sales. If you want to take bad pictures, include a poor description, and offer restricting return policies, then you can. EBay will let you do this without penalty. They will recommend that you take good pictures, include detailed and accurate descriptions, and offer favorable return policies, in order to get more sales and at higher prices, but they don't make you do this. It's up to the seller to choose how professionally that they want to run their eBay business.

This difference in the buying experience has brought a lot of buyers, and subsequently sellers, over to the Amazon marketplace.

This is not meant to scare you. It is meant to make sure that you take selling on Amazon seriously. Before you jump in with both feet, read the Amazon rules for sellers. If you are unclear on something, ask questions online or contact Amazon. They have email and phone support. They want you to succeed, but if you are going to play in Amazon's sandbox, you will follow the Amazon rules.

Amazon is so passionate about customer service that they will even block new sellers in the Toys & Games category going into the fourth quarter (Christmas selling season). Don't worry, new sellers who use FBA are excluded; another perk of FBA! Wouldn't blocking new sellers reduce their profits and their bottom line? Possibly, but Amazon is not going to let some new seller start listing on Amazon in a category that sees a huge spike in sales and take a chance on that seller not delivering the promised goods to the customer. A new seller may get overwhelmed with the process and ship orders late, or offer items that they later find out that they can't fulfill and be forced to cancel orders. It's also possible that a new seller is someone who is trying to take advantage of the huge surge in fourth quarter sales to try to get away with fraudulent activity. Whatever the case, it poses a risk of a poor customer experience. Amazon is not going to take this risk as they would rather ensure the integrity of the Amazon marketplace than try to bump their bottom line every chance that they can. I applaud them for this as it builds a stronger customer base that has confidence to continue to buy from Amazon time and time again. It also keeps sellers out who are not able to perform at the high standards that Amazon requires. This is a good thing for existing sellers as well as  keeping Amazon's business growing, which, in return, benefits third party sellers.

If you are selling using FBA, you have less to worry about compared to merchant fulfilled sellers. If you are 100% FBA, then you can't really ship something late because Amazon is doing the shipping. You can't be penalized for canceling orders because Amazon is managing your inventory levels. Just label your inventory properly, price your items competitively, and describe your items accurately and you're pretty much in the clear (still, read the rules!).

Even if something does get messed up like the seller gets the wrong item or the shipment arrived later than the expected delivery date, if it is an Amazon order, Amazon will take responsibility. This includes removing any negative feedback that is related to the fulfillment experience (imagine eBay doing that!).

Here are the reasons that Amazon will remove negative feedback:

The feedback includes obscene language.

The feedback includes personally identifiable information.

The entire feedback comment is a product review.

The entire feedback comment is regarding fulfillment or customer service for an order fulfilled by Amazon. (Feedback which qualifies for removal under this rule will not be removed, but a line will appear through the rating and the statement, "This item was fulfilled by Amazon, and we take responsibility for this fulfillment experience" will be added.)

If you sell used books and media items where you have to select a condition other than 'New', then you have the possibility of receiving negative feedback if the buyer disagrees with your grading of the item. For this reason, I've always recommended grading very conservatively in order to give your buyer something that exceeds their expectations.

If you are 100% FBA and only sell items in 'New' condition, then it is actually pretty hard to get negative feedback. Still, it will happen. When it does, do what you can to keep the customer happy. You can contact them through the Amazon website and if you are able to rectify the situation you can ask them to consider removing their negative feedback. Good customer service will pay off (just look what it's done for Amazon!) and maintaining a high feedback rating will inspire greater buyer confidence and attract more buyers.

Under no circumstances should you only offer customer service or offer to return an item in exchange for removing negative feedback. Run your business as a professional and take your customer service seriously. Take care of any issues and only after the customer is satisfied should you ask them to consider removing negative feedback.

**The Amazon A-to-Z Guarantee**

http://www.amazon.com/gp/help/customer/display.html?ie=UTF8&nodeId=537868

From Amazon:

> What is the Amazon.com A-to-Z Guarantee?
>
> We want you to buy with confidence anytime you purchase products on the Amazon.com website or use Amazon Payments. That is why we guarantee purchases from Amazon Marketplace and Merchant sellers when payment is made via the Amazon.com website or when you use Amazon Payments for qualified purchases on third-party websites. The condition of the item you buy and its timely delivery are guaranteed under the Amazon A-to-Z Guarantee.

The Amazon A-to-Z Guarantee is the buyer's ultimate protection against a seller who may not be following the Amazon rules. You do not want to have A-to-Z Guarantee claims opened against you. This should be used as a buyer's last resort so a seller should have had ample time to correct any customer service issues with the buyer prior to the claim being opened. There are many types of A-to-Z Guarantee claims, but here is an example to show you that Amazon means business:

If you list a toy like a Star Wars Lego set on Amazon, you can't put in your description notes something like, "most of the pieces are there, and Darth Vader is missing. AS IS." This is not eBay where the listing for the item is what it is. On Amazon, you are listing on a specific product page and your item better match that description 100%. If a buyer received this partial Lego set and opened an A-to-Z Guarantee claim against you as a seller, you would not only lose and be forced to issue the buyer a full refund, but the buyer would not have to return the Lego set to you. Ouch.

How do you avoid A-to-Z Guarantee claims? Simple; follow the rules! Read them and follow them. I have never had an A-to-Z Guarantee claim opened against me and I don't plan to ever let that happen. I'm sure Amazon also keeps track of A-to-Z Guarantee claims against sellers and could ban a seller if they receive too many.

There are lots of rules and there is not enough space to list and discuss them all in here. The current Selling on Amazon rules can be found here:

http://www.amazon.com/gp/help/customer/display.html/ref=hp_sn_sell?nodeId=1161232

Here is a link to the FBA homepage:

http://www.amazonservices.com/content/fulfillment-by-amazon.htm

## Chapter 16 - Sales Rank Explained – What It Is, What It Is Not

Products listed for sale on Amazon have what is called a Sales Rank, or more recently, a Bestsellers Rank. One thing to always remember is that Amazon does not have to provide this information. Currently they do provide it and it is a piece of data that sellers can use to decide the products they want to stock and sell on Amazon, either through FBA, or by shipping their orders themselves.

There is a lot of bogus information out there about what Sales Rank means. Many sites will tell you that Sales Rank will tell you how fast an item will sell. This is not true at all. They will say that an item with a lower Sales Rank (lower being better as in the #1 seller is better than the #100 seller) will sell faster or is a 'better seller' than the other. Again, simply not true.

**Sales Rank is actually very simple. It is an indication of recent sales. Nothing more.**

Now that you know what Sales Rank is, how do you use this piece of information? How can you decipher the data at your disposal to make the best buying decision? This is what I want to teach you.

**Sales Rank Means Different Things in Different Categories**.

There are a lot more books listed for sale on Amazon than there are toys. At the time of writing this book, there are 32,000,410 book listings and only 963,514 toy listings. So a book with a 100K Sales Rank is in the top 0.3% of all book listings. A toy with a Sales Rank of 100K is in the top 10%. Huge difference (30X+) as you can see. You have to read Sales Rank differently in different categories.

**When Items Don't Sell, Sales Rank Gets Higher and Higher and Higher...**

If an item has not sold in a long time, then the Sales Rank will gradually get higher and higher until the item sells again. Try to think of Sales Rank this way; when an item sells on Amazon, the Sales Rank will 'spike'. If you were charting Sales Rank over time on a graph, you would see a literal spike in the graph.

Here's a simple and inexpensive experiment that you can run to test this and see for yourself. Find a high ranking item sold through FBA. Make a note of the Sales Rank at the time that you purchase it. Then watch the Sales Rank jump (Amazon updates Sales Rank every hour). You'll see that high-ranking item all of a sudden has a good Sales Rank!

A book that hasn't sold a single copy in two years may have a Sales Rank of over 2 million. Buy it once and it spikes to 80K, for ONE SALE. One sale in TWO YEARS. Now compare that to the book that has sold one copy every month for the past two years. It may have a Sales Rank of 80K and it has sold one copy a month, every month, for two years. So twenty-four copies compared to one copy. SAME SALES RANK. Is it starting to make sense now? Sales Rank is just a snapshot in time.

**How To Use Sales Rank**

When you decide what items to buy to sell on Amazon, you should use Sales Rank as one piece of information that you have at your disposal. You should also look at the item itself. If you scan a 1994 tax planner guide that comes back with a 'good Sales Rank' of 100K, should you buy it without thinking or should you stop and consider all of the dynamics at play. The book has a Sales Rank of 100K. This only means that it has sold one copy recently. Nothing more. Who bought it? Who knows? Several scenarios come to mind. Maybe it was purchased by mistake? Maybe a buyer has $21 in their Amazon shopping cart and needed a $4 FBA book to get to $25 for Free Super Saver Shipping? (This can be cheaper than paying shipping on a $21 order.) Who knows? Do you really think someone is going to buy it again? You should look at the market price vs. your cost to determine if the margin is high enough to warrant the risk of laying out inventory dollars for the item. This is where you can make the judgment call with your head that while it may have a recent sale, it will likely not sell again for a long time.

You may be asking, "Wouldn't items with lower Sales Ranks be better items to sell?" The answer is yes, but let me explain why the answer is yes. Items with a low Sales Rank mean that they have sold recently. The lower the rank, the more frequently they have sold recently. Think spike after spike after spike, each time getting a better and better Sales Rank. This is a good indication that the items will sell again. This is why lower sales rank items are generally considered 'better' to sell on Amazon.

Always remember that just because something has been selling well, doesn't mean it will always continue to sell well. Think about fads that come and go. They may be selling like crazy one month and dead in the water the next. Many items are also seasonal, meaning they sell well during some times of the calendar year, and perhaps not at all during other times. Think Christmas lights.

You can use all the data at your disposal, including Sales Rank, to evaluate items but it is ultimately up to you to learn how to read that data and how to use it to lower your risk and help you make the best buying decisions.

## Real World Examples

I have an item on Amazon and I created the listing using a purchased UPC. I'm the only one who has ever sold this item. I get the emails when they ship out. We don't sell a ton, but I check Sales Rank every now and then. I've seen it as low as 4K and as high as 40K. So is it a 4K item? Or a 40K item? I sold fifty units in five months, so say ten a month or one every three days. Even with a steady sales rate OVER TIME, the sales rank fluctuates tremendously between sales. 4K Sales Rank would be after selling two in one day. 40K Sales Rank would be after not selling any for a week or more. This product is listed in the Office Products category on Amazon.

Another item I sell for which I created the product page took two months to get the first sale. I have been the only seller of this item (and still am). This item is in the Home Improvement category. It went from 0 Sales Rank to 14K Sales Rank. A week later it was at 70K Sales Rank. Two weeks later, 90K Sales Rank. It will sink lower until it sells again at which time it will spike to 10K-14K Sales Rank and then slowly drop again until the next sale.

It has sold one unit in the entire history of Amazon (although you could say in three months). Say you scanned this item and the margins were attractive. Was it a good item when the Sales Rank was at 14K? But not a week later when it's at 70K? Do you see why you cannot let Sales Rank dictate what you buy and don't buy? Will it ever sell again? Probably, but Sales Rank has nothing to do with it. Sales Rank will continue to climb (sink?) as other items sell and jump above its Sales Rank. When it sells again, it will jump up and then slide back down.

Here is another example from the Home Improvement category:

Sold item on 6/30/11, in the Home Improvement category. This was a merchant fulfilled item. I am the only seller and have been the only seller since I created the product page.

As soon as I got the email, I checked Sales Rank. It was 170,999. A little later, 9,183. Same item has a Sales Rank of 170K one hour and the next hour the Sales Rank is at 9K. This huge difference over just one sale.

If you base buying decisions only on sales rank, is this a bad item in the morning but a good item in the afternoon?

## More Data to Consider

Last time I sold this item was 6/5/11. So it took 25 days of no sales to get to 170K. So for simplicity, say this item sells once a month, every month. An item with this sell through rate can have a Sales Rank as high as 170K and as low as 9K (and anywhere in between) depending upon when you look at the item.

## The 10 Million Ranked Book

Bob Willey from the FBAForum Yahoo Group sold a book that he forgot that he had listed. It was listed as a merchant fulfilled book and he listed it almost three years prior to the sale. Once he received the email that it had sold, he checked the Sales Rank. It was 10,042,312! He emailed me after he received the order and I anxiously waited to see the new Sales Rank based on this single sale. It jumped to 94,060 after JUST ONE SALE.

Bob listed this book on 5/23/08 and it sold on 7/18/11 so it took over three years to sell. There is no telling how long it will take to sell again.

I hope this explanation and these examples help your business use Sales Rank appropriately to make the best buying decisions.

## Chapter 17 – Risk Management

Every item that you purchase for resale will represent some degree of risk. After all, there are no guarantees that any item will ever sell again. Even the number one selling book has the possibility of completely dropping off in sales.

The idea is to use as much information as possible that you have at your disposal to make the best buying decisions. The better your information, the better buying decisions that you'll make, and the lower your risk will be.

Because you don't know exactly what has sold before, you have to use the information that you do have access to in order to make good buying decisions. This data includes Sales Rank, competition, margin, and good old-fashioned intuition.

**Sales Rank**

In the previous chapter we talked about what Sales Rank is as well as what it isn't. When an item has a good Sales Rank, that means that it has had recent sales. Recent sales are a good indicator that the item will sell again.

**Amazon Sales Histories**

Amazon does not provide any histories of their sales. This policy comes from their legal department so I would not hold out on seeing anything like this anytime soon.

**Competition**

You can also use your competition to gauge if an item should be sold online. If there are a lot of sellers, especially FBA sellers and the margin is good on the item, then it's more than likely a good item to sell online.

Why? Well, you are using the fact that multiple other sellers also believe it to be a good product to sell online. You can piggyback on their knowledge, or at least use it to help you make your buying decision.

**Margin**

Always consider margin when deciding what to buy. If the item has a large margin of profit, then you have more room to take risks. If the item has less margin, then you want to make sure that the item will sell quickly. The amount of margin in an item can dramatically alter your buying decisions. Remember, you're going to find items at steep discounts that will have high margin for you but that other sellers are selling with lower margin because their costs were higher. These are all things to consider when managing your risk when making buying decisions.

## Chapter 18 – It's a Margins Game

This book is listed in the Recommended reading section at the end of this book:

How to Sell at Margins Higher Than Your Competitors

By Lawrence L. Steinmetz & William T. Brooks

It will change the way that you see price, competition, and margin. When selling on Amazon as a reseller, you have to consider margin above all other factors. You've probably heard people say that 'they'll just make it up in volume.' This is a recipe for disaster when you stop, sit down, and run the numbers. Here is a simplified example that they use in this book:

Consider a business that makes a product on which they enjoy a 35% margin. It costs them $65 to produce and they sell it for $100. They do an even $1,000,000 in sales in order to break even. Their margin covers the entire business overhead including salaries.

These simplified numbers mean that they spend $650,000 on producing 10,000 units with a cost of $65 each. The margin of 35% or the profit of $35 on those 10,000 equates to $350,000 to cover overheads.

This is their break-even point. While they are not turning a profit, they are not losing money and providing employment to their workers.

If the CEO all of a sudden says that they want to lower price and cut margins and attempt to 'make it up in volume' with no other business plan for sustainable growth, here is what will happen. Everyone at the company will work harder and make no additional profit.

The complete breakdown is explained in detail in the book but what you will find is that in this example with these numbers, by cutting their price by 10%, they will have to do double their work to make and sell twice as many units in order to make the same amount of money and break even. Conversely, if they raised price by 10%, they could sell half as much (lose half of their sales), work half as hard, and make the same amount of money.

For some reason, many struggling retailers who, in a last ditch effort to get back on track, try to lower prices and make it up in volume. Does it ever work? Nope. All of those struggling retailers are now out of business.

When you learn the vital importance of margin and price over volume, you'll learn to protect price and margin and work smart while your competition works hard.

An example that I like to use is when you hear people talk about how much money they make online. Someone may make the claim that they made $100,000 and how awesome they are and laugh at someone who only made $50,000. What they forget is that it is not the total profit that makes a business successful or not; it's the effort behind those profits. It's not a fair comparison when a seller who makes $100,000 profit on high volume, low margin items compares themselves to a seller who makes $50,000 with low volume, high margin items. When they claim that they are so much better because they made twice as much money, I would tell them that they should have made TEN TIMES as much money because they actually worked TEN TIMES harder!

## Chapter 19 – The 'Race to the Bottom' & 'Chasing the Next Sale'

There are two common phrases that you may start hearing when you are selling products online. These are the 'Race to the Bottom' and 'Chasing the Next Sale'. These are both the result of sellers who too often don't understand the marketplace dynamics at play and the factors that go into each buyer's decision-making process. They are the result of sellers who think that they can only compete on price and that price is king. They believe that the seller with the lowest price, even if only by $0.01, will be the only seller to get sales on Amazon.com. If you've read this far in the book, I hope that you see how this is simply not true. Buyers do not buy based on price alone and how cutting price is not a sustainable long-term business strategy.

As mentioned in Chapter 6, price, supply, and demand are constantly changing. Each time you look at the Amazon marketplace, you are only looking at a snapshot in time. As time goes by, things will change. Sellers will sell out, demand will rise and fall, supply will come and go and all the while price will be affected. Sometimes prices will go up and sometimes prices will go down.

Racing to the Bottom and Chasing the Next Sale are NOT strategies that I recommend. I want you to understand what causes these things to happen so that you do not get caught up in a downward spiral that negatively affects your margins and profits.

### The Race to the Bottom

The race to the bottom happens when sellers repeatedly undercut each other in an attempt to be the lowest price. It's a shame that this happens because so many buyers do not buy based on price alone, so sellers who repeatedly undercut only hurt their own businesses.

This can also happen when multiple sellers use automated repricing programs. The sellers may have poorly implemented pricing rules without safeguards to prevent lowering prices too much, or the repricing programs themselves are just poorly designed and written. These programs can go off in succession and result in a downward spiral of price, margins, and profits. A profitable item can be reduced to not profitable in a very short amount of time for no good reason other than aggressive sellers competing to see who can make the LEAST amount of money. This is not a strategy that I promote for obvious reasons.

I suppose this is good for the buyers of these products, but this is not an attractive set of circumstances for sellers.

Smart sellers need to learn to avoid the race to the bottom and also be able to identify it when it happens. Some sellers will even buy up their entire competitors inventory when this happens and items are listed for sale well below the equilibrium market price. See how supply, demand, and price just always seem to work things out in the free market? ☺

**Chasing the Next Sale**

Chasing the next sale happens when sellers don't stop to consider that items will sell throughout the year. It sounds very simple and logical that items will sell throughout the year and that a product is not just going to sell one more unit and then never sell again, doesn't it? You'd never know it the way that some sellers compete so aggressively on price. They are determined to be the absolute lowest price and 'chase' that next sale. They will lower their price (and reduce their margins) in order to undercut any and all competitors until the item sells.

I believe this to be a shortsighted strategy. It may be an item that sells 300 units every month on Amazon.com. Does it really matter if you are the first sale of the month or the last? What is the incredible motivation to be the 'next' sale? Personally, I prefer to sell at higher margins when I make the sale. When you stop and consider the number of units of each product that will sell on Amazon.com each month, being overly concerned with who is able to get the 'next sale' starts to sound pretty silly.

Some sellers will even lower their prices to levels where they are actually losing money on every sale just to be 'the next sale'. I'd rather not sell at all than sell items like this. $0 profit is $0 profit, but it is more profit than taking a loss on an item. If you see other sellers doing this, just leave them alone. Let them sell out at their low prices. Time will tell which sellers will remain in business.

## Real World Pricing Example

I was working with an FBAPower user over the phone and we were also using remote screen sharing software so I could watch what she was doing. She was getting used to the FBAPower workflow as I walked her through it. Here's what happened next:

She entered a book and it showed that it had a Sales Rank of under 12,000 (this is a very good Sales Rank). She graded it VeryGood, and then came to the FBAPower pricing popup screen. The lowest merchant fulfilled net price was $9.95 in Acceptable condition. Amazon was selling it for $19.95. There was one other FBA seller in Good condition priced at $14.95. I thought for sure that she would click on the $14.95 FBA price but instead she clicked the $9.95 price. She wanted to match her FBA listing in VeryGood condition against a merchant fulfilled Acceptable condition offer. I know, you're probably wondering what was she thinking. Don't worry; we were on the phone so I offered her some advice on pricing FBA items. I suggested that she match the $14.95 price and that it was pretty much a guaranteed sale at that price due to the popularity of the item and her specific condition compared to her competitors. This was a price 50% higher than the lowest price. I was surprised when she did not like my advice, after all, my advice was intended to help her make more margin and more profits on her inventory. She started to tell me how I didn't know what I was talking about and how important it is to simply get the books listed and sold and how speed was everything and how she had no time to stop and look at prices and how she always just matches to total lowest price regardless of condition. Yikes! She was chasing the next sale on a 12,000-ranked book, and as an FBA seller no less! It seemed like I was in for some trouble, but I really wanted to help her learn to price her items well. I tried some simple explanations about understanding the Amazon buyer and the advantages that FBA sellers enjoy over their merchant fulfilling competitors. She did not want to hear it. She proceeded to tell me how she has been selling books online for three years and she knew what she was doing and the three seconds that I recommended she take to stop and look at the competitive pricing information was just too long and it would slow her down too much. I tried again with some helpful information about how it may only be a few dollars, but how it can really add up over time. She came back at me again telling me how she does $350,000 in sales every year and that she knows what she is doing and has no interest in any other pricing strategies. I'll admit that my frustration level was rising a bit at this point although her bottom line didn't really affect me personally. In a pretty stern voice I told her that my advice would increase her prices, margins, and profits by an estimated 50% meaning an additional $175,000 on her $350,000 business. The phone was silent for a few seconds. I had finally gotten my point across. We finished our discussion on how to price FBA items and I'm happy to say that she is still a customer of ours and she is enjoying higher margins.

## Chapter 20 – What Makes a Product Good for Resale

I'd rather teach you to fish than just give you a fish so in this chapter we're going to talk about why there are no lists of good products to sell online. A product is not good for resale because it is on a list; it is good for resale because of all the factors surrounding that product. If I had a list of products that were good for resale, it would benefit you more to learn WHY those products are on that list.

You have to learn this business and not just blindly follow every expert out there. This includes me as well! I want to teach you this business and how to use the required tools to become successful. It won't do either of us any good if I just tell you what to do and then you go do it without ever learning WHY this all works the way that it does. As soon as I stopped telling you what to do, your business would fail. This is not the position that I want to be in and it should not be a position that you want to find yourself in, either.

When you make buying decisions, you need to make them with confidence. You know the risks involved and the rewards that match those risks. Things to consider:

**Margin**

Personally, the number one thing that I consider is margin. Review Chapter 18 to be sure that you have the proper view of margin and volume. When margins are high, you can take more risks.

**Brand**

Good, popular brands will have a better chance of having strong demand as well as lasting demand over time as people trust and prefer brands with good reputations.

## Category/Type of Item

Some categories will be better to sell in than others. Consider the Toy category that was discussed in Chapter 12. Categories that have the same characteristics as the Toy category will respond in a similar way to the market forces of supply and demand.

## Homeruns Or Singles?

A lot of sellers hear all of the homerun stories about buying 200 items for $5 each that are selling for over $100 on Amazon and while homeruns like that do happen if you are out in the stores and doing this business, they are rare. Don't think about only trying to hit homeruns. Just like in baseball, you'll score a lot more runs if you hit a lot of singles than if you only try to hit homeruns. The best part about this is that singles are easy and don't slow you down in your search for homeruns.

A deal isn't a deal just because someone says that it is a deal. There are so many things that can differ between two resellers looking at identical items. If the item sells online for $70 and one reseller finds it for $50, it's not a deal. But if another reseller finds it for $20, then it is a deal. So you can't just put items on a list, because you need to have a price point at which the product becomes a deal. Since every product can become a deal at a certain price point, the 'deal list' would be a list of every product ever! A list like this is not useful which is why you need to carry FBAScout for accurate data, learn this business, decide how you want to run your business and take action.

# Chapter 21 – Sourcing Products – Retail vs. Online

Sourcing products is probably the number one topic that people want to talk about and it is obviously very important. There are many places to source inventory. In the previous chapter, we talked about what makes a product a good deal to sell online and how there is not just a list of products that are good to sell online. We'll take that a step further and discuss different sources of products and the advantages and disadvantages of both.

First thing that I want to mention is that there are big differences between retail stores and their online counterparts. Knowing these differences will allow you to properly evaluate the market dynamics at play. Knowledge is power and knowing the differences here can give you the information to find deals that your competition overlooks.

## Home Depot vs. HomeDepot.com

I am very familiar with this relationship for reasons that you can probably guess from reading the beginning of this book. It may surprise you to know that Home Depot and HomeDepot.com are run completely separately. You cannot buy from HomeDepot.com and then return the product to your local Home Depot (at least not at the time of this writing). Products available at your local Home Depot may or may not be available on HomeDepot.com. Same thing for HomeDepot.com; they will carry products that are not available at your local Home Depot store.

How does knowing the differences help you as a reseller? Let me explain.

First, let's consider demand for certain products. You will undoubtedly see large-scale advertising campaigns on TV, on the radio and in print. These advertisements create demand for those products. Those products are only available in a limited supply for limited sales channels, namely Home Depot Stores or HomeDepot.com. Now add to this situation the dynamic that the product is also a house brand (discussed later in this chapter).

You now have demand for a product with limited distribution channels. Sure, HomeDepot.com can ship anywhere in the country and most of the population lives in close proximity to a Home Depot store, but consider these possibilities:

Customers who have never ordered a product online (and don't plan to start).

Customers who do not live near a Home Depot store.

Customers who are unaware of the house brand relationship so they look elsewhere for the product.

Neither HomeDepot.com nor Home Depot stores have unlimited supply of the product so when they sell out, supply is gone but demand remains. If you have some of that supply, you can now meet that demand and you are not bound by any pricing agreements. Your price is set by the simple market forces of supply and demand. Thanks to the Internet, you can offer your supply on several sites such as Amazon or eBay (shipping eBay orders through FBA is covered later in this book in Chapter 32).

Here's an example that surely plays out somewhere in the country:

A husband and wife are watching TV. The husband sees the Home Depot commercial and says to his wife that he would like that product for a Christmas gift. She makes a mental note and the next day goes on Amazon.com and purchases the product from an FBA seller. Done.

Why not go to Home Depot? Maybe she doesn't live near one. Maybe she didn't even realize it was a Home Depot commercial and she just remembered the product. Maybe Amazon is the first place that she considers for purchases. When she finds it on Amazon, she buys it and her shopping is done. Maybe going out shopping is the last thing that she wants to do.

Maybe she did note that it was from Home Depot but when she went to the store, she found out that they were sold out. Maybe she doesn't realize that HomeDepot.com even exists. Even if she did, HomeDepot.com may be sold out, or they may not even offer the product (some products are only sold in retail stores).

Once she finds it on Amazon for a price at which she values the item, she makes the purchase and the transaction takes place. She got what she wanted and the seller got what they wanted.

She may be paying more than retail in order to get her hands on a popular product that is not in stock at the regular MSRP. If she wants the item at this point in time, she has to pay the premium price on the secondary market. She may be paying this premium price knowingly or unknowingly. The facts of the matter are that price is set by supply and demand and a transaction only takes place when the buyer values the item more than the price and the seller values the price more than the item.

## House Brands

House brands are brands that have partnerships in place with retailers. Some brands are even owned by the retailer. One of the most famous house brands is Craftsman tools. They are sold exclusively at Sears. I'm sure you are familiar with many brands that are called house brands, but you just didn't know that they were house brands. Ryobi tools at Home Depot is another house brand.

What happens is that these retailers like Sears and Home Depot put on their national advertising campaigns and create nationwide demand for their products. The supply is limited to certain channels such as the local stores and the company's website. There will be many reasons why the demand will not be able to reach the supply. Not everyone lives near a Sears and Sears.com may be sold out or not even carrying the product at all.

This goes for all kinds of products, not just power tools. It even works on grocery items. Have you heard of Trader Joe's? I use this example because it is easier to understand. If you haven't heard of Trader Joe's, I'll tell you this: People are crazy for Trader Joe's! It has very loyal shoppers who prefer their Trader Joe's branded products like salsa or olive oil. It is not unreasonable to assume that there are people out there who have a special preference for certain Trader Joe's products. Some of those people who at one time lived within shopping distance of a Trader Joe's have since relocated to another part of the country where there are no Trader Joe's. Now when they cook dinner, the only thing that they can think about is how they wish they had their special Trader Joe's olive oil. This is the DEMAND. They decide to go online and see if it's available from Amazon.com. THERE IT IS! You understood that this demand existed and you met that demand with your supply (if you live near a Trader Joe's) and you sent some supply to FBA. They are happy and purchase the olive oil, and you are happy and put the profit in your pocket.

This example doesn't work because it's Trader Joe's olive oil, it works because of the brand association, the dynamics of personal preference, and real world factors such as moving across the country. If you find other items that have these same characteristics, then you'll find more items that are good for Retail Arbitrage.

This strategy works for all kinds of products including Canadian exclusives. There are the same types of products available in Canada that Canadian buyers prefer. There are many Canadian ex-patriots living in the USA who shop on Amazon and prefer FBA sellers. If the products were made available on Amazon.com, they would purchase them. This is the DEMAND. You can meet this demand if you have access to the supply (either by importing in bulk or by living in Canada and using some creative FBA strategies discussed in Chapter 32).

Examples of this type of supply and demand abound. Here is another one with a double twist; consider 'snowbirds' who live in the northern states during the summer and then travel to the southern states during the cold, harsh winters. They surely have favorite items that are only local to them during certain parts of the year. If you can provide the supply of those 'southern' items that they cannot get while they are up north or the 'northern' items that they cannot get while they are down south, then you are able to match up supply and demand with a profitable transaction. Supply and demand do not have to be very big when you have the power of the Internet bringing them together.

## Retail Exclusives

There will be some products that are not sold online and are only sold as retail exclusives. There will be buyers (demand) who want these products (supply) who do not live near a store that sells them. These buyers may be more than happy to buy online if there was a seller selling the items. Out of all of the potential buyers who make up the total demand, some of them will value the item at a higher level than the others. Don't think that you have to sell to all of them; you just have to sell to the buyers who value the item the highest as long as this price that they are willing to pay is high enough to hit your target margins.

Retail deals are my favorite deals because you can find deals with sky-high margins and you are truly able to capitalize on knowledge being power. YOU know about the deal because YOU went out and found it. You'll have less competition on deals like this, at least until someone else finds the same deal.

Online deals can be more risky because they are public and anyone can get in on them while the website still has supply to sell. This can lead to increased supply on the secondary market, which of course will drive prices down (at least temporarily).

**Retail Advantages**

Deals are only accessible to those who make the trip to the store.

Not everyone will be aware of the deals.

Low lead times; you can buy and list as merchant fulfilled the same day as well as buy and send to FBA in the same day.

Items can easily be returned if warranted.

**Retail Disadvantages**

Quantities can be limited.

Requires time and effort.

**Online Advantage**

Quantities can be higher than at retail (purchase 200 units instead of just 20 units).

You can purchase items and have them delivered to your door.

**Online Disadvantages**

Increased lead times (shipping time in transit) can lead to changed market dynamics by the time your products are available for sale.

Deals are 'public' meaning that anyone can find the deals and get in on them. This can increase the secondary market supply and drive down price.

The online returns process can be more difficult and cost money (return shipping).

There is much more information about retail deals and online deals found later in Chapter 24 and Chapter 26.

## Chapter 22 – Purchasing TAX FREE for Resale

Quick question: Who is responsible for paying sales tax on retail items?

The buyer? Well, sort of. The correct answer is the END USER. The end user is the buyer who buys the item to use. There may be other buyers along the way, but it is only that last buyer, the end user, who pays the sales tax. As you are likely well aware, end users who buy online only pay sales tax on in-state purchases or on online purchases where the website has an in-state presence, or 'nexus'. This is one reason that Amazon was able to become so powerful. By not having to collect sales tax on interstate purchases, their prices have been lower than if buyers purchased the same items in-state and had to pay sales tax.

When you buy items at retail or even at book sales and thrift stores that you intend to resell, then you are not the end user. You are a reseller. Resellers do not pay sales tax on items that are destined for resale.

Resellers who resell to in-state buyers are required to collect and remit sales tax on those in-state purchases. In a simplified example where you sell to all 50 states equally, you would only be collecting taxes on 2% of your sales, or from one out of fifty states. The other 49 states, or 98% of your sales, are sales on which you are not required to collect or remit sales tax.

This is not cheating or tax evasion; this is knowing and following the law. Knowing the law and the rules of resale will allow those who know the law and the rules to work smarter than their competition. Remember, knowledge is power? It applies here as well. People who buy and sell retail products who don't follow this one simple rule will have product costs that are much higher than yours. This means your margins are higher and you make more money. Over the long run, your business will thrive and they will be working too hard.

**Here's how it works:**

Every state will be a little different, but they will all be very similar. Search for your local comptroller's office. They likely have their own website. You can call or email and explain what you want to do. Tell them you are a reseller and you want to know what is required in your state to purchase tax free for resale. They will know exactly what you are talking about and will be able to help you. You may be able to do the entire thing online. When I first started, I had to actually go to the comptroller's office to fill out paperwork. Now the process in Texas is completely online.

Once you have your state tax ID number, you have to know how to use it. Some states will have a form that you can print out and present to the retailer. Some stores will just want the number for their records. Some stores will want to see the actual tax ID certificate so you may have to carry it with you. Some stores, like Home Depot, require you to set up a tax-free account in their computer system. This can be more difficult to initially set up, but it is actually the easiest to use. Once your account is set up, you just have to tell them the purchase is tax exempt and give them your phone number and they can pull up your account.

You may be asking if purchasing tax-free is only for local retailer purchases or can online deals be purchased tax-free? The answer is that anything that you buy online for resale can also be purchased tax-free. It can be a little more complex, but here's how to do it:

Many websites that you can buy from will already be tax-free so don't worry about those. Let's use an example of a site that has a local presence in every state, HomeDepot.com. There is no way to checkout at HomeDepot.com without paying sales tax (they may change this at some point, which would be awesome, but currently you have to pay the sales tax on all online orders). After you purchase, you contact HomeDepot.com and explain that you are a reseller and that the items that you purchased are for resale. They will send you the paperwork to file for a refund of the sales tax. You fill it all out and include copies of all relevant documents such as your tax ID form and they will refund the sales tax that they charged back to your credit card. Not as easy as just not paying it at checkout, but still very worthwhile to process.

Another option is to claim sales tax credit when filing and remitting your sales tax records. Each state may vary, but when you file your sales tax records each month, there should be an option for entering an amount for purchases on which you were claiming sales tax credits. So even if you pay tax at checkout because you didn't have your sales tax ID or just checked out and paid sales tax in the interest of expediency, you can still claim the sales tax credit so that your purchases net out as tax free.

In my experience, it is a much better idea to not pay the sales tax when you purchase than to pay it and then try to get it back. Keep your business as simple as possible!

This is all a method of lowering your costs. The lower your costs are, the higher your margins will be. Simply knowing the rules allows you to have lower costs than your competitors. It's awesome.

If you live in an area where you will be purchasing tax free for resale from several different states, be sure to talk to your accountant or tax professional to be sure that you are following the rules for each state and filing any required reports properly.

As with all laws, they can change. This information is accurate at the time of this writing. Laws may change so be sure to check online for the current rules to be sure that you are following them.

## Chapter 23 – Coupons, Discounts, Rebates, Rewards & Cashback

When you are buying items for resale, your margin is dependent on your product costs. The lower you are able to get your costs, the higher your margins (and profits) will be. There are many ways to lower your costs and even though some of these methods may only be 1-2%, when you do them all, the discounts add up and become significant. When your costs are significantly lower than your competitors, then you are in a much more powerful position as well as in a lower risk position in the event that prices decline.

Some strategies outlined in this chapter work better for retail deals and some work better for online deals. Use as many as you can on each and every purchase regardless of where you are purchasing your inventory for resale.

### Coupons

There is no shame in using coupons! Coupons are easy to get and easy to use. I recommend getting on the mailing lists and email lists for the retailers that you are purchasing from so that you will be updated and alerted for their current discounts and available coupons. Home Depot and Lowe's will periodically simply mail you 10% off coupons for being on their lists.

### Discounts

There are many ways to get additional discounts at retail stores. Some stores give 5-10% discounts for senior citizens or military personnel on certain days of the week or month. All you have to do is ask at the store if they have any special days. If they do and you qualify, be sure to shop more on those days to lower your costs.

You'd be surprised how many times you can get an additional discount by just asking. This will have more likelihood of success if you are making a large purchase or offer to make a large purchase. You might as well try this on every large purchase if the products are already good for resale. Since you are buying them anyway, any additional discount would just be icing on the cake. And if they don't give you a discount, it's no big deal. It never hurts to ask.

**Rebates**

You'll find many products with all kinds of different rebates. Some rebates will be for cash and some may be for products. Some may be on the spot rebates and some may require a form to be mailed in.

Instant rebates are the best kind because they often have no restrictions and there is nothing else to do later. Nothing to pay for now and wait for later, and no waiting for any products that you intend to sell.

A typical restriction of rebates is a limit on the number of rebates that can be submitted per person, or per address or household. Is there any way around this? You bet there is, and it's not anything tricky. When we would find a product with an attractive rebate for resale, we would read all of the fine print. If there was no limit listed but it was still a mail-in rebate, we would contact the company issuing the rebate to be sure that there was no limit. We prefer email for this type of communication so that you have something in writing.

If a rebate has a redemption limitation, we would simply ask if they would waive the limit if we purchase a large number of items. Sometimes they will say no, but you'll be surprised how many times they will say yes. It never hurts to ask and you'd be surprised how many people would never consider asking for an exemption to their rules. So if you think outside of the box and pursue ways to do deals that other resellers do not, you'll be the one reaping the rewards. Less competition will mean that you'll be able to maintain higher prices and margins.

Another bonus of rebates is that they are only available for a limited time. This means that only the resellers who are able to capitalize on the deal within the limited window of time for which the rebate is valid will be your potential competition. Ideally a rebate may come and go without other resellers even noticing the opportunity.

## Credit Card Points & Rewards

The odds are that you'll be making most of your purchases on credit cards for convenience. You might as well get and use cards that give you points, miles or other rewards. Different cards will cater to different types of rewards programs so find one that matches your personal preferences. We use the Southwest VISA to rack up free Southwest flights and the Amazon VISA to get Amazon gift cards. Our American Express gives us Home Depot gift cards that we use to buy even more products to resell. We have a card that has great rewards for restaurants gift certificates as well as cards that help us maximize our discounts at the gas pump. My favorite card (no longer available) was the Home Depot Rewards MasterCard. It gave us 3% back in the form of gift cards. When spending big bucks at Home Depot, getting 3% of all of those dollars spent back in gift cards each month was just icing on the cake. I would get strange looks sometimes when checking out at Home Depot with a huge flat-cart loaded up with power tools and handing them gift card after gift card after gift card. Once I told them that we buy a lot on the Home Depot Rewards MasterCard, they knew exactly what was going on. I miss those gift cards ☺.

## Stack & Exploit

When I say exploit, I mean it in a good way. I mean it in a way that follows all of the rules but all of those rules are in MY favor. You'll find times when the retailer will have a promotion that coincides with a manufacturer's rebate. Deals like this can be incredibly lucrative but you do have to do your homework and make sure that there are no exceptions such as 'This offer cannot be combined with any other offer' type of stuff. The good news is that you can do all of your homework before ever spending one penny so you always know what you are getting into. Find these types of deals, validate exactly how it will ring up at the register, and if it's a deal, pull the trigger. The more complex or creative the deal, the less of a chance that another reseller will figure it out and get in on it. This means that you'll have less competition, which will keep your margins (and profits) healthy.

**Cashback Sites**

If you are already buying products online, you might as well get the best price in order to lower your costs and maximize your margins. A great site to squeeze every last drop out of discounts is FatWallet.com. They have an entire section about cashback from online retailers that you may already be purchasing from. You might as well go through the cashback process to get every dollar that you can.

Details about their cashback program can be found here:

http://www.fatwallet.com/cash-back-shopping/

## Chapter 24 – Retail Deals

Retail deals are awesome and this is where you can buy great products and make serious profits with nice, high margins. Personally, these are my favorite kinds of deals because it's like a treasure hunt! Retail Arbitrage opportunities exist in every store; you just need to have the tools and information in order to identify them. You are able to purchase items at set prices whose sales are dependent on the LOCAL supply and demand and move that supply to the online marketplace when price is determined by the ONLINE supply and demand.

Scouting at retail is also a much less competitive environment compared to library sales and book sales (covered in Chapter 30). You are able to scout pretty much any time of day and at your leisure. No elbow jabs, no pushing and shoving. Well maybe on Black Friday, but you know what you're in for if you go out scouting on Black Friday, so you can't really complain about that.

Buying from retailers is so much fun because when you buy at the retail level, you are not bound by any kinds of pricing agreements or Minimum Advertised Price (MAP) guidelines. Retail purchases can be sold anywhere, to anyone, for any price.

**Ultimate Backup Plan**

Retail deals can be very low risk because since you are buying from a retailer, you have the ultimate fallback plan of simply returning the product to the store. I obviously don't recommend doing so because this would mean that you are spending your time on non-profitable activities, but it is a nice safety net, especially when first starting out. If you do return products, be sure that you are within each store's specific return policy guidelines and that the items are in the same condition as when you purchased them.

**Any Retailer, REALLY!**

When I say any retailer, I really do mean it. We have bought items from the big retailers that come to mind when you think retail stores like Wal-Mart, Target, and Home Depot. But we have also purchased items at the pharmacy and grocery store. Pharmacies and grocery stores always have that little toy aisle that usually has some pretty cheap stuff. I don't know where they get it, but sometimes they'll have brand name, popular in-demand toys for sale at ridiculously low prices. I don't need to know where they got them in order for me to buy them and send them to FBA. The cool part is that you can do scouting like this while you are at these types of stores anyway. Buying groceries? Check for toys. Picking up a prescription? Check for toys. You may be surprised at what you find.

**Scalability – Buying Multiple Quantities**

Retail deals can be very attractive because you are able to buy items in multiple quantities. Each time you find a winning product, the number of items that you are able to buy multiplies those profits. Instead of finding ten used books to sell and only finding one copy of each, you can find ten products to sell but have ten units of each. So you now have 100 profitable items to sell instead of just ten. The effort required to list these does not go up by a factor of ten because you still only have ten DIFFERENT products. If sending to FBA, all you have to do is list the ten products and print multiple labels.

There are so many places to go to find profitable items for Retail Arbitrage. Many people who live in mid-to-major metropolitan areas will have access to multiple locations of the same retailers. This is how you can again MULTIPLY your profits without multiplying your efforts. Those ten items that you bought at Big Lots are likely sitting on the shelf at another Big Lots across town. It's even easier now because you just have to go in and pick them up since you have already done the initial scouting. But still, take your FBAScout in case this other store has some different products that are too good to pass up.

**Negotiating Deals**

Remember that retail stores want to sell things. You can simplify it this way; they sell boxes. Big boxes, small boxes, light boxes, and heavy boxes. They want to sell boxes and as a reseller, you want to buy boxes (to resell of course). There is nothing stopping you from negotiating with the store management on prices or quantities. I encourage you to build relationships with store personnel as they can come to see you as a place to move inventory that they do not want (but that you want, at the right price). All store managers have monthly budgets with which to mark down products that are slow moving, or for any other reason at their discretion. They may be overstocked on an item and be willing to mark down products if you are willing to purchase them. You'll find that as you build these relationships, stores will CALL YOU with potential deals!

**Deals are Based on Numbers**

When you are discussing potential deals and negotiating prices or quantity, always remember that this is strictly a numbers game. Don't be afraid to remind the store personnel of this fact. This should never be a high-pressure sales decision. A deal is profitable enough for you when the deal meets your individual target margins and risk tolerances. Also, never think that you have to buy more inventory than you are sure than you can afford.

If the deal is a deal, do the deal. If the margins aren't there, don't do the deal. Don't ever chase a deal or feel that you have to purchase something to justify your trip to the store. It's better to leave without making money than to leave with the potential of losing money. Always remember that you have limited funds with which to buy inventory. Don't put yourself in a situation where all of your funds are tied-up in mediocre inventory and then find yourself with no way to purchase the great inventory.

## Loss Leaders & Special Buys

Retailers even sell some products that they actually lose money on. These are called loss-leaders. They are primarily designed to get shoppers in the door so that in addition to buying the loss-leader product, they also purchase other items that are more profitable. Some retailers will also get 'special buys' that are often only available in limited quantities. They will get special buys for special events such as grand openings and holiday weekend sales events. These special buys are at prices that are below the normal, equilibrium market price. This means that they can sometimes be resold on the secondary market for a higher price.

## Taxes

The only real rules that you have to follow when buying and selling retail products are the tax laws. These are covered in Chapter 22. Know when you have to pay tax and when you don't as well as when you have to collect tax and when you don't. If you are ever unsure, consult a CPA with specific knowledge of your state's tax laws.

## Clearance Items

Clearance items are a good place to start because their prices will already be lower than the normal retail prices. Some stores will have special tables for clearance items. Some stores will simply change the price on the shelf. Some stores re-label their shelves with different colored price tags such as red or yellow in order to attract the attention of buyers while shopping. When you know what to look for, you can train your eyes to see the clearance deals as you walk down the store aisles. Keep notes for each store about how they price and label clearance items so that you know what to look for each time that you shop at the store.

## Chapter 25 – Retail Secrets

When I was working for Bosch Power Tools and calling on Home Depot (currently the second largest retailer in the US behind Wal-Mart), I learned a ton about how retailers worked. These aren't really secrets in the sense that nobody knows them, but this information is really only useful if you are a store employee or a reseller. This is powerful information that will enable you to absolutely CRUSH your competition in terms of lowering your costs and being able to acquire large amounts of inventory efficiently. You want to be running an efficient, high margin business. If your competition wants to run an inefficient, low margin business, that's up to them. I'll teach you to work smart; leave it to them to work hard.

**Learn the Policies of Each Store**

Each store will operate differently but all will be similar. They will all have a return policy that you should be aware of in the event that you ever return items to the store. Some are 30 days, some are 90 days, and some have shortened return policies for certain items like computers or electronics.

Some stores will aggressively beat another store's advertised prices and some will simply price match.

One of the most powerful policies related to price that most resellers overlook is a store's policy of refunding the difference in price if the price on an item drops within a certain time-frame from the original purchase date.

What this means is that if you bought an item for $100 and ten days later the price drops to $50, you can go in, usually with only your receipt, and they will simply refund $50 back to your credit card. How sweet is that! Paying attention to price drops, even after you have purchased the items for resale can get you some nice refunds. This all goes back to your bottom line by lowering your costs, which increases your margins.

It's so easy to do. Just keep all of your receipts organized by retailer and by date. Learn the store's price matching policies. When it gets close to the cut off date, it's time to check for any price drops. Here's another secret; you don't even have to go to the store to check. Just call the store and use the numbers on your receipt to have customer service check on in store prices. Only after you have verified that there were any price drops do you actually go to the store.

## Learn How Each Store Works

Each store will have little differences in how they operate, but most stores are using some pretty sophisticated inventory programs that show real-time inventory levels. This means that if you find an item on the shelf that is a good item for resale, that the store's computer system will know exactly how many they have on hand (assuming that the on-hand quantity in the computer is correct). It never hurts to ask; remember, stores WANT to sell you things! You may find two but the computer may show that they have ten. Those other eight may still be in the back and you would never know unless you ask and have a store employee check.

Many stores are also networked together so that one store can see the inventory levels at other stores. Some will only have access to other local stores, such as stores in their district, and some will show inventory levels for any store anywhere in the country. Home Depot was like this; I could be in Texas and tell you on-hand inventory levels for any specific store in California or Florida. This means that if you find a deal at one store, you can check other stores in the surrounding area right from that first store. It's all about efficiency. By doing this, you can see exactly which stores have the most inventory. Now you can spend your time focusing on the stores with the most inventory FIRST.

## Store Numbers

Each store will have a unique number most commonly called the store number. You should make notes of any known store numbers for stores that you frequent. It will make it easy for you to keep things organized; when you talk with store personnel about different stores, they will be familiar with what you are talking about.

## Store Folder/Records

You should make some kind of notebook that contains information about the stores that you frequent. This should be information like address, phone number, store number, and even the names of the store personnel that you meet and talk to. This will help you be more efficient when tracking down deals as well as help you build relationships at the store level.

## SKU Systems

Each store will use some kind of numbering system with which to identify products. Most of these will be called SKUs (pronounced skews). When you are familiar with how a store identifies its own inventory, it will be easier for you to talk to the store either in person or over the phone about their inventory levels.

## How to Tie Up Deals Without Ever Leaving the House

When you are organized and knowledgeable about the deals and the stores that sell the deals, you can quickly tie-up large amounts of inventory without ever leaving your house. You can work smart and efficiently while your competition drives around aimlessly from store to store only to find out that they went to three stores that were already sold out. They would have known this if they had the SKU number and called the stores before heading out.

Many stores will let you purchase items over the phone. The first step is to call and verify inventory levels on the items that you are looking for. This is why understanding the SKU systems in place are very helpful. If the store confirms that the item is in stock, then see if you can reserve the items so that there is no possibility of the items being sold while you are traveling to the store. Some stores will let you reserve items, but the better way is to straight-up pay for the items over the phone. This is much more official and will prevent the stores from 'accidentally' selling the items to someone else. Sometimes you don't even have to pick up the items right away so you can sit at home and call multiple stores and tie up large amounts of inventory. Items that are already paid for will be held in a will-call area and you can pick them up at your convenience. I do recommend picking your items up as soon as you can.

If the deal is lucrative, don't worry about trying to pay tax-free over the phone. While this can be done, it is not always the easiest thing for the stores to do. In the interest of speed, just get the items paid for and tied up so that you can either make more calls to other stores or go pick the items up. You can always refund and repurchase the items tax-free when you are at the store picking them up. Some stores can also just take your receipt and refund the tax on the spot.

**When to Call, When not to Call**

Calling a store to check on inventory levels or to purchase items over the phone is a brilliant way to tie up inventory without running all over town blindly, but it does have some drawbacks. By calling a store, you can alert the store employees to the deal. Store employees love a good deal as much as everyone else so there is the possibility that as soon as they realize that the deal exists, they will purchase the items themselves or even call their friends to get in on the deal. This is more of a concern in categories such as computers and electronics. Everyone loves a good clearance deal on laptops, as they have a high perceived value and are more universally utilized. Compare this to vacuums or jigsaws where even at a super low price, not as many people will be interested.

Sometimes there are straight up price mistakes where stores accidentally have a low price on an item. This can be incredibly lucrative for obvious reasons. It's rare, but it does happen. If the price is an error, you would want to lay low so as to not alert the store to the mistake. This is a time where you would not want to call around and check inventory levels. If the price is what it is and you check out and pay the cashier, then the mistake is the store's responsibility.

## Go Where Other Sellers Don't Go

Earlier in Chapter 12 we talked about how I was able to just waltz into Sears and purchase Nintendo Wii accessories at the peak of the pre-Christmas rush on the Nintendo Wii. Everywhere else was sold out, but the thing to take away from this example is that people go to the stores that they THINK will have the items that they want to buy. Best Buy and Toy R Us are the first places that many buyers think of for video games, but many people do not think of Sears (to be honest, I didn't think of Sears at first, either).

I have always had great luck finding hard-to-find items still in stock at stores that are in rough locations. Not all stores are in the nicest parts of town, but I can't name one store that I would not feel safe shopping at during the day. If it's a part of town that your competition does not frequent, this will mean that that you'll have less competition at these types of stores. Sometimes your competition is just lazy. There is much more on your lazy competition at the end of this book in Bonus #7.

Oftentimes these stores have slower sales volumes as well, which means that toys can sit on the shelves for longer periods of time. As a toy becomes harder and harder to find, you go to a store like this and see that you'll find the toys that have been sold out everywhere just sitting there waiting for you.

## Chop Shop: The Parts are Worth More than the Whole

We did this with power tools that we bought from Home Depot and Amazon.com to sell on eBay. Just like an automotive chop shop that takes a car and sells all of the parts for more than the value of the car as a whole, we would buy power tool combo kits and sell each part individually. This way we could get maximum value by selling the batteries to someone who only wanted the batteries and the drill to someone who only wanted the drill.

Why would someone want a cordless drill without batteries and a charger? Well, they probably already have a bunch of batteries and chargers, especially if they use their tools at their job. Maybe the drill out of their combo kit broke, or was lost, or even stolen. Maybe they just want two drills for times when they have an extra helper.

A typical DeWalt combo kit would include a drill, circular saw, reciprocating saw, flashlight, two batteries, a battery charger and a case (yes, we even sold the case separately). You may be able to pick up tools where some parts are more valuable than others. By selling in pieces, you can maximize the value of each piece rather than trying to find a buyer who wants to buy everything at once. Chop shop selling works for many different products that are sold in groups but are able to have their parts resold individually.

We've done countless deals through Home Depot and Lowe's. Power tools are a pretty safe bet in terms of holding their value. A drill is still a drill even if a new drill model comes out. Does it still drill holes? If yes, then it's still a drill and has value to someone who needs to drill holes. They do not drop in value the same way that electronics do when new models come out.

This 'chop shop' dynamic works for more than just power tools; the power tools category is just an easy example. Anything that you can buy that comes as a package composed of smaller, sellable parts, can be sent through your 'chop shop'. Stores like Sam's Club, Costco, BJ's, and other membership-based bulk-buy stores sell all kinds of products like this. A multi-pack of shampoo can be broken down into individual bottles or a 'special-buy' toy with a bonus DVD included. Don't always think that items have to be sold in the exact same manner in which you purchase them. When you think outside of the box and get creative, you find there are opportunities right in front of you; opportunities that your competitors are missing.

## Chapter 26 – Online Deals

Online deals are awesome because you can often just order up a ton of profitable inventory and have it delivered right to your front door. This beats driving around to dozens of different stores in terms of simplicity, but there are some important differences to be aware of.

Websites can sell items that they do not have enough of to distribute at the retail level. This means that you will find items on a retailer's website that are not available in the actual stores. This is because Home Depot has over 2,000 stores and if they have an item that they only have 700 left of, it doesn't make sense to try to distribute them all at the store level. They throw the remaining 700 units on HomeDepot.com at a hot price to be done with them.

If a deal is really good, then it will be purchased quickly, not just by resellers, but also by regular buyers who just want the item for personal use. This means that online deals can disappear quickly so sometimes you need to ACT FAST to get in on a good online deal.

### Online Deals are More Visible

Because online deals are online, anyone with a computer can find them. If more people find them, then the odds are that some of those people will be resellers just like you. This means that you'll have competition on the secondary market. While increased competition can lead to lower prices, at least short-term lower prices, there are several strategies that can be used to maintain your target margins.

### Ryobi 12V Auto-Hammer

Here is an example of an online deal that I did. It was sent out in the HomeDepot.com marketing email. This item was the Ryobi 12V Auto-Hammer. It retailed for $99 at the store level. It had been released the previous Christmas season and this deal was sent out in May. This item had been selling for $59 on HomeDepot.com previously and for this promotion they dropped the price to $19.88. I can only assume that these did not sell very well for Home Depot.

If you spend $249 you got free shipping. I did have to pay sales tax at checkout, but I was able to get that refunded later.

Here is the receipt:

More saving. **More doing**.    Welcome Chris, (Sign Out) Seekonk, MA is your LOCAL STORE    LOCAL AD

| SHOP ALL DEPARTMENTS | SEARCH ALL | | GO |

Home / My Account / Order Information

## Order Details

**Order Number: W105993779**

| Order Status | Order Date |
| --- | --- |
| Complete | May 17, 2010 |

### Items To Be Shipped or Delivered

**Merchandise: 1 Item(s)**

**Item Details**

| | Description | Status | Qty | Total |
| --- | --- | --- | --- | --- |
| | 12-Volt Auto Hammer<br>Model CAH12QLX<br>Store SKU 928609<br>Internet/Catalog SKU 202614871 | All Shipped | 250 | $14,750.00 |

Free Shipping on Most Orders over $249

**Shipping Method**

| Shipping Address | Tracking Number | Shipping Method | Provider | Total |
| --- | --- | --- | --- | --- |
| Chris J Green<br>319 W. 3rd St.<br>Irving TX 75060 | 1Z40E36V0339923279 | Standard | Standard Ground | $0.00 |

**Promotion Code**

Free Shipping on Most Orders over $249 See Details

| | |
| --- | --- |
| Merchandise Subtotal | $14,750.00 |
| Shipping Subtotal | $0.00 |
| Savings | -$9,780.00 |
| Sales Tax | $410.03 |
| Estimated Total | $5,380.03 |

HomeDepot.com had A LOT of these in stock. I had to set a limit as to how many I would purchase. I don't remember why I chose 250; it was probably because it was a fairly round purchase number of $5,000.

I was aware that other resellers would find this deal. How many of them would be in the position to drop $5,000 on 250 units? Probably not too many, but it's possible. After they were delivered, I checked the Amazon product page. It was easy to see that other sellers had received theirs as well! Price had plummeted. It was down to a price of $27.95 + shipping from merchant fulfilled sellers. I knew that price would come back up because this lowered market price was temporary and based on a short-term spike in supply. The sellers who were selling these did not have an unlimited supply at this artificially low cost of $19.88. As these other resellers sold through their inventory, the price would return to a normal level. I held onto my 250 units until October and then I sent them all to FBA at a price of $84.95. I was the only FBA seller and sold every one of them for $84.95 before Christmas.

Plug this item into the Amazon FBA Revenue Calculator and you'll see a payout of $70.75 at this price. At a price of $19.88, a profit of $50.87. Multiply by 250 and get a total profit of $12,717.50. Of course there were a few returns and the inbound shipping costs, but those are small percentages of this total profit.

Compare this to the profit that my competition realized at their silly prices of $27.95 + shipping. This example goes hand-in-hand with what we discussed in Chapter 19 about 'chasing the next sale' by believing that you absolutely have to be the lowest price. It's like all of the sellers are in one room and one seller says that they are willing to make $5 profit and then another stands up and says that they are willing to only make $4 profit. They do this until there are only sellers left who are willing to make no profit at all. It will even get absurd and sellers will lower their price to where they are actually losing money on each sale. This is a game that I do not play and I don't recommend that you play either. Actually, I don't know why anyone plays this game but in a free market society, people are free to play this game if they choose to do so.

## Ridgid 24V Combo Kit

Here is another deal that I did from HomeDepot.com. This was for Ridgid 24V combo kit. This one was destined for the 'chop shop' as the pieces of this kit were much more valuable separately than as a whole kit.

## Why This Deal Worked

This deal worked because of several factors. First, Ridgid power tools is a house brand at Home Depot. This means that these tools enjoyed a vast distribution when they were available in the retail stores. Home Depot stores stopped carrying these, but that didn't mean that the demand for the tools or replacement batteries went away. That demand still existed but it could not find any supply at the local store level; these buyers had to go online to the secondary market. Ridgid also stopped making these particular tools (at least periodically), but because there were already many people out there who had purchased them, there were people who still wanted support for them. If their batteries died, they wanted to buy more batteries. They did not want to go buy an entire new cordless drill kit.

The batteries alone in this kit sell for over $100 each.

Here is the receipt. You can see that nice, big sales tax number that I had to pay at checkout (don't worry, I had it refunded). I actually bought 200 of these on three separate purchases (120, 40 and 40) so that I would not overload any one credit card.

## Shipping Confirmation

The Home Depot
More saving. More doing.™

Dear Chris J Green,

Thank you for your order with homedepot.com. your order number is W103241855. Follow this link to check on the status of your order. We are pleased to inform you that we have shipped one or more items.

Shipping Date: Mar 23, 2010 11:59:59 PM EST
Order Date: Mar 19, 2010 4:01:01 PM

**The Home Depot Emails**

Sign up now to receive exclusive offers, promotions, home improvement tips & more.

▶ Sign Up

| Quantity Ordered | UPC Code | Product Description | Unit Price | Return Policy Line | Quantity Shipped | Amount |
|---|---|---|---|---|---|---|
| 120 | 648846053509 | 3 Piece 24 Volt Combo Kit | $199.00 | A | 120 | $23,880.00 |

Ship to Address
319 W. 3rd St.

Irving
TX, 75060

| | |
|---|---|
| Merchandise Subtotal | $23,880.00 |
| Shipping Total | $0.00 |
| Sales Tax total | $1,970.10 |
| Shipped Order total | $25,850.10 |
| XXXXXXXXXXX1000 AMEX | $25,850.10 |

These kits were big and it was an adventure when they were delivered. They were stacked to the ceiling.

We chopped these kits into every single piece that we could. Run the numbers yourself on this deal. You can still search for these items and see market prices on eBay and Amazon.

This kit includes:

Ridgid 24V drill

Ridgid 24V reciprocating saw

Ridgid 24V flashlight

TWO Ridgid 24V batteries

Ridgid 24V charger

Ridgid big-mouth tool bag

There are many strategies that you can take on deals like this. It may depend on how quickly you need to see the sales come in to pay that bill from HomeDepot.com. You could take a hot price on some pieces to cover the product cost and then sell the rest for pure profit. Or take your time and sell over a longer period of time and earn a higher return. Your individual business goals will affect which strategies work best for you.

Because this was a higher price point deal, any competitors would be limited by either how much space they had (imagine receiving a purchase like this if you lived in a small apartment?) or your available funds (not everyone has $39,800 to drop on inventory for resale). You will always have the risk of competition. It's up to you to take steps to run your business profitably. Don't ever fear your competition. Learn to evaluate all of the dynamics at play on all deals and you'll be able to out-maneuver them along the way. Remember, you work smart; let them work hard.

**Buy from eBay, Sell on Amazon**

EBay may not be the first place that you consider as an online retailer, but there are deals to be found on eBay. All you need to do is find someone who is happy with a price that is low enough for you to sell on another channel and make money. Amazon and eBay are very different channels that attract very different types of buyers. This means that different items will sell for different prices on each site.

You can find items whose eBay market price is low enough that they could be sold on Amazon for a nice profit. Why is the eBay seller not selling on Amazon? Who knows? Maybe they live in their own little eBay-world and still don't realize that Amazon.com sells more than just books. When it comes down to it, if they are happy with the price as a seller and you are happy with the price as a buyer (and reseller), then deals can be made. You may just stumble upon a great source of inventory that can be easily replenished.

When we were selling on eBay, we would get inquiries from resellers in the UK. They wanted to buy power tools from us to sell in the UK. These were tools that were not available at all in the UK but that still had some demand. This demand had no supply to meet it so these UK resellers came to us to get the supply. We made a deal that was profitable for us and at a price that left room for profit for them as well. We were happy to do it. Profit is profit and sometimes you're more than happy to get in, get paid, and get out. We weren't in love with any of the products; they were just items to resell.

## Chapter 27 – Online Secrets

There are not as many online secrets as there are with retail stores, but there are still ways to get better prices than what you see at first glance. Like we talked about in Chapter 23, you can get on the email marketing lists for online retailers that you are buying from. They will send you special promotions, coupon codes, and other information by email that you can use to lower your costs at checkout.

Many online retailers have built in chat programs so you can communicate with someone when you are deciding what to buy. This is a great feature to use to ask for a discount on an item. You can negotiate here as well. If they do not give a discount on a small purchase, ask if they would take off 10% if you make a large purchase. This doesn't always work, but when it does it can save you a nice chunk of change.

You can also keep track of any price matching policies that the websites may follow. If you buy an item for $100 and a few weeks later the price drops to $75, some sites will credit you with the difference. The only requirement is that you have to ask. So keep track of websites that offer these types of price matches and bookmark the products. Check on them prior to the end of the time window for price matching and alert them for any potential refunds.

### Deal Websites

There are several websites out there that consolidate and post deals for retail products at the best price (which is of course below the regular retail price). They are primarily geared towards consumers looking for the best price on products that they want to purchase for themselves. Two of the most popular sites are FatWallet.com and SlickDeals.net. These sites are community driven, where users will post deals.

Of course some deals are good for personal purchase because the price is artificially low. If the price is low enough, then those items will often move into the secondary market where resellers are able to turn a profit.

## Website Monitors

There are programs out there that will check on website pages at regularly scheduled intervals to alert you of any changes in the html code of the page. Why would that be useful? How about when a website offers a product at a price attractive to resellers but they sell out. You can set up a page monitor to send you an email alert as soon as the item is back in stock as indicated by the html of the page being updated. This allows you to get the jump on deals without having to camp out in front of your computer clicking the refresh button all day.

## Daily Deal Sites

There are a number of websites that have temporary price drops on certain items including Amazon.com. The Amazon Gold Box Deals can sometimes be at prices that allow for arbitrage opportunities. There are sites that offer special deals on certain products that are only available until sold out. The biggest of these is Woot.com where they sell one product per day at a significant discount. When they sell out, they don't sell anything else until midnight the next night (CST). Woot.com does have a limit on how many you can purchase, so you won't be able to load up with hundreds of any particular item. They also sell toys under kids.woot.com.

Of course you should always be using the tax-free strategies even for online purchases that were outlined in Chapter 22 as well as the cashback strategies from Chapter 23.

## Chapter 28 – DealsDoneRight.com

DealsDoneRight.com is our membership-based deal sharing site. It can be seen as the destination for all things resale. Think of it as resale for the sake of resale. There are so many places to acquire inventory and there are so many ways to sell inventory that you should never feel as if there is only one model to the business.

You can buy at retail stores, thrift stores, garage sales, manufacturers, wholesalers, or even directly from China. You can sell on Amazon, through FBA, on eBay, or even on Craigslist.

The information on DealsDoneRight.com goes beyond even the scope of this book with a team of contributing experts who specialize in this exact business model of Retail Arbitrage.

The site will include:

Actual retail deals sorted by retailer that you can go and pick up yourself. These deals show you profit and margin so that you can pursue deals that match your business goals. These deals are verified and shared by our network of trusted deal hunters. Information will be included to check store stock levels without ever leaving your home.

Actual online deals that have been carefully screened for high profit margin and fast turns.

A network of trusted deal seekers from all across the country will provide these deals. Deals are available in abundance! Do not let yourself have a mindset of scarcity! These are the real-deal, only at your local store, get them while they're hot deals. These are the deals that you can get in on when you have the information. The same deals that you miss out on because you simply did not know that they were there.

With DealsDoneRight, you'll know they are there and the rest of this book will show you what to do with them.

DealsDoneRight will also include a retailer database of store return policies, clearance/markdown schedules, and in-store reward programs.

**Seminars, Tutorials, Classes, and Resources**

When you are a member of DealsDoneRight.com, don't think that the only deals out there are the ones on our lists. There are more deals out there than anyone can pick up. When you are out at Big Lots picking up the deals shared on DealsDoneRight.com, take your FBAScout and Scanfob™ 2002 and check on other products!

Members can make money with DealsDoneRight.com in three different ways:

The first way is to buy and sell the deals that are posted.

The second way is to be a Deal Bounty Hunter. We pay for good deals to share. You don't have to buy and sell a thing to make money with DealsDoneRight.com. You can just go out and find good deals. Report them back and get paid cash money for every qualifying deal.

The third way is to refer new members.

Now, you may be concerned that sharing deals like this could lead to a drop in price on Amazon.com and that's a valid concern. There are strategies that can be used to maintain price and margin even though supply on Amazon may spike. The first thing to remember is to not panic. Total supply is constant. The supply has just been transferred from local stores to Amazon so it is only the Amazon supply that has spiked. The only way that the Amazon price goes down is if Amazon sellers drop price. It only takes one seller to drop price and potentially start a pricing war. Sellers are free to sell for whatever price that they are comfortable with, but I always encourage sellers to consider if dropping price is necessary to get sales or not. It is then up to each individual seller to price their inventory the way that they choose.

Even if price drops due to an increase in the supply on Amazon, this increase in supply is only temporary. Sellers do not have an unlimited supply of any item that is purchased at a clearanced or a discounted price. Over time, sellers will sell out, supply will go down, and prices will go back up. Sometimes a 'buy-and-hold' strategy makes sense. Retail deals and online deals can be purchased by anyone and not every seller will always be an educated FBA seller or a DealsDoneRight member. There is nothing that you can do to make sellers set prices; you just have to work with the things that you can control. Stay cool and use your understanding of the market forces at play in order to make pricing decisions for your inventory.

Another strategy to consider is using Multi-Channel Fulfillment in order to list and sell on eBay but fulfill your orders through your Amazon FBA inventory. Remember, it is only the Amazon supply that has spiked, not necessarily the eBay supply. This is discussed in greater detail in Chapter 33.

## Chapter 29 – Used Books & Media – Still Easy Money

While true Retail Arbitrage is still a young, emerging business model, there are still plenty of opportunities in the first categories to be scanned like crazy: books and media items (DVDs, CDs, etc.). This is one of the more competitive markets due to the high number of sellers who have been using book and media scanning services for many years. Even with this higher level of competition, you can still carve out a nice little business for yourself by learning what to look for, what to avoid, and how to work smart and not hard.

When deciding what products you want to source to buy and sell online, it is important to look at the margins specific to the category. The margins in used books are huge! When you can buy books for $0.50 and sell them for $80+, the return on your investment is sky-high. It can make this category very attractive and it is actually one of the best categories to start in because of the low cost of inventory.

When deciding between used books and retail items, remember that you don't have to do one or the other. You can do both since they are both profitable. It will depend on the sources in your area as well as the level of funds that you have available with which to purchase inventory.

The differences in categories are not limited to just the margins on the products. Retail stores are open every day, while you may only have book sales or library sales periodically. You can purchase multiple units when buying from retail stores, while used book purchases are likely going to be single items.

When it comes to booksellers, you can think of them two ways. There are real booksellers who know all about first editions, collectible books, antique books, and other stuff that a scanner could never tell you. Then there are books-as-widgets sellers. These sellers scan barcodes and make buying decisions based on the available pricing data and the cost of the book. They treat books as just an inventory item that they can flip for a profit.

There is a distinct dichotomy between these two groups. Real booksellers often do not approve of books-as-widgets sellers because they believe them to be cheating and having no real knowledge or love of books. They have a point but the reality is that books-as-widgets sellers are here to stay so we all might as well get along. I'll freely admit that I am a books-as-widgets seller. I do not have any in-depth knowledge of books. If I find myself in a place where there are collectible books that require more research and evaluation, I'll happily call another bookseller that I know who deals with that sort of thing. I don't even ask for a finder's fee or commission; I'm happy to give them some profitable books. Their business model is much different from mine. This is not my business mode and that's OK. Time is limited so I do what I like doing and other sellers can do what they like doing. They use their knowledge and experience and they are able to buy books and sell them to collectors who collect rare books. They also list and sell on other book selling sites that are better suited for the collectible market. Amazon.com is often not the first place that true book collectors go to for collectible books.

## Still Easy Money to be Made

Selling books is easily the most competitive market that you can currently sell in. While this can sound like something to avoid, if you know what you are doing and you have the right data with which to make buying decisions, you'll soon find that your competition simply leaves so much good stuff behind that you might as well add used books and media to your Retail Arbitrage business model.

## Even Bookstores Are Great Sources for Inventory

You may think that you could never go to an actual bookstore and be able to purchase books for resale, but this is actually a great place to get great books to sell online. Sure, stores that sell new books will know and price their inventory differently than a library sale where everything is usually a flat price per book, but a local, physical bookstore has limitations that will affect the price at which their books will sell.

Even stores that buy and sell used books such as Half-Price Books are not able to get top dollar for every book that they process. Why? Because they are only able to sell to people who are walking in the doors of their local store; they are not reaching the international marketplace. Some $100 book that is only of interest to someone living in India will likely never sell to a walk-in customer for $100 while sitting on the shelf at a local store in Pawtucket, RI. That supply and demand will never meet. After a while, the store decides to put it on the clearance shelf for $1 where you are more than happy to buy it.

Some stores do sell online as well, but if they don't use FBA then they will have different qualifications about what they will list online. They may see a book as not worth their time while you see it as an easy moneymaker. Also, if they don't understand Sales Rank, then the items that they consider to be good matches for online sale will be very different from what you, an educated FBA seller, understand to be good items to sell online. Consider this as well; if they don't understand the Long Tail then the items that they choose to sell online will again be very different from what you consider to be good books to sell online.

What it comes down to is that it is extremely unlikely that any one place is able to funnel each and every item that they sell to the optimal sales channel. Sometimes the optimal sales channel for them is the clearance shelves or tables where they are happy to sell to you for $1 each.

## More Competitors? Or Lazy Competitors?

There is a whole section at the end of this book about Your Lazy Competition in Bonus #7. When you realize the human nature of your competitors, you'll see why good books will so often be left behind.

Bonus #3 also talks about why no one can take over an entire market and be everywhere every time a thrift store puts out new books.

## Why Books Are Awesome

Books are awesome because they are easy. They are easy to find, easy to scan, and easy to process. They are also CHEAP. This is one reason why many new sellers start with books. You get a lot of books for $100 and the margins can be sky-high. When you only pay $0.50 for a book, the price doesn't have to be very high in order to earn a high return. Just wait until you find your first $100 book. If you get out and hit the stores and book sales, it really won't take very long.

## CDs of artists not on iTunes

Are compact discs (CDs) a dead media format yet? Where do people go for music now? Many people go straight to iTunes. This change in the supply and demand means that more demand is getting its supply online. Less demand means lower prices and this is true for most CDs. Today's generation wants their music instantly on their computer and is not going to wait for a CD to arrive in the mail. Are there any exceptions to this market force? You bet there are.

Not all musicians are available on iTunes.

Garth Brooks, Def Leppard, AC/DC and Bob Seger, among others, do not currently offer their music on iTunes. It was only recently that The Beatles put their music on iTunes. This means that anyone who wants Garth Brooks on their iPod or iPhone has to buy an actual CD and rip the songs to their computer. Demand for Garth Brooks hasn't changed, but the supply is much different than the supply for artists on both CD and iTunes. This limited supply forces the prices on the secondary market up and keeps them strong. Go search Amazon.com for used Garth Brooks CDs to see what I mean.

Remember, Garth Brooks CDs are not good for resale because they are on a list of items that someone says are good for resale. There are specific market forces that make this a true statement. Learn to spot and understand the WHY behind this phenomena and you'll be on your way to a successful resale business.

## Will Kindle Kill Books?

I thought about just writing in 'Nope' and moving on to the next section but then I thought that wouldn't flow with the rest of the book. Every time I give you an answer, I want to explain WHY it is the answer. The reason that Kindle will not kill books is because even though e-books are growing, and in some cases overtaking regular books in sales, sales of regular books are also growing on a year-over-year basis. This is the key set of data to consider.

For books to go away on any noticeable level will take an entire generation or more. Could I be wrong? Sure. There's one way to tell. When you read the e-books vs. regular books sales articles, always be sure to dig a little deeper and compare the physical book sales year-over-year. If they are the same or better, then books are here for a while. If they are declining consistently, then books as a market will be shrinking. If there is a decline, it will most certainly not be an overnight shift. It will be slow, measurable, and easy to adapt to.

## Using FBAScout Optimally

When using FBAScout for books and media items, there are some strategies that you can use to be as efficient as possible. First, understand that there are items in the book category that have not just hundreds but THOUSANDS of offers. When an item has that much supply, the price is inevitably going to be low. Sometimes the market price for a book with a ton of offers will be so low that you would lose money if you sold it for that price, even if you got the book for free. Just because some sellers want to play this losing game, doesn't mean that you should. I recommend that you stick with higher-margin items. Lots more info about low price books is covered in Chapter 31.

When you scan an item that has so many offers, you will see something like this:

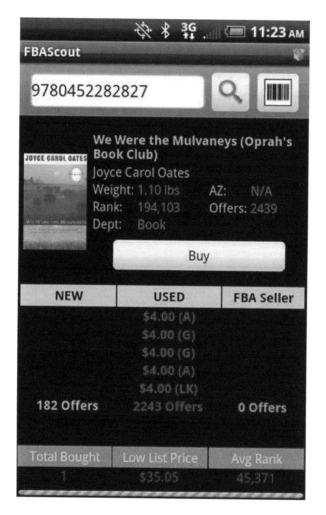

You'll get the product image and details as well as the lowest merchant fulfilled prices. These $4.00 prices mean that this is a book that merchant fulfilled sellers are selling for $0.01 + the flat $3.99 shipping credit charged in the book category. A merchant fulfilled seller cannot sell this book for a lower price; this is as low as they can possibly go.

When you see items like this where there are so many offers (in this case, 2439 different sellers), and sellers are already at the absolute lowest price, then you can bet with certainty that there are FBA sellers selling at prices that are simply not profitable. When you see this, you know that you can move on and scan another item.

You do not have to wait for all of the data to load. Just scan another item. Here you'll see a new item scanned and the pricing data all returned because there were only 53 offers.

FBAScout is still running in the background and will alert you when the pricing data is compiled. You'll see a screen like this when the pricing data is ready:

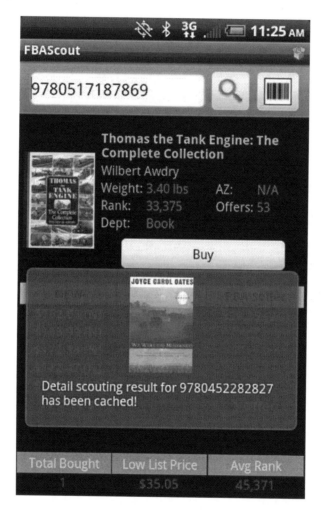

After you see this popup, you'll know that the pricing data is ready if you still wanted to review it. Your choice, but most of the time it will not be worth your time to do so.

If you do want to check it, just scan the barcode again and you'll see the completed data as shown below.

I explain this to you here so that you can scan books as fast as possible. Train yourself what to look for in books and remember the forces of supply and demand and how they affect price. If supply is sky-high, price will be low. If there are already a ton of sellers that have raced to the bottom, then it's probably an item that is not profitable, even at zero cost. Stick to the higher-margin stuff.

## Chapter 30 – Book Sales, Thrift Stores, Estate Sales & Garage Sales

Books can be found in many places. The most common places will be book sales, library sales, thrift stores, estate sales, and garage sales. Each of these places will likely have a very low price per book. You will also find all kinds of media items like CDs and DVDs as well as some toys and games.

Used board games can be quite valuable and you can sell used games on Amazon in collectible condition. For a game to be considered collectible, it should be out of print, meaning that it is not currently manufactured anymore. However, it may still be available in new condition. This can be a great category to scout for because many Amazon sellers, especially booksellers who only focus on books, will pass right over games. Factory sealed games are best because you know that all of the pieces are there. If you are selling a used collectible game, you should be sure to double check that all of the pieces are present and accounted for. If the item is valuable but missing pieces, then sometimes it is worth contacting the manufacturer about purchasing the missing pieces. If a game is missing the instructions, you may also be able to simply print out a copy of the instructions from the manufacturer's website. If you include instructions that are not 100% original, be sure to note this in the item description. If a buyer wants to return the item for any reason, including the reason of simply wanting the original instructions, take the return.

### Running into Other Scanners

When you are out scouting at book sales, and other places, you will inevitably run into other scanners. You know they are out there because you see the stickers covering the barcodes on books nudged away just enough to see the barcode. Over time, you will run into other scanners face to face. What do you do? Do you get nervous? I used to. I used to think to myself that they probably already got all the good books or that they may see me as a threat and possibly act hostile. This is silly of course. When you do run into other scanners at sales or in stores, I encourage you to be nice and take the high road. You will find that many scanners are paranoid and secretive and will most certainly not look you in the eye or even talk to you. That's OK; just leave them alone and stick to your plan. But by being nice, you will eventually run into other nice scanners who see a world of opportunity and abundance and not a world of scarcity. These relationships can pay off both personally and professionally.

I like to describe books scanners this way:

The rare North American 'book scanner':

Feeding habitats include thrift stores, library sales, and garage sales. Although can also be found at estate sales and even retail stores.

Most speak fluent English, but when approached by strangers or startled, will result to code words, or even silence. If asked questions, will often give vague answers to throw you off of their tracks.

Always protective of their food supply (books). Eye contact is rare. They will bite.

**Book Sale Strategies**

The most common place to get information on book sales in your area is http://booksalefinder.com/ If you are planning to go to a sale that is not a close drive, my advice is to call ahead and confirm the date and location. As with anything, sometimes there are errors.

When going to a book sale, I recommend bringing a box. Some people bring little fold-up handcarts and some people bring bags. Find what works best for you. I prefer just one box and when I fill it up, I take it to the holding area and get another box. Most sales will have a holding area where you can keep stacking your books. Just put your name on the box and keep on scanning.

## Friends Night or Preview Night

Most book sales or library sales will open the sale early to members of the Friends of the Library. You have to be a member and membership usually cost $10-$20 for an entire year. In most cases, you can join at the door, so for booksellers it's more like an entry fee to the sale since they likely won't really be involved with the Friends of the Library organization. On preview night, get there a little early. Some people will get there very early and stand in line for hours. That's one strategy I suppose, but it's not mine. I just get there a little early.

Bring your tax ID. They know that they attract booksellers and dealers who are buying books to resell and they know that they don't pay tax.

Bring cash or a checkbook! You may not carry a checkbook around much anymore but you'll find that many book sales are not set up for credit cards. If you don't have enough cash, you may find yourself searching for a way to check out.

You will see other scanners there. Some will be nice and some will be mean. Some will be clueless, and some will be know-it-alls. Your job is to be one of the nice scanners. Once the doors are open, scanners will run to their book section of choice. Some people go for certain categories of books over others. While there are good books in practically every category, there isn't really a hierarchy or map of where to go first. You may just want to go where the other scanners are not just to avoid the crowded, competitive environment.

You'll probably scan like crazy like everyone else for a couple of hours and then you'll look up and see that many of the other scanners have already gone home. Why? Good question. They may actually believe that in the few hours that the sale has been open that every single book in the sale was scanned, evaluated, and either purchased or passed on based on the collective buying criteria of each and every bookseller at the sale. Maybe they do not use FBA and therefore have the limitations of space and time and can only add a fixed number of books to their inventory without being overwhelmed. Maybe they have limited funds with which to buy books. Whatever the reason, I assure you that all of the good books are not taken after the first two hours of a book sale. Be patient, thorough, and most of all, not lazy.

Easy trick: when book sales run out of room on the tables and they still have more boxes of books, they often put them under the tables. Anxious book scanners who run around frantically from section to section will often overlook these.

The book sale may also have many more boxes of books that are not on the sales floor at all but still in the back. As books sell, they will bring these boxes of fresh, un-scanned books out to fill in the holes left by the books that have sold. This is why coming back the day after the preview sale can yield some great books.

On the last day of the sale, they will be looking to really get rid of some books. Everything that doesn't sell has to be either packed up, donated, or disposed of somehow. Many sales will do a flat rate sale by the bag or by the box. Books don't have to have very high sale prices on Amazon when you can get them for ten cents a piece. Books that you can turn a profit on when your cost is close to zero will be plentiful on the last day because so many scanners only take the highest dollar books and leave these other books behind. If they do not use FBA, then these books would not make sense in their business, but since you are selling using FBA, you are able to earn a nice return on these books.

Some libraries sell online and that's OK; they are their books, right? Most book sale and library sales will tell you if they are selling any books online. You can then use this information to decide if the book sale is an attractive one to go to. If they sort and sell some of their books online, then there will be fewer books in the sale that are real winners.

Libraries that do sell online may cause your competition to stay home so it can work to your advantage to go to these sales. Even though some good books will already be pulled, there will still be good books that they missed. It is not likely that they have 100% efficiency when sorting books for online sales or for the physical book sale. It would also be rare for a book sale or library to be selling using FBA. If they are not using FBA then they will run into the same limitations that we talked about at the beginning of this book regarding space and time. These restrictions will factor into which books are removed for online sale and which ones don't make the cut. Many of those that don't make the cut for them will still be easy moneymakers for you.

## Secret Book Sales

Sorry, there aren't really any 'secret' book sales, but there are more book sales than just what you see on Booksalefinder.com. When you attend book sales in your area and you see the same booksellers at every event, you can quickly come to the conclusion that everyone is getting the book sale information from the same place. The main site that most booksellers use is Booksalefinder.com. The good news is that most of your competition never thinks outside of the box and they just rely on this one site to tell them where to go to buy books. Booksalefinder.com is great, but not every library contacts them about their sales. There are many libraries that have no idea that Booksalefinder.com even exists, but they are still having their book sales. How do you find them? I'm glad you asked!

Pretty much every town in the USA has a local library and odds are that each and every one of them will have a book sale at some time during the year. How do you find these libraries? It's pretty easy actually; just search online. Enter a city, state, and the word 'library' and you'll have contact information for pretty much any library in the whole country.

Some will have an email address and you can send inquiries about if and when they are having a book sale. Some may only list a phone number and you would have to call them to find out if and when they are having a book sale.

These can be some of the most lucrative book sales because you have a greater chance of being there with little to no competition. You will find that most of your competition is lazy and that means that they will take the easiest road only, even when the other roads are really not that hard. They will rely on Booksalefinder.com listings only and never take that next step.

One site that has compiled a list of additional book sales is BookSalesFound.com. They are a member-ship based site that boasts offering information on more sales than what you'll see online from free sites.

**Thrift Store Strategies**

There are so many thrift stores out there and so many of them are run differently. Some put new books out daily and some put color-coded stickers on their books to track how long they have been on the shelf. Some stores pull old books that have not sold from the shelves and some stores leave them on the shelves indefinitely.

Sometimes your competition will be lazy and not scan the books on the bottom shelf, or they won't consider the VHS category, or browse the toys and games section. If your competition doesn't do it that means that the good stuff will still be there when you get there.

Pay attention to sale days such as 50% off certain colored items or 50% off certain categories such as books. Most will have a discounted senior citizen's day. Some will have coupons, club cards, or rewards cards. Treat thrift store purchases the same as retail purchases. Use your tax ID to purchase tax exempt. Some small thrift stores may not be familiar with how to do a tax-exempt purchase. Evaluate the situation and if it seems like it will take longer to figure it all out than it is worth in savings, just pay the tax and move on. Your time is valuable and you should be sourcing products and not standing idly at the register. You can always file a credit later.

Be nice to the thrift store employees. This is so important that I wrote a whole bonus (#6) at the end of this book about how being nice not only makes you feel better, it helps your business.

Some may even be selling their own books online either as merchant fulfilled or through FBA. Even if they are, I find it very unlikely that they were able to catch every good book before they make their way out to the sales floor. There is no way that they checked every UPC, every manually entered ISBN, or every title. Sure, they may have found some, but there is no way that they got them all.

**Estate Sale Strategies**

It's easy to Google the estate sales in your area. A few companies will likely run them in your area so you should get to know them and get on their mailing lists. They likely have a website as well so that you can be aware of all upcoming estate sales. Feel free to tell them that you buy and sell books and build up a win-win relationship with them. After all, they want to sell books and you want to buy books. You may not always agree on price and that's OK; it's business, not personal.

Estate sales will likely be better sources for older, collectible books. You may decide that this is a market that you want to learn if you find yourself able to purchase quality inventory.

They may even start calling you when the estate sales are over and they still have books to get rid of.

**Garage Sale Strategies**

You never know what you'll find at garage sales, but odds are you will be able to find some books. Books usually do not sell well at garage sales so you should be able to get them for a good price. You can also make the seller an offer if you buy all of their books.

Scanning books out in the open at a garage sale can draw attention to what you are doing. There will be times when a seller may not want to sell to you if they learn that you are checking prices online and realize that the books are actually valuable. Most sellers could care less, but some may change their mind and decide to keep the books themselves.

Even if a garage sale doesn't have any books out, you can always ask them if they have any books for sale inside. It may have never occurred to them to pull out books for their garage sale. You'd be surprised what doors will open for you just by simply asking.

There are many ways to intentionally look for garage sales that will have books for sale. When you are viewing the garage sale listings on Craigslist, enter the search terms 'books'. Once you find some promising listings, take the addresses and use Google Maps to map out the most efficient route to cover all of the garage sales on your list. Be sure to stop at any other garage sales along the way that were not posted on Craigslist.

There are even apps for iPhone and Android that will help you locate listed garage sales by your desired search terms and map it all out for you using GPS. Fancy stuff.

# Chapter 31 – Penny Books Explained

You've probably seen the books listed for sale on Amazon for $0.01. These are called 'penny-books' because they sell for one penny. This is the absolute lowest price that a merchant fulfilled seller can charge. In the book category on Amazon, buyers are charged a flat $3.99 on the book to cover shipping. So to purchase a penny book, the buyer pays $4.00 to have it delivered. Does the seller get $4.00? No, Amazon takes their commission, which in this case is 15% of $0.01 which equates to zero. They also take what is called the Variable Closing Fee, which is $1.35. So the seller receives $2.65 and they have to ship the book to the customer. After the shipping costs and any other costs involved such as packing materials, labels, overhead and labor, the penny book seller gets their profit.

Here is a screenshot of a penny book transaction from a seller's perspective. You'll see the total received is $2.65.

**Transaction Details**

Order Payment for Order 105-3975423-3669826 (view details of this order)

Transaction date: **Sep 7, 2011**

**Shipping Address:**

**Billing Country**
US

**Product charges**
Obeying Jesus: The seven commands for every disciple    Qty: 1    $0.01

**Amazon fees**
Variable closing fee:    $-1.35

**Other**
Shipping:    $3.99

**Transaction Total**    $2.65

The seller now has to package the book, label it, and ship it to the buyer. If the book is one pound or less, then the USPS Media Mail rate is $2.41. This leaves the seller with $.24 and they still have to package the book and get it to the post office. I don't know about you but this does not look like how I want to spend my time.

Sellers can increase their margins on orders like this by getting bulk rates from the USPS. You need to be shipping about 300+ books a day and be pre-sorting all of your packages for the USPS to get these rates.

This is a business model that some sellers choose and while it is technically profitable, I greatly prefer the business model outlined in this book that enjoys much higher margins and much less effort.

When you take penny books to FBA, they become $4.00 FBA books. This is because FBA sellers MATCH the net price of their merchant fulfilled counter parts. Here is an example showing all FBA fees and the total net payout. You'll see that instead of chasing around $0.24 and tying myself down and shipping my own books, you can put an FBA label on a book, and turn it into $1.17 - $1.41 as you'll see in the two examples below. Not bad if you have a source of cheap or free books AND you can process them fast enough to make it worth your time.

All of these payouts and numbers should also be considered against the inbound shipping fees that will be variable to your account based on your geographical proximity to the assigned Amazon fulfillment center. Other costs will be boxes, packing material, tape, labels, and of course, YOUR TIME and EFFORTS.

$4.00 FBA books only works if the books are lightweight because of the weight-based fees involved of $0.40/lb. Once inexpensive books get heavier, it makes less sense to send them to FBA.

# Retail Arbitrage

Here is an exact payout showing all FBA fees and a final payout of $1.41. The only variable fee here is the weight based fee. This book has a listed weight of 5.6 ounces. At $0.40/lb., you get $0.14 for the FBA weight based fee.

**Transaction Details**

Order Payment for Order 105-7616005-0333062 (view details of this order)

Transaction date: **Feb 24, 2011**

**Shipping Address:**

**Billing Country**
US

**Product charges**

| | | |
|---|---|---|
| Blind Promises (Steeple Hill Women's Fiction #60) | Qty: 1 | $4.00 |

**Amazon fees**

| | |
|---|---|
| Commission: | $-0.60 |
| FBA per unit fulfillment fee: | $-0.50 |
| FBA weight based fee: | $-0.14 |
| Variable closing fee: | $-1.35 |
| **Transaction Total** | $1.41 |

Return to View Transactions

Conditions of Use | Privacy Notice   © 1996-2010, Amazon.com, Inc.

Here is another example where the weight is different. This book has a listed weight of 15.2 ounces so at $0.40/pound for the weight based fee, you get $0.38. All other fees are fixed. The additional weight of this item affects the payout and lowers the payout from $1.41 to $1.17.

This example shows how an Amazon Prime member purchased this book and paid an ADDITIONAL $3.99 to have it shipped overnight. If you need any more proof that some buyers are willing to pay more for an identical item than other buyers, then remember this example. This buyer paid a total of $7.99 for a penny-book. This shipping service does not affect my payout at all. You'll see that they paid an additional $3.99 shipping and that Amazon took out a $3.99 shipping chargeback. This buyer could have purchased this book for less and received it at a later date, but they chose to pay more and get it delivered the next day. These are the customers that you can reach as an FBA seller. Merchant fulfilled sellers simply cannot market themselves effectively to these customers.

This $4.00 penny book business works if your FBA competition has not lowered the price to a level below $4.00. As long as prices are still in the $3.75+ range, then it can make sense to do $4.00 FBA books. Any lower, and it starts to simply not be worth your time to process them.

Merchant fulfilled sellers cannot price their items lower than the $4.00 net price because they cannot enter a negative price to be added to the $3.99 shipping credit. This hasn't stopped FBA sellers from undercutting each other and making FBA books even cheaper than penny books. You'll see sellers with prices down in the $2.30 range. Most of these sellers are 'racing to the bottom' and 'chasing the next sale' as discussed in Chapter 19.

There is the strategy of selling dead stock at a price that will make you lose less money than if you had to pay Amazon to remove or destroy the items. If it costs $0.50 to remove an item, the seller would rather sell at a $0.40 loss to avoid paying any additional FBA storage fees. It costs $0.15 to destroy an item so they would rather lose $0.10 on the sale than to pay the $0.15. While true, my advice would be to never put yourself in this position by submitting such low margin and highly competitive inventory. There are more productive things that you can do as a seller instead of chasing nickels and dimes.

You may now be asking what these sellers are thinking and if there is any money to be made in a business model such as this. The answer is yes, but while there is profit, the profits are very small in relation to the efforts. Run the numbers yourself and consider the value of your time. If a penny book that sells for $4.00 through FBA only nets $1.17 and you drop price to $3.00, then you are doing a lot of work for only $0.17. Just considering the inbound shipping costs of postage, boxes, and labels should make you pass on inventory like this even if you could acquire the items for free. This doesn't even address the fact that you would actually have to take time to list, label, and pack it up into an FBA shipment. Your time is valuable!

I only explain all of this to you here so that you understand what your competition is up to. It is not recommended to compete on this level. The margins are razor thin and the risk of losing money is probably about equal to the odds that you'll end up working for free.

## Chapter 32 – International FBA & Advanced FBA Techniques

FBA is not just for US-based Amazon.com sellers. At the time of this writing, FBA is available in the USA, Japan, Germany, France, and the UK. You can bet Amazon has plans to roll out FBA in more countries soon.

### FBA in Canada

Here is how you can sell on Amazon.com using FBA even if you are located in Canada. First, you need an Amazon.com seller account, a US bank account, a US credit card, and a US address (get a P.O. Box). All of these things can be done online. The easiest way is to get the credit card from the same bank where you open your US bank account. Once you have all of these pieces, you can open your US Amazon.com account just as if you were physically located in the US.

So even though you are in Canada, you can log into your Amazon.com account and prepare FBA shipments as though you were located in the US. You can even print UPS labels. But what address should you use for your 'Ship From' address? How will UPS charges be calculated?

Here's how to do it. Sellers have figured out that it is more cost-effective to print US postage from the US Post Office website at USPS.com and then physically take their shipments across the border. There are companies that have sprung up to help Canadian sellers get their online orders to their US customers. One of these companies that services the Toronto area is http://chitchatsexpress.com. For a fee, they will take bulk loads of shipments across the border for their customers. You can use services like this to get your US bound FBA shipments delivered through UPS as well.

Preparing FBA shipments that will be delivered to the US FBA warehouses will be prepared just like any other FBA shipments. You will need a US address for Amazon as a 'Ship From' address; Amazon will use this address to assign the fulfillment center and for UPS to calculate accurate inbound shipping charges. If you are using a border courier service, ask them what they recommend. They may be dropping off their shipments at a UPS store right over the border and you can use that store's address. If taking them over the border yourself, use the address of wherever you drop them off such as a UPS store or UPS drop off location.

This strategy works well for Canadian sellers who live near the border, but any seller can choose their own shipping service and send products to US FBA warehouses to be sold on Amazon.com. This also applies to any country where you can use FBA. US FBA sellers can send products to Japanese FBA warehouses and German FBA sellers can ship to UK FBA warehouses. The same account requirements exist for each country-specific Amazon seller account. Amazon even promotes this practice and will help you set up your international accounts. Use the Contact Amazon pages on each country-specific Amazon site if you need help getting your accounts set up.

You may have additional inbound shipping charges if you are getting your products to a US FBA warehouse from Canada or any other country. Take these additional costs into account when deciding what products to send to FBA.

**Direct to FBA**

There is no reason why you have to be the one to send your products to your Amazon FBA account. Anyone can send products to your FBA account as long as they are prepared correctly and labeled properly. As your FBA business grows, you may find yourself working with suppliers who are willing to label your products for you and send them to your FBA account directly. They may have an integrated solution, or you may have to train them from scratch. FBA labels, packing slips, and UPS labels can all be saved as HTML files or PDFs and emailed to your supplier. You can even print them out yourself and send them to your supplier by UPS or USPS.

## Risks

Finding companies that will send directly to your FBA account can be awesome because it eliminates duplicated shipping charges, reduces product lead-time, and allows you to not have to be tied down to receive and process FBA inventory shipments. While there are rewards, there are also risks involved in a relationship like this.

These Risks Include:

Teaching your supplier how to use FBA and potentially inviting a new competitor

Losing a source of product if they decide to sell directly themselves

Trusting someone else to properly prepare your FBA inventory

In my experience, if you work with reputable companies, this type of relationship can be a real win-win. The risk that a company may decide to get into selling directly to consumers is real, but I think that you'll find that most companies do not want to add direct consumer sales to their businesses. There is a reason that so many companies do not sell directly to consumers and instead rely on distributors, wholesalers, and retailers to get their products to the end users. This is just not what they want to do; they are focused on other parts of their businesses.

## Chapter 33 – Multi-Channel Fulfillment – List on eBay, Ship From FBA

Multi-Channel Fulfillment is an amazing tool that is often overlooked. Your FBA inventory is not locked to Amazon as a sales channel. You can still list on other sites and fulfill those orders with your FBA inventory. It is a common misconception that FBA is for Amazon only, and while Amazon and FBA certainly go hand-in-hand, a seller's items are not tied to the Amazon sales channel once they are stored in an FBA fulfillment center.

This chapter has two "Aha!" moments. The first is that you can ship your FBA inventory to fulfill orders that you receive from any channel such as eBay or your own website at very competitive rates (likely less than what it costs you to do it yourself). Using Multi-Channel Fulfillment allows you to sell on any sales channel and still fulfill your orders needing only access to a computer. You don't need to store your own inventory, multiple sizes of boxes, print labels, or go to the Post Office every day. You get the orders, and Amazon ships them out. This goes on whether you are at home or on vacation. Once you get your inventory to an FBA fulfillment center, you can manage it from anywhere on the planet! "Aha!"

The second is the big one; how to LEVERAGE this new information into increased margins and a more efficient business model. Using Multi-Channel Fulfillment properly can truly revolutionize your business. You can lower your overhead in shipping costs, labor costs, and warehouse costs, while at the same time increasing your margins on every item that you sell. This is because of the extremely competitive costs associated with Multi-Channel Fulfillment. I'll explain how to do this after the fee breakdown.

This is truly a win-win-win situation that most sellers would not believe is true:

**Win #1: Increase margins and profits (higher payouts per item)**

**Win #2: Reduce work (outsource storage, picking, packing, and shipping)**

**Win #3: Improve customer satisfaction (shipments arrive faster)**

This would seem like a magic potion from business fairly-land, but it's not; it's simply learning how to use the available tools optimally. Run the numbers (shown below) and take the steps to streamline your business.

**Fees Involved**

Yes, there are fees involved but these fees are fixed and known upfront for Multi-Channel Fulfillment orders. Since they are your orders and not orders on the Amazon website, there is no Amazon commission.

Multi-Channel Fulfillment Fees

The Multi-Channel Fulfillment fees consist of a per-order 'Order Handling' fee, a per-unit 'Pick & Pack' fee, and a per-pound 'Weight Handling' fee. These fees can be seen here:

**Fees for Multi-Channel Fulfillment orders**

Orders placed through other sales channels

| Shipping Method | | Standard | Expedited (Two-Day) | Priority (Next-Day) |
|---|---|---|---|---|
| **Order Handling** per order | | $4.75 | $7.75 | $14.75 |
| **Pick & Pack** per Unit | | $0.75 | $0.75 | $0.75 |
| **Weight Handling per lb.*** | First 15 lb. | $0.45 | $0.55 | $1.50 |
| | + next 16-70lbs | $0.45 | $0.70 | $1.75 |
| | More than 20lbs | See Oversize Media and Non-Media | | |

**Example**

**Digital Camera sold using Multi-Channel Fulfillment**

The example below is a guide in evaluating FBA only. Amazon does not warrant the accuracy of the calculations.

- Weight: 2 lb.
- Dimensions: 7" x 6" x 3" (.073 cu. ft.)
- Shipping method: Standard

| Fee | Calculation | Amount |
|---|---|---|
| **Order Handling** | 1 order x $4.75 | $4.75 |
| **Pick & Pack** | 1 Unit x $0.75 | $0.75 |
| **Weight Handling** | 3 lb* x $0.45 | $1.35 |
| **Selling on Amazon Fees** | N/A | |
| **Total** | | $6.85 |

*Multi-Channel Fulfillment Weight Handling: Total shipment weight is calculated by adding a dunnage factor of 10 percent to the combined total of the individual Unit weight of each Unit in the shipment, then rounding up to the nearest pound.

You can calculate your Multi-Channel Fulfillment rates prior to sending inventory to FBA. You can also experiment with your FBA inventory by making 'pretend orders' and reviewing the rates for Standard (Ground), Expedited (2-Day Air), and Priority (Overnight) shipping services.

I just did a 'pretend order' in my Amazon seller account on a five pound item. Total fulfillment fees (includes picking, packing, boxes, shipping, etc.) are as follows:

Standard (Ground): $7.75

Expedited (2-Day Air): $11.25

Priority (Overnight): $23.00

This is for anywhere in the USA. It is not based on zip code; it is based on fixed fees and weight. Once these costs are known, you can then price your items strategically on other channels (more on this later). For comparison, here are the UPS Published Rates and Daily Rates for a five-pound shipment from Massachusetts to Washington State:

Ground Published: $13.98 – one week in transit

Ground Daily: $9.76 – one week in transit

2-Day Air Published: $44.25 – two days in transit

2-Day Air Daily: $35.04 – two days in transit

Overnight Published: $77.00 – one day in transit

Overnight Daily: $67.04 – one day in transit

Remember, in addition to being more expensive to ship it myself, I would also have to store the product, be home to process orders, keep boxes and other packing materials on hand, pick and pack my own orders, print shipping labels, and then get my boxes to UPS or the Post Office. Easy choice if you ask me!

## Inbound Shipping Fees

To use Multi-Channel Fulfillment, you have to get your items sent to an FBA fulfillment center. They have to be labeled properly with special barcodes so that Amazon can properly identify your items. You are able to use Amazon's partnered UPS rates for inbound FBA shipments. These are the best rates around. Depending on where you are located and what fulfillment center your items are going to, this will be about $.20 – $.60 per pound.

## Storage Fees

Amazon does charge storage fees based on unit volume. These rates are very low and can easily be managed by only sending in enough supply to match your sales volume. Many sellers find the storage rates to be so attractive that they want to send their entire inventory to FBA. It is recommended that you only send in a maximum of one year's supply at a time. Amazon does charge a Long term Storage Fee of $45/cubic foot for items left in FBA inventory more than one year. This fee does not apply to single units for each item so you can still send in Long Tail items (items that will sell, just not very often). Just only send in either one unit at a time for slow-moving, 'Long Tail' items, or a maximum of one year's supply.

Removal Fees

If you no longer want to have your inventory in Amazon's fulfillment centers, you can request to have your items returned to you or destroyed. You can have your items returned to you for $.50 per unit for regular items and $.60 per unit for oversize items (this includes shipping). If you want Amazon to simply remove and destroy your inventory items, the cost is $.15 for regular items and $.30 for oversize items.

**"Aha!" Moment #2 – How to LEVERAGE Multi-Channel Fulfillment**

Having access to Multi-Channel Fulfillment at Amazon rates is a very powerful thing. Imagine UPS came to your small, fledgling eBay business and said that you can now have Amazon's UPS rates for all of your shipping needs. Impossible? Does this sound too good to be true? You could lower your shipping costs drastically without having to be a big shipper? This is essentially what you get by using FBA's Multi-Channel Fulfillment. Your shipping costs have just decreased meaning that your overall margins have just increased. Your shipping and order fulfillment rates are now significantly lower than your competitors; use this to your advantage! Here's how:

There is more to a purchase than 'just the item'. There is more to a transaction than just price; even on commodity-type items where you and your competition sell the exact same item. Consider the ways to differentiate yourself as a seller on eBay: feedback, return policy, a well-designed listing page (or not), and shipping options/speed (among others). The shipping is where you can now trump your competition by offering your customers something that they simply cannot offer (at least not at the price that it costs you).

There are several strategies that you can use. Since your shipping rates are now lower than your competitors', you can beat them on price and still make the same profit per item. This is an 'apples to apples' comparison. You may now be able to sell at a price that is profitable for you, but not for them. This may cause them to stop selling a product and you will not have to compete against them anymore (and prices will rise). You can also set up barriers to entry to new competition who can't figure out how you are able to make a profit on your items since they don't know that you are using FBA Multi-Channel Fulfillment.

Another strategy to use would be to offer premium shipping such as 2-Day Air on your products at the same price that your competitor charges for Ground shipping. This makes it a 'rotten apples to fresh apples' comparison. You are both selling apples and for the same price, but you are able to offer the customer MORE than your competitor can. If a buyer on eBay is buying a commodity-type item and they can get it for $100 from you in two days or they can get it from your competition for $100 but will have to wait a week or more, who do you think will get the sale? You are able to maintain margins and take the lion's share of the sales by offering your customers more but not increasing your overhead. This will drive your competition crazy, as they will think that you are paying high shipping rates to ship 2-Day Air and must not be making any money. Let them think that all they want; just keep it your little secret.

**How to Increase Margins with Multi-Channel Fulfillment**

The previous examples are valid ways to use Multi-Channel Fulfillment, but personally, I don't recommend these strategies, especially for small sellers. You are able to capture more sales, but that also comes with more work. I prefer to increase margins and differentiate myself as a seller from my competition and not compete solely on price. What I'll show you below is how using Multi-Channel Fulfillment allows you to effectively market your items at higher prices, while keeping your overall fulfillment costs the same. This increase in margin goes directly towards your business' bottom line.

This book is in the recommended reading section at the end of this book:

How to Sell at Margins Higher Than Your Competitors

By Lawrence L. Steinmetz & William T. Brooks

It will change the way you see price, buyers, and your competition. It is worth every penny. I only wish I had read it before I started selling on eBay when I used to try to compete solely on price!

Above we talked about how you can use Multi-Channel Fulfillment to stop fighting in the 'apples to apples' comparison game. When you can change it to an 'apples to oranges' comparison, you can then market your oranges against your competitor's apples (even though the actual items that you both sell are the exact same). You can make your oranges more attractive for the same price and capture sales, but I prefer to position my oranges as a premium seller. I can offer the same commodity-type item as my competition, but with faster shipping and charge more for it. I can charge more because I am offering more (fast delivery options vs. slow delivery options). You will find customers that will see the difference and the added value that you provide with your oranges and they will pay you more for it. This is how you increase your margins on the same items that your competitors sell.

On eBay, you can also now add the Get It Fast option to your shipping settings. I recommend offering 2-Day Air shipping for free and factoring in your fulfillment costs into the price of your item. Then, just calculate the difference between Expedited (2-Day) and Priority (Overnight) and make that the upcharge for Overnight shipping (or round it to something nice and clean like $9.95). Again, these are options that your competition simply cannot offer at a competitive price. EBay makes these options available because they know some buyers want their items FAST and these buyers are willing to pay more to get their items fast. They even let you sort search results showing only items with the Get It Fast option, essentially making your competition disappear, regardless of their prices. You are able to charge more because you are offering more. Here are two images I made to promote my eBay listings. Feel free to use them if you like.

Check out this example with costs and fee breakdowns. Note the increased Return On Investment (or ROI). This is the key.

| RIDGID 24V Battery | Comp Low | Comp High | Locomodem FBA |
|---|---|---|---|
| Sales Price | $97.50 | $97.50 | $119.95 |
| eBay Final Value Fee | $8.78 | $8.78 | $10.90 |
| Paypal Fees (est. 3%) | $2.93 | $2.93 | $3.60 |
| Listing Fees | $0.50 | $0.50 | $2.00 |
| Shipped UPS Ground | UPS Ground | UPS Ground | UPS 2-Day Air |
| 3 lbs., Residential | | | |
| Shipping Costs | $9.52 | $13.59 | $10.15 |
| Boxes, tape, supplies, etc | $0.50 | $1.50 | $0.00 |
| Inbound FBA Shipping | $0.00 | $0.00 | $0.50 |
| NET | $75.27 | $70.20 | $92.80 |
| | | | |
| Cost (Hypothetical) | $50.00 | $50.00 | $50.00 |
| | | | |
| **Margin $** | **$25.27** | **$20.20** | **$42.80** |
| **Margin %** | **50.5%** | **40.4%** | **85.6%** |

$17.53 – $22.60 more on each transaction and 35.1% – 45.2% higher margins.

This isn't even an 'apples to apples' comparison! In addition to making more money per sale, I'm doing less work AND my customers get their items faster. But don't just take my word for it; run the numbers yourself.

It's all about the perceived value of what you are offering. 2-Day Air shipping is incredibly valuable, especially to a buyer who needs their items fast. It would normally cost $30-$40 for 2-Day Air shipping on that five pound item, but they get that value from you for less. This is what makes your items more attractive than your competitor's.

This is not a volume game; it's a margins game. Sellers who consistently make the most margins will thrive in the good times and survive in tough times. Sellers who ignore margin and try to 'make it up in volume' will work way too hard for too little of a reward. Always run the numbers!

Different channels may fare better by using different strategies. Learn the customer base of each one and market your items appropriately. What works on eBay may not be the best strategy for your own website. A combination of these strategies is also something to consider.

**Limitations:**

FBA Multi-Channel Fulfillment is currently only for domestic orders, although I would expect that Amazon is working towards adding more international options. If you get a lot of international orders, you may want to consider keeping some of your items on hand to ship yourself and only sending a portion of your inventory to Amazon's fulfillment centers.

(The fees included in the examples in this chapter were accurate at the time of writing. As with any service, fees may increase or decrease over time. Always check the most current fee schedules on Amazon.com and eBay.com).

# Chapter 34 – So Why Isn't Everybody Doing This?

Or as Kat Simpson of Kat's Kloset would say, "So, what's the catch?"

It's a fair question! When you understand how easy the principles of this business are, you may think that there must be so many people out there doing this that there's no room for you to join in all the fun. If you have this mentality then you need to snap out of it! The only people out there who want you to have this mindset are the people who are already doing this and fear competition. They know that there are so many easy deals out there and they want them all for themselves. They have a mentality of scarcity instead of one of abundance.

But you don't just have to take my word for it; you can grab your smartphone, get in your car, and go out and see if everything written in this book isn't 100% true. You can see for yourself if there are items in your area that you can buy locally and sell online for a profit.

You can also join any of the many online groups where sellers are actively helping each other and sharing their success stories. Need help? Just ask!

This business is fun and financially rewarding, but it is still a business and requires real work. Real work means that some people will not do this business even if they know how it works.

All of my friends and family know exactly what I do. Well, they sort of know what I do because trying to fully explain resale and FBA is not always the simplest conversation. They know that I go to stores and buy stuff to sell online. If they looked around my house they would probably think that I'm not a very big seller since I don't have a lot of inventory. That, of course, is the power of FBA. When I try to explain this business to them, it usually goes right over their heads.

Every now and then a friend or family member will ask me to teach them how to get started in this business. I'm happy to teach them, especially if they can pick up deals that I simply cannot. I'd rather someone that I know go get a deal and make some money than for it to sit there unclaimed or go to another seller that I don't know.

Some people are not comfortable with any kind of risk and that's OK. This business does have risks, but those risks are both small and manageable. When you understand the principles and dynamics of this business and use all of the information available to you, then this business is as close to a risk-free business model as I have ever seen.

Just having the knowledge presented in this book is simply not enough to make instant profits. A person has to take this knowledge and apply it. They have to go out and find items to resell. They have to make that first purchase. They have to prepare that first FBA shipment.

Even though people understand this business, not everyone takes action. Not everyone has the time to pursue the resale opportunities that they find. They say that they don't have the time but it's really just an excuse. They could find the time if they were serious about this business, but they may be too comfortable in their regular full-time job to see the opportunities in front of them.

Not everyone has the available funds with which to buy inventory. Knowing the information in this book is great, but if someone is unable to purchase any inventory for resale, then their business won't get very far. Some people may now possess this knowledge but find themselves living in a location with no signs of civilization (retail stores) or they may not even have a car in order to go to the stores.

If a new seller has a goal of $5,000 profit per month, every month, but they only have $500 with which to buy inventory, then they are setting themselves up to fail. You have to run the numbers! Set your goals and back out the numbers. Make these goals realistic and attainable so that you don't simply discourage yourself for any reason other than unrealistic expectations.

Take this simplified example: say you have a goal of making $5,000 per month in profit. If you sell items with 100% margin (meaning that you are doubling your money), then you have to be able to spend $5,000 per month. Is this something that you are comfortable with? Do you have $5,000/month to spend on inventory?

This needs to be run like a business. A $5,000 purchase is a big deal, but train yourself to look at it differently. This is your business spending $5,000 on inventory and not you personally spending $5,000. As sales come in, turn these profits around into more inventory. Keep it snowballing as your sales increase and your revenue grows.

Remember, even if another seller buys some inventory, they may not be able to purchase ALL OF IT. Some of the deal examples that I showed you in this book involved some pretty big numbers and not everyone will be either comfortable with purchases that large or financially able to make these large purchases. All this means is that there will never be a time when other sellers take all the opportunities. It's simply not possible. So even if someone else is doing this business, they are not doing it at a scale that in any way prevents you from finding plenty of deals in your area.

The lifestyle of a self-employed entrepreneur is great, but it's not for everyone. Many people like the reassurance of that static paycheck every two weeks. That steady paycheck also comes with steady hours and a steady schedule. This is probably the number one reason that people do not do this business. They are so used to something else that making any kind of switch from their regular routine is just too much of a change for them to make.

The business of resale, especially resale with FBA, is the perfect one to start because you can start small while you keep a full-time job. Are you willing to take the steps required to start building a profitable side business? Not everyone is. It is up to you to actually get started.

This side business can quickly grow into something big and lucrative. So big, in fact, that it may soon take over your regular job and make you 100% self-employed! Getting to this point means that you took lots of steps along the way. Unfortunately so many people never take these steps. No one has to take these steps; there's nothing wrong with a regular full-time job. But if you want to take control of your schedule and start capitalizing on the opportunities all around you by learning and applying the principles outlined in this book, then you have to actually get out there and do it! Some people won't and that is their choice. What is YOUR CHOICE? I can't make you get started; only you can do that. I can write chapter after chapter and book after book, but only you can take the steps toward building this business for yourself.

Basically, don't worry about everybody else. You'll only psych yourself out of this business, which is only good news for your competition.

## Two Kinds of Critics

As you read this book and decide what kind of reseller you want to be, I encourage you to share and discuss this business model with friends and family. You may find someone who wants to partner up (which would be great, especially when you are first starting out) and you may find critics who say that this business is not possible.

Some critics will not believe this business model works even if you show them examples and payouts and bank accounts. There are plenty of naysayers out there.

Some critics KNOW that this is a powerful business model and will attempt to steer you the wrong way to prevent competition. You may run into another reseller who tries to sway you from continuing with your business when you run into them at a store or book sale. They'll say things like how there are no good books anymore and how they are probably going to stop doing this business because there is no money in it anymore. Boo-hoo. If they actually believed what they say, would they be out scouting?

You may find critics online who say that this business is dried up and that there are no opportunities out there anymore. They want you to believe them so that you get discouraged. The theme of this book is EDUCATION. This business doesn't work because I say it works; it works because it actually works!

Understand the ins and outs of this business as well as the WHYs and HOWs and you'll be able to decide FOR YOURSELF if this business is legitimate or not. Don't listen to other people and don't just listen to me! Take what I write in this book and TEST IT FOR YOURSELF. Then decide what you're going to do. Hard work and due diligence is rewarded.

## Chapter 35 – Summary – Go Feed Your Amazon Monster!

Well there you have it. That's pretty much everything that I know about Retail Arbitrage, selling online, and FBA. I'm sure I could fill more pages with stories of running into grumpy booksellers and retail store adventures, but I have to stop writing at some point. ☺

Once you grasp the fundamentals of this business you'll see that it's a fairly simple process of scouting, listing, and selling. Then just repeat the process. You'll also see that this really isn't all that difficult. The business that you set up is almost like a machine that is on autopilot. This machine cranks out more if you put more into it. Work harder, it produces more. Work less, it produces less.

Since you do have to put dollars and products into this business machine that you've created, I like to refer to it as 'Feeding Your Amazon Machine', or to make it more memorable, 'Feeding Your Amazon Monster'. You have created a monster (the good kind) and you have to feed it. You wake up each day and what do you have to do? Feed your Amazon Monster! The more you feed it, the more it grows. You can even give it a name. That way when your friends and family ask you what you are up to, you can just tell them that you are feeding your monster; his name is Sparkles.

After you try to explain to them what you do, and they look at you like maybe you're the one whose name is Sparkles, just hand them this book. It will make your life much easier.

I truly believe that anyone can take the knowledge contained in this book and start a successful Retail Arbitrage business at whatever scale they are comfortable with. You can work extremely part time hours and make some extra supplemental income, or you can go full steam ahead and make this your full time (and very profitable) business. I've listed many sources for inventory as well as reasons why no one can possibly ever take over all of the deals out there in the bonus sections at the end of this book. There are likely many more sources and creative ways to find inventory that I have not even considered. Keep on thinking of new ways to run this business and you'll continue to learn and grow.

My final piece of advice is this; find trustworthy people, work with them, and stay with them. The hardest thing to find is people that you can trust. If you are working with people right now that you do not trust, then I would recommend that you re-evaluate those relationships. When you surround yourself with people that you can trust, then you are free to talk about ideas without fear of being undermined. I read on message boards where people will not even tell their own friends and family about their online business. They are worried that they will learn the business, become a competitor, and put them out of business somehow. It's a shame that some people feel as though they cannot share this business model with friends or family because they fear that they will be inviting a ruthless competitor. If you are truly afraid of this happening, then you are hanging around people that you do not trust. This will severely limit how successful you can make this business or any other venture. Finding someone that you can work with and bounce ideas off of will help your business grow.

One of the biggest reasons that FBAPower works and has enjoyed great success is because of the level of trust enjoyed by everyone on the FBAPower team.

I wrote this in the Introduction and I'll write it here as well:

If you have any questions about this business, I invite you to call or email me directly.

214-298-6866 – yes, that is my cell phone number and I invite you to call. I'm Eastern Standard Time so please consider the time when calling. Also, please read the whole book before you call. ☺

If you prefer email: chris@scanpower.com

For general technical support for FBAPower, FBAScout and FBARepricer please visit http://www.scanpower.com as well as the support & help pages at http://help.scanpower.com

Or send an email to support@scanower.com and someone from the FBAPower support team will be happy to help.

I wish you nothing but great success in this exciting business. If there is anything that I can do to help, I'm just a phone call or email away.

To your success,

*Chris Green*

Chris Green

Director, ScanPower.com

When you are done reading this book, feel free to sell it back on Amazon using FBA!

## Bonus #1 – How to Compete Against Amazon

If you sell on Amazon long enough, you will run into Amazon as a competitor. This can be intimidating! Competing against Amazon is not something to take lightly. They are able to sell at margins and prices that they find acceptable but that most sellers would not. This can cause them to lower price to a level at which you may feel that you can no longer compete. They may even sell items at a loss. They also have advanced algorithms and monitoring tools in place behind the scenes that allow them to 'dial in' exactly what they want to sell the item for and how to position themselves against their competition.

It's Amazon's site and they make the rules. The best that you can do is to understand the rules and compete in the best way that you can.

Here are some strategies to effectively compete against Amazon.

**Hold Price**

Sometimes Amazon is selling at a price that you simply cannot match or even beat. When you find yourself in this position, sometimes it is best to just hold your price and see what happens. Amazon has been known to sell out of a product, both temporarily and permanently. When this happens, buyers will have to look to other sellers for the product. There is a big difference in an item being $49.95 and IN STOCK and being $49.95 and OUT OF STOCK. If Amazon is out of stock, then your $59.95 price might look pretty good.

Here's another scenario that can happen. Remember that price is set by supply and demand. Price is also only constant at one point in time. As time goes by and supply and demand change, so will price. Price may be low today but higher in the future (consider popular toys at Christmas time, seasonal products, or when Oprah recommends something). If your business model supports it, simply holding price and seeing how the market develops can be a strategy that pays off instead of instantly liquidating inventory at the first sign of Amazon competition.

**Play the Up and Down Game**

This can be fun. Amazon is bound by the same limitations of the physical world as the rest of us are. So even though they are monitoring prices and competitors on products that they sell, they cannot do it instantly. It takes a while for the computers to sync up, calculate changes and implement those changes. There are windows of opportunity that you can take advantage of if you know how the game is played. I learned this from experience. It cost me money the first time, but I learned the system, so it was tuition that I was more than willing to spend.

I was selling a cordless screwdriver with a market price of $19.95. I had fifty units and I received these for free as a bonus for purchasing a separate item that I was also selling. I labeled the items and sent them to FBA when Amazon was also selling the item. I priced mine at $18.95 to get the sale based on price. I sold some and then Amazon dropped to $18.95. As a buyer myself, I would choose to buy from Amazon over a third party seller so I dropped my price to $17.95. I got a few sales and then noticed that Amazon was now $17.95. We played this game until the price was $6.95! I was frustrated but since my cost was zero, I was taking it all in stride and trying to figure out how to play this game to my advantage. The first thing that I thought of was that I should buy up all of Amazon's stock at $6.95, label it and send it all back to FBA and be the only seller at $19.95. This could work, but it would be risky as Amazon could likely get more in stock from the manufacturer so this would leave only a small window of time where they were out of stock and I could get all the sales at full price.

At $6.95 I was not happy since I was really just giving them away. I only had a few units left, so I raised the price back up to $19.95 to prevent sales at the $6.95 price while I thought about what to do. You can probably already guess what happened next; Amazon raised their price to $19.95! Lesson learned! Amazon will compete on prices GOING DOWN, but they will also stay competitive when prices GO UP! So we played our little game again when I cut price by $1 and got a few sales until Amazon caught up. These sales were at a profitable level (not down at a silly $6.95 price). Unfortunately, by now I had sold out of my fifty units and while I did make profit on the items, I didn't make as much as I could have if I had known how Amazon reacted to competition from the beginning. And what did Amazon do when I sold out? They raised price back to $19.95.

## Use Multi-Channel Fulfillment

As mentioned in Chapter 33, you can use Multi-Channel Fulfillment to fulfill orders from any number of other sales channels such as eBay. Not all buyers buy from Amazon, even if they have the best price. Some buyers still think that Amazon only sells books and some buyers simply don't like Amazon and want to spend their money elsewhere. The market price on Amazon.com can be unprofitable for you but don't let this stop you from listing and selling on other channels where the market price is still at a profitable level. The online markets are not efficient; Amazon may sell an item for $100 that sells on eBay for $150 or vice versa. Sell your items on the sales channel where it makes the most sense and remember that the Amazon price is set by the Amazon supply and demand. Those are both only pieces of the overall supply and demand.

Another thing to remember is that even when Amazon sells an item, they face some of the same limitations that all sellers face. That includes possibly selling out of a popular item. When Amazon sells an item and then they sell out, the secondary market takes over. Odds are, if Amazon has sold out, that the item is popular and the market price is too low. Price on the secondary market will rise in situations like this when demand outpaces supply. Sometimes you can predict when this will happen. A good strategy for this is to raise your price in order to not compete with Amazon while Amazon has the item in stock in anticipation of Amazon selling out.

In the event that having Amazon as a competitor no longer makes the item profitable to sell, sometimes it is best to get out and just move on. There are so many opportunities out there to take advantage of, so don't get caught up on one product. Stay smart and watch your margins.

## Bonus #2 – Creating New Product Pages for Items NOT on Amazon

When you are buying items to sell on Amazon through FBA, FBAScout will give you the complete pricing picture so that you can make the best buying decisions and lower your risk. But sometimes you will find an item that FBAScout shows is not in the Amazon catalog at all. So now what do you do? You have less information with which to make a buying decision. Less information means higher risks, but higher risks can also mean higher rewards.

You may find an item that shows no match in the Amazon catalog, but it's an item that you've seen on national TV. Or maybe it's a different version of a product that already exists and is selling well on Amazon. Or it's a store exclusive of a strong brand like 'Toys R Us Exclusive' Barbie doll or an 'Only At Target' Disney Cars Giftset. Consider as many pieces of information that you can and then make a decision to either purchase the item in order to create a new product page on Amazon or to move on. If you find yourself thinking too hard about an item, I recommend moving on. There are too many good deals out there to worry too much about a single item. If the item is intriguing, think about it later. It will still be there tomorrow. Don't slow yourself down and miss other opportunities because of indecisiveness.

Knowing if an item is sold on Amazon or not is a powerful piece of information in itself. You now know that if you were to list this item on Amazon, that you would be the only seller. As the only seller, you would be the one who sets price since you would not have other sellers to compete with. When you set price, remember that people put different values on items. Some buyers will value an item at $50 that other buyers only value at $10. When you control the entire supply available on Amazon, you can market your items to the Amazon buyers who place the highest value on the item. Remember, it's not about volume; it's about margin.

Over time, if the item is bringing you good profits, the odds are that another seller will find this same opportunity. As competition enters the market, prices will change. Keep selling the item as long as you are making profit margins that are acceptable to your business model. If an item attracts too much competition and the price falls to a level that is not profitable, simply stop selling the product. That is one of the best things about Retail Arbitrage; you're never tied to a product long term. You have complete control and you can react quickly to any sudden market changes.

To make a new listing for an item that shows no match for the UPC, first do a title search on Amazon.com for the product. There are times where the product exists on Amazon but it is simply not tied to the UPC. If you do find a product page for the item, look it over very carefully to be sure that it is an exact match (or not). Some products vary only slightly and those slight differences can be very important.

If the product does not exist, then you can start the process on Amazon of creating a new product. You'll be asked to enter the UPC for the item as you create it.

If you want to create a product page for a product that does not have a UPC, then you'll have to buy a UPC. When I first started selling on Amazon, I had no idea that you could buy a UPC, but as soon I learned this little trick, it was off to the races! Creating Amazon product pages out of thin air for any product that you wanted to sell is an amazingly powerful thing to do. I would do this for special power tools that were only available as part of a combo kit at retail stores. If a buyer wanted to buy this particular tool, they could buy the $500 combo kit and pay for a bunch of stuff that they don't really need, or they could buy it from me for $100 on Amazon. Did I sell to everyone who wanted this tool? No, but I sold it to the buyers who valued it at $100.

Here are a couple of sites that sell single UPCs. You get a price break if you buy in bulk:

http://www.singleupc.com/

http://www.qualityupc.com/

You can also search online for many other websites that sell UPCs. They are also sold on eBay of all places.

Like we mentioned earlier, other Amazon sellers can piggyback on your newly created listings. There is not a whole lot that you can do about it if they are selling the exact same product that you are selling. Amazon is not eBay, where each seller makes his or her own page for each product. Amazon is one page per product and all sellers list their price and descriptions on this one page.

What you can do is make it difficult for other sellers to match your newly created product pages exactly. If other sellers are not offering the EXACT same item, Amazon will stop them from listing on the product page. There are a few ways to do this. One way is to bundle a low cost item with your original item. You may be selling a poker chip set but you also bundle in a special low cost card protector. For another seller to list on your product page, they would have to be able to acquire and bundle the exact same card protector.

You can also create new product pages for custom bundles of complimentary products. Skip McGrath of http://www.skipmcgrath.com has had great success with this method. He was selling knife sets and cutting boards separately but the competition was forcing prices down to non-profitable levels. Rather than give up on the products, he bundled them together under a newly purchased UPC and sold his bundles for more than if a buyer purchased the items separately. You may already be thinking, "Why would a buyer do this?" It's been a theme throughout this book that FBA sellers enjoy a premium position in the Amazon marketplace as well as how buyers do not always compare every possible option when making buying decisions. A buyer sees Skip's bundle, likes the price, buys it, and gets on with their life. This happens every day on Amazon.

Skip has also had great success with working with companies to sell their products online and give Skip the 'Amazon Exclusive'. This type of agreement means that Skip will be the only one that the company allows to sell their products online on Amazon.com. This type of agreement can help you maintain margins on Amazon by blocking potential competitors. This is good for you as a seller and it is also good for the company who may not want their product or brand to be watered down by sellers who drive price down unnecessarily. If you are able to set up some Amazon exclusive product lines, you can enjoy a nice profit while not always being concerned about price and competition.

**Things to look for to find potential 'Amazon Exclusive' items:**

**Not Currently on Amazon**

This is key of course. Like we talked about earlier in this book, Amazon customers want to buy from Amazon as their preferred place to shop. As more and more products become available, more and more customers will be able to do a larger percentage of their overall shopping online.

**Small Companies**

Small companies who do not sell on Amazon or do not sell online at all are good to approach for Amazon exclusive agreements. They will be more receptive to new and innovative ways to get their brand or products distributed to consumers. As with any agreements that you enter into, be sure to make a win-win type of situation.

## Destination-type Products

A product that is a destination product means that buyers will want it regardless of price. The buyer needs the product or wants the product and this need or want is greater than their desire to get the product at a low price or discount.

Grocery & Gourmet Food products can be good destination products because people who use them may put an above-average preference on a particular item and this personal preference can override price sensitivity in the buying decision process.

Creating new products or new custom bundles is a great way to carve out your own niche on Amazon. If you have special knowledge about a product or groups of products, you can make new product pages for items that are attractive to buyers. If these are things that your competition cannot match exactly, then you'll have your own set of listings on which you will enjoy exclusivity.

Here's one more trick about creating new listings. More importantly, this is how to gauge which items warrant creating a new listing. When you see reviews online or in magazines for new products or Top Ten Lists for certain products, you can bet that there are many people who will see and read these articles. Consider products reviewed by Consumer Reports magazine or featured on Yahoo.com. These magazines and websites have readerships in the millions. When they make a Top Ten List for their readers that feature products like the top ten curling irons under $50, you can bet that there is a sub-group of those readers out of the entire group of readers who will want to purchase that number one rated product. Out of that sub-group of readers who want to purchase that product, there is a sub-group of readers who want to purchase that product online. Out of that sub-group of readers who want to purchase that product and want to purchase that product online, there is a sub-group of readers who want to purchase that product from Amazon.com. Out of that sub-group of readers who want to purchase that product, want to purchase that product online, and want to purchase that product from Amazon.com, there is a sub-group of readers who want to buy from Amazon directly or from an FBA seller because of preference, trust, FSSS (Free Super Saver Shipping) or Prime shipping options. Out of that sub-group of readers who want to purchase that product, want to purchase that product online, want to purchase that product from Amazon.com, and want to purchase from Amazon directly or from an FBA seller, there is a sub-group that will value the product at different levels. Some will want to buy the product for the listed price, some will only want the product if they can get it at a discount, and some will buy the product regardless of price because they want that number one rated curling iron regardless of price. They see something in a magazine or on a website and they have to have it from Amazon or an FBA seller. Those are the buyers that you can reach that your competition cannot.

When you see these articles and lists, check to see if the products are listed for sale on Amazon or not. If not, you may have just stumbled upon a new opportunity. I can pretty much guarantee that when articles like this run, it creates demand for the specific products on Amazon.com. If there is no supply, then the demand doesn't go away, it just doesn't enter into a transaction. If you can spot trends like this, and you can identify a source for the supply (either from the manufacturer or sourced at local retailers) you can be the seller who brings the supply to Amazon and is able to capture this demand at high margins.

## Bonus #3 – Why No One Can Take Over

The thought may have crossed your mind. You may run into another reseller when you are out and about, scouting for products to sell. You may think that someone already has your neck of the woods 'covered' and that they are already getting all of the good deals. Let me tell you that the scenario of you running into another online seller may be real, but the scenario that they are able to scoop up all of the available deals simply is not possible.

There are a few restrictions in place that affect every online seller. They are the limited number of hours in a day, the amount of money that they can spend on inventory, and their physical capacity to transport products. Not to mention the sheer impossibility of being able to scan every item at every store. Some stores carry hundreds of thousands of different products. Calculate the time to scan each one and you start to see the scale of what we are talking about.

**Hours in a Day**

There are only 24 hours in a day and there are only so many hours that some stores are even open. Online sellers can only be at one place at one time.

**Disposable Income to Invest in Inventory**

Some online sellers will have more disposable income with which to buy sellable inventory than others. Those sellers with less to spend on inventory will want to spend that money on the BEST products to sell online. There are varying degrees of deals to be found. Some items are good, but some items are great! Sellers with excess funds will have the option to buy both good and great deals and buyers with limited funds should focus on only the best deals. Both business models are profitable.

## Capacity to Transport Products

I've run into this one several times. I'll find so many good products that they simply will not all fit in my vehicle to transport them home. I'll fill up five carts at Toys R Us and then have to re-evaluate the items and only purchase the great ones. The good ones have to go back for another trip or another day.

## Different Target Margins

Similar to disposable income and transport capacity, having different target margins has to deal with how a seller chooses to run their business. When you compare the return on your money using Retail Arbitrage compared to what the bank gives you, it's easy to see why people start to get excited about this business. Some sellers will be happy making a 50% return on their money and some sellers will only want items that give a 300% return. Both are profitable and it is up to each seller to decide how they want to run their individual businesses.

A competitor who only buys the highest margin items will be leaving behind plenty of good items for other sellers.

## Different Risk Tolerances

Different sellers will have different tolerances for risk. Some will take more chances on items that may not be fast sellers but have sky-high margins and some sellers may only want items that they feel will sell through in less than 30 days. Some will be willing to take chances on new products that are not in the Amazon catalog and therefore have less information regarding previous sales and competition. Each seller decides how they want to run their business and some will make riskier moves than others. Risk should not be seen as a bad thing; big risks often lead to big rewards. It is important to analyze all available information and only take calculated risks that you are comfortable taking.

Because of these different risk tolerances, different sellers will purchase different items for their resale businesses, even if out shopping side-by-side.

**Different Knowledge**

Different sellers will have different knowledge about different stores and products. Some will have a previous background giving them an advantage in certain categories and some will have been selling online for a long time and have gained experience over the years. Some will be brand new and will miss easy deals due to their lack of knowledge. This dynamic will always be changing and it is important for you to keep on learning and gaining experience.

**Right Place, Right Time**

This will happen to you at some point. You'll be in a store just as they are marking down items for clearance pricing. Or you'll look up in the overhead and spot a stack of toys that has been sold out everywhere and is a hot item. No one seller can be everywhere all the time. Don't psych yourself out and take yourself out of the game and think that this won't happen to you. Keep on scouting and keep your eyes open for deals and look for opportunities and you'll have plenty of success stories to tell your friends.

## Bonus #4 – The ZERO RISK Way to Start

Don't worry if a lot of this is going over your head. This is pretty high-tech, cutting-edge stuff. The business described here is one that was simply not previously possible in such a low-risk, efficient manner in which it exists today.

Running an online Retail Arbitrage business this way is new and exciting and it can be difficult to explain. We're talking about a lot of new technologies and market dynamics that might not always make sense. LEARN as much as you can and when you don't understand something, ASK! There are many online groups that are more than happy to help new sellers 'get over the hump' of getting started. The world's largest FBA seller group is the FBAForum on Yahoo Groups.

http://finance.groups.yahoo.com/group/FBAForum/

It is moderated by Bob Willey who has been running his own successful online business for many years selling books, media, toys and anything else that he can get his hands on. Only requirement? It has to be profitable! Odds are, your question has already been asked, so check the message archives first. There is a wealth of information available. If you still can't find your answer, post it to the group. This group is known for being positive and helpful; there are no stupid questions!

Once you have all of your questions answered, you may still be wondering what to buy to resell. That's OK; it's normal to be cautious when just starting out. You are actually laying out your hard-earned cash for inventory. Here is how to start RISK FREE.

Get the free trial of FBAScout for iPhone or Android. If you use up your free 250 scans and you're still not ready to subscribe to the service, use the Amazon app. It's not as comprehensive, but it's better than nothing.

As you scan items and compare your costs to the Amazon market prices, you'll find some items with healthy margins. When you find something that you have confidence in, BUY IT. Use your credit card and KEEP YOUR RECEIPT. Take it home and list it on Amazon as Merchant Fulfilled (not FBA). Set your price where you are happy with the profit after all fees. Now sit back and wait.

One of two things will happen, both of which will not cost you money. You'll either get sales, which means you have to ship your orders out yourself as they come in. Or you won't get any sales. Getting sales means PROFIT in your pocket. If you don't get sales, and your confidence in the product goes down, simply delist your items and RETURN the product to the store with your receipt. Be sure to follow the store's return policy. Most stores will give you at least thirty days and I've never heard of a store having an issue with new items being returned in new condition with the receipt. Your refund will go straight to your credit card and even out your balance. This method is truly ZERO RISK. You either make money, or you are right back where you started with a little extra knowledge in your head, but either way you did not lose a penny.

There are some downsides to this model. You would have to be home to process and ship your own orders. You would have to go to the Post Office or find a UPS drop off location. You would not get the boost that FBA sellers see because your items would not be eligible for Amazon's free shipping programs like Free Super Saver Shipping and Amazon Prime.

## Bonus #5 – The Pixar Effect

Pretty much everyone knows Pixar. Pixar has brought us movies such as Toy Story, Cars, and Finding Nemo among others. Each of their movies has been wildly popular and when a movie is popular, the merchandise that goes with it is popular as well.

What is interesting about Pixar movies is how they stand the test of time. Pixar movies have spanned generations (and will continue to do so). Never in the history of entertainment have movies remained so popular for so long. In 2011, kids are still watching Toy Story for the first time. Toy Story came out in 1995! Name one other kid's movie that is popular the same way as Toy Story is sixteen years after its release. If you grew up in 1988, were you turning off Transformers and G.I. Joe to watch movies from 1972? In 1995, when Toy Story came out, are you still watching movies from 1979? Not likely. This is newly charted territory.

So what happens when a movie stands the test of time and its popularity spans generations? The merchandise stays popular long after the retail stores stop carrying it and move on to the next big thing.

There are a few reasons for this. The first is that they are just great movies. Kids and adults both enjoy watching Pixar movies. Another reason is the unprecedented access to various forms of media. People now have a near infinite amount of entertainment choices. With the Internet and services like TiVo and Netflix, people have access to practically every movie ever made at any time.

Having access to such a wide variety of media means that people can now discover shows that they would never have realized existed before. Have you ever heard of Pingu the Penguin or Oswald the Octopus? Me neither, until Netflix 'recommended' them because of the other shows that my kids watch on the computer. Now that kids can discover and watch shows that would normally be considered obscure at best, and for all practical purposes, non-existent, it creates a demand for the toys and related merchandise. This newly found demand would never be able to find the supply without the Internet. Prices for these toys, which can only be found on the secondary market, are sky high. But guess what? Some parents are willing to pay them. Remember, price is set by supply and demand. Supply may be small, and demand may be small, but some of the buyers that make up that demand have a much higher personal perceived value for the items. They are willing to pay higher prices for the items in short supply and the sellers are more than happy to sell to them at these prices.

Now consider this; someone whose first trip to the movies is to see Toy Story 3 can come home and delve into the entire history of Pixar movies instantly. Kids are not limited to what is on live television or what is available to rent at the local video rental store anymore. As they watch Finding Nemo, they tell their parents that they want some Finding Nemo plush toys, but they are not available in the stores anymore. These dynamics create a lingering strong demand for Pixar brand toys on the secondary market. Pair this DEMAND with sellers being able to make their SUPPLY known by listing online, and these toys are exchanged on the secondary marketplace at prices that both sides are happy with. This continues long after the movies have left the theaters.

Remember that Toy Story came out in 1995, A Bug's Life in 1998, Monsters, Inc. in 2001 and Finding Nemo in 2003. You can still find some Pixar brand merchandise from these movies in the stores today! Kids today are just as fascinated with a movie that came out back in 2003 as they are with the newest releases, but retail stores can't carry EVERYTHING that kids want because of physical limitations.

People are not limited to just what toys are on the shelf at the local store since they can now go online and find practically anything that their heart desires. Kids used to be limited to just what was available at the local toy store. Then you had mail order catalogs, and now you have Amazon.com.

Just a few generations ago, old store stock of toys from ten years ago would not have much value. Even those collectors (DEMAND) who did put a high value on the items (SUPPLY) had limited ways to find the items and complete the transaction. In today's marketplace with the Internet, eBay, Amazon, Craigslist and other sites, supply meets demand and buyers and sellers of even the most obscure items can transact business.

There is also the incredibly valuable branding of Pixar movies and characters. Pixar brand items can command a huge premium over identical, non-branded items. This goes for sippy-cups, bed sheets, pool toys, etc. The exact same item, but you pay more for the Pixar ones. Why? Because parents are willing to pay more to get their kids what they want.

Want proof? I sold Lightning McQueen Boo-Boo Buddies for $19.95 on Amazon.com through FBA. Non Lightning McQueen Boo-Boo Buddies sell for around $7. Almost three times the price premium for Lightning McQueen. I can also give you proof as parent and a buyer. One car from the Cars movie retails for almost $4. How about a regular Hot Wheels car? About $1. I'll give you one guess which one my little boy prefers and which one we end up buying. Yup, Lightning McQueen.

All of this is a fairly recent phenomenon and will extend well beyond Pixar. Understanding why this works will help you to stay ahead of your competition and recognize opportunities that your competitors will miss. It will also help you price your items properly to maximize your margins.

## Bonus #6 – Attitude is Everything

I don't believe in karma, but I do believe that people will treat you the way that you treat them. If you're nice to people, they'll be nice right back to you. If you are rude, then don't expect much in return. This is a valuable chapter because in this business you will interact with other people. How you interact with them can determine your success level in this business.

When you are at a retail store, you will cross paths with store employees. If you are scanning barcodes and your little Scanfob™ 2002 keeps going beep, beep, beep, they may ask you what you are doing. I always tell people to explain exactly what they are doing. Tell them that you are comparing online pricing information because you want to buy products to sell online. Store employees want to sell you things; that's what retail stores do, sell things. You tell them that you buy things, and many times they will try to sell you things. They just need to know what you want to buy. If you tell them that you like clearance items, they may lead you to a previously undiscovered aisle of clearance items.

If a store manager sees you buying a large amount of items, they may ask you what you are doing out of curiosity. They will be happy to see so many items being purchased. After all, they are running a retail store. You can often use this as an opportunity to explain what you do and ask for a discount. Make them an offer such as if you buy $1,000 will they take off 10%? Or if you fill up three shopping carts will they give you 25% off? Can't hurt to ask and they just might take you up on it. If you give them the cold shoulder and act paranoid and secretive, do you really think that they will go out of their way to offer you a discount? Me neither.

You may run into store employees or managers who are concerned about what you are doing. After all, they may have never seen someone come in and just start scanning all kinds of barcodes in their store before. They may think that you are price shopping for a competitor. It's their store and it's OK for them to ask what you are doing. This is where being honest and truthful counts. When you tell them what you are doing, it is very likely that they will be more than happy to just let you shop.

There may be rare times when a manager asks you to leave and you'll have to gauge the situation on a case-by-case basis. If the situation looks like it's not going to be resolved, just leave and find another store. You may want to return to the store another time and talk to the store manager one on one so that they truly understand what you are doing and you can answer any questions for them. Again, niceness goes a long way. Remind them that they want to sell things and that you want to buy things. Hopefully everyone is able to work it out.

When it comes to books at book sales and thrift stores, being nice goes incredibly far. If you are polite, look people in the eye, leave the books just as neat as when you found them, and buy a bunch of books, then you'll make friends at the book sale. They know that people come in and buy books to sell online. You may find the odd person who takes offense at this practice but the majority will see you as a book buyer and them as a bookseller. You should be good friends.

When you have a positive attitude, good things just seem to keep happening. If you grumble about, talk down to people, and make a huge mess out of the book stacks as you scan, do you really think that the people working at the book sale are going to go out of their way to help you? But if you are nice and courteous, don't be surprised when they pull out fresh boxes of books from the back and give you first shot at them. They may even cut you a deal on your books when you check out.

At thrift stores, books are often not very good sellers. If you come in and buy a cart full of books, their eyes will light up! That cart full of books is not only money in their register, but also books OUT OF THEIR STORE.

Thrift stores want stuff selling so that they can put out more stuff. If you are buying stuff, they will like you.

I've told many, many thrift store employees exactly what I do. I haven't found one yet that has turned into a competitor. I find buying used books and selling them online through FBA to be not only profitable, but also fun! Not everyone does though. Make no mistake, this is a business and it is work. It also requires a commitment and some expensive equipment to start (although the startup costs for this business are pennies when you consider the income potential). More often than not, I'll explain what I do and chat with them for a little bit. They are more curious than anything. Many times they have offered to go in the back and bring out some more books for me to go through. Why? They want me to buy more books! Do you think they would offer to do this if I acted like I was too good to talk to them? Or simply ignored their questions? Not a chance.

Being nice pays off in this business as it does in life. I am not suggesting that you fake being nice to advance in this business. Life is too short for that. Be nice, be happy, and be positive. Life is too short and books are too plentiful to worry about a world of scarcity and be in a bad mood all day.

Not entirely related, but I always recommend giving an additional donation to the library sale when you check out. I usually try to round up around $20 so if my total was $181, I'd write them a check for $200. Running a book sale is a lot of hard work! It's not a ton of money, but every little bit helps and it's going to a good cause.

## Bonus #7 – Your Lazy Competition

Oh how I love my competition! I know that they are out there even though I don't run into them very often. I see the scrunched up stickers that used to cover the UPCs on books that are pushed out of the way just enough to scan the barcode. I know that they have been there before although I'm never sure exactly when. I do know that I always find a ton of good stuff when I go out. I really can't remember ever leaving a store without buying something to sell online.

So, am I just getting lucky? Is there just always fresh stock when I'm at the stores? Not likely, I'm just not lazy. The number one thing that causes sellers to not make as much money as they could in this business is being lazy. They want it all to be easy. If it's not easy, they won't do it. I can see the allure of liking things easy, but the work that they are trying to avoid is not that hard! I think it's great that they are lazy. Your job is to not be lazy.

So what do they do that is lazy? Well, several things and these are all things that mean that they miss good books. This is good news for anyone who is not lazy and that's what I'm trying to teach you here.

One thing that they don't do is manually enter ISBNs. ISBN stands for International Standard Book Number and it is the 10 or 13 digit number that is often found above the UPC on a book. Some older books have no UPC on the back and they just have the ISBN. If not on the back, then it will be on the back of the title page. Books published prior to 1970 do not have ISBN numbers. Manually entering a 10-digit number into FBAScout is not hard (actually I use the voice recognition feature on Android. I get weird looks sometimes but that's OK), but I suppose it's harder than just scanning a barcode. So since lazy scanners don't enter ISBNs, there are always lots of good books left behind for me to scoop up with a few manual ISBN searches. Manual entry is simply not that hard and because so many of your competitors just don't do it, it means that you'll always be able to find good stuff.

Book sales are a place where my lazy competition really baffles me (but trust me, I don't mind at all). So many times at a book sale, my competition will hit it hard at the beginning and then after about two hours, 90% of them will leave the building. I read it online all the time where book sellers will say that there is no point in being at a book sale after the first two hours because all the scanners will have taken all the good books by then. I don't find this to be plausible. It's simply not possible due to the size of some book sales and the behavior of some scanners. Run the numbers on how many items are at the sale, how many items you can physically scan per hour and how many other scanners are at the sale. I think you'll find that the idea of everything being scanned and checked is pretty preposterous.

You'll see so many scanners picking and choosing books with UPCs to scan and never once entering an ISBN. They don't even scan every UPC in a section; they only selectively scan UPCs. If one scanner goes over one section then all other scanners assume that all of the good books in that section will have been taken. I really don't know why they think that. That scanner may only buy items with a sales price of $20+ and a Sales Rank of under 500K. This would leave a TON of good stuff left behind.

Also keep in mind that not everyone uses FBAScout. If they use an inferior service that does not provide accurate information, they will make poor buying decisions. They will make both kinds of poor buying decisions; buying books that will prove to be unprofitable as well as passing on books that are profitable.

Also remember that different sellers have different business goals. They may have a more limited amount of funds with which to invest in inventory and will therefore be more selective in the books that they buy. They also may not use FBA which would mean that they are dealing with space restrictions in terms of how many books they can physically add to their inventory as well as time limitations for listing new items and processing their orders. As an FBA seller, you have neither of these restrictions so your profit targets will be much, much different.

Remember, don't be lazy!

## Bonus #8 – How To Run A Book Drive Fundraiser

If you are selling using FBA, then you have no limits on storage as long as you are sending in inventory that is selling and not just sitting around. You may want to consider a book drive fundraiser. They are very easy to do and there are several ways to do them. The first thing to consider is that you have to present a win-win situation to whoever you are working with for the fundraiser. You can approach a group such as the local Boy Scouts, the high school band, a non-profit organization, or a local church.

You have to agree on the terms of the fundraiser. Basically, who does what?

A typical agreement could go like this:

You work with the local Boy Scouts who will collect books over a period of four weeks. They could be going door-to-door asking friends, family and neighbors for book donations. They could leave flyers on neighborhood doors or special bags or boxes for the book donations. All books are brought to one central location for pickup.

This works because collecting books is something that they can do; it's not hard. It works because you are providing an outlet for them that turns their book collecting efforts into cash. They don't want books and they don't want to try to sell books. They are collecting books because they know the terms of the fundraiser and it works for them to generate funds for their group.

You could sell all of their books on a consignment basis (discussed in Bonus #9) but I would strongly recommend coming to an agreement to take possession of the books in exchange for an agreed upon sum. You could pay by the book, by the box, or by the pound.

You are taking a risk in doing this because you will be buying books unseen. You will get some junk, but you will also get good ones. The Boy Scouts are doing the work of collecting books. They need to get paid for their efforts during the fundraiser. You need to be sure that the terms of the agreement of the fundraiser allow you to purchase unseen books at a price at which you can make a profit. If it's not a win-win, then the fundraiser falls apart.

My recommendation to make this fair to the groups who collect the books is this: In addition to paying them the flat agreed upon rate (by book, by box, or by pound), you also pay an additional $1 (or more) for any book that you find that you would have purchased yourself if you had found it at a book sale. Some may say that this is not necessary but I believe it to be fair.

So a typical payout could go like this: Boy Scouts collect 2,000 books and you are paying $0.15/book, no questions asked. Or maybe you pay $5/box. Or $0.12/pound. You tally the books and cut them a check on the spot. Then, as you process the books, you keep track of the valuable books and you later write them another check for these books. These are just examples; you'll have to find prices that work for your specific fundraiser.

You may be worried that you'll get a lot of books that are simply not suitable for listing and selling online, let alone sending to FBA. To prevent this and make the fundraiser a win for both sides, you can do as much as you can to qualify the donations. You can do this by preparing a special flyer for people to hand out and use to promote the fundraiser. This flyer lists the types of items that are acceptable.

You may have qualifications such as:

Books have to have a barcode on the back

Books have to be in good condition (no moldy or water damaged books)

You can make exclusions for types of books (examples: mass market paperbacks, microwave cookbooks, or encyclopedias)

You can make exclusions for certain authors (Tom Clancy, Danielle Steele, etc.)

Here is an example label that I made to be affixed to boxes that could be handed out to be filled with book donations. You can use it as a guide to make your own.

If you are partnering with a non-profit or church, you may be able to give out paperwork for tax donations. Discuss this with the non-profit or church, as they should be familiar with the process. Also be sure to get permission to use the name of the group, non-profit organization, or church on any paperwork or flyer pertaining to the fundraiser. For example, you cannot say that you are raising money for The Special Olympics without their permission.

Also, be sure to keep meticulous records when doing fundraisers.

## Bonus #9 – How To Run An FBA Consignment Business

You'll soon find that there is absolutely no shortage of things to sell online or buyers waiting to buy them. You may start to talk to and network with people who already sell online but maybe not on Amazon or maybe they sell on Amazon but they don't yet use FBA.

Once you are selling on Amazon using FBA, you will soon realize that you have no scaling restrictions anymore. You can grow as big as you're willing to grow; you just need more things to sell.

One thing to consider is running a consignment business. A consignment business is fairly straightforward. You partner with someone who has things to sell but who doesn't want to do the selling themselves. You, in exchange for doing the actual selling of the item, get a percentage of the proceeds. It's a win-win situation. The consignee is able to sell items and get paid, and you, the consignor, get more items to sell and earn a return for your time and effort.

Running a consignment business without FBA would be labor intensive in respect to the commitment in both time and storage. You could fill up your garage, your home, your shop, or a warehouse with other people's stuff to sell. If you have to ship all of the orders yourself, you will quickly be tied down to this business. Personally, this is not what I would want to do when FBA is out there waiting for me with open arms. ☺

As long as the products that you are selling on consignment have Amazon product pages, then you can list them on Amazon and use FBA for the entire process. What you need to know is how to keep track of whose inventory is whose when you are only using one Amazon account to sell items belonging to multiple people. The way to do this is with an identifier in your SKU prefixes.

**Here is an Example:**

Say you are selling books on consignment for an ex-college professor that you know named Mr. Ted. You would assign SKU numbers to their books beginning with TED. Simple enough, right? Then, when you get your detailed payout report from Amazon, you can sort the entire report by SKU number. This will group all of the TED SKUs together in one block. Copy and paste this block of SKUs into another Excel file where you can add up the totals for Mr. Ted's sales. You can then calculate their individual payout based on whatever terms you agreed upon.

We did consignment with our local library when we lived in Texas. Our agreement was 50% of the net payout (meaning ½ of the total that we received from Amazon after all Amazon and FBA fees). Their portion of the payout averaged about $10-$15 per book that was sold through our consignment agreement. They were very happy with the program as they were previously getting only $1 per book at their book sale. They dramatically increased their profit per book while doing no additional labor themselves. Win for them. Win for us because we were able to locate an additional source of sellable inventory.

When you use FBA to run a consignment business, there are really no limits to what you can do if you use your imagination and get a little creative. I put together this site to advertise our consignment services to both libraries and thrift stores.

http://www.bookoutsourcing.com/

Feel free to use it or copy it.

I've read online about people who get upset when they find out that a bookseller has partnered with a local library to help them sell their books online. They get mad that one of their sources is gone and how dare that bookseller do something like that.

My response to them would be that there is absolutely nothing stopping them from doing the EXACT SAME THING. They could just as easily have talked to that library about partnering with them to sell their books online. They say they are upset that their source may be gone but I think they are actually upset at themselves for not working with the library and are misdirecting their frustration. Maybe I'm wrong; remember I majored in economics, not psychology.

Consignment with your local library is not the only thing you can do. How about consignment with your local thrift stores? Remember, when you are an FBA seller you have no space constraints so you can handle huge amounts of inventory. Just get it processed and sent to FBA. You could run a consignment business for every thrift store in your area. Don't get mad if you hear someone else is doing it because there is nothing stopping you from doing it yourself!

It's a difference in how you see the world around you. Do you see it as a land of scarcity? Or do you see it as a land of opportunity and abundance? I know the way that I see it!

**Downsides to FBA Consignment Businesses**

There are downsides to an FBA consignment business. It can be a lot to keep track of, especially if you have multiple consignees. You'll be responsible for monitoring their inventory items on FBA, calculating fees, avoiding Long Term Storage Fees, and all of the other details of selling on Amazon.com.

As I mentioned earlier in the book, there are downsides to FBA and those downsides apply here as well. Amazon or UPS may lose or damage your inventory. You may want to consider some additional types of business insurance to protect you and your consignees. You are also at the mercy of Amazon customer service for returns. A customer may return an item to you long after you have paid out your consignee for the item. Amazon will then debit your account for the purchase price leaving you in negative territory and you still have the item in unknown condition. Do you ask for a return of the consignee's payment? Or do you debit their next payout? There are different ways to do it, but be sure to consider these possibilities before entering into an agreement with someone.

These are all things to take into consideration when you decide if an FBA consignment business is the right thing for you. You may decide that buying inventory from people at a discounted price is a better strategy. They get paid instantly instead of slowly over time and you get the items at a discount but they are now solely your responsibility to sell. You do the selling and you keep all profits. To me, this is a much simpler way to run an FBA business.

## Bonus #10 – How To Get More Books Than You'll Know What To Do With

You're going to see that getting more books than you would ever possibly know what to do with is actually not hard. I've done several of these methods myself and while they are all profitable, they are not for everyone.

They are not for people who want a ton of freedom and flexibility. You may be able to partner with one of the sources listed below and get a constant stream of inventory to sell, but now you have to be around on a regular schedule and process the stuff fast enough to be ready for the next load. You'll get pallets of unsorted inventory but not all of that inventory will be good to sell online. You'll have to get the stuff in, process the items to get the stuff that you want to list online, and then figure out what to do with the rest of it. Sell it? Donate it? Recycle it? Whatever you do, you'll have to move it and I can tell you from experience how fun it is to move heavy boxes of books around that you know are nothing but junk.

You may also live in a studio apartment and while pallet after pallet of unsorted books may sound like a dream come true, if you don't have the space with which to receive and process this type and quantity of inventory, you will be overwhelmed very quickly.

### Clothing and Shoe Donation Bins

You may have seen these bins in parking lots around your town. They have signs that say that they want your clothing and shoe donations. These companies send the clothing and shoe donations overseas in big cargo containers after they are picked up and processed. Well, trust me when I say that these bins get a lot more than just clothing and shoes. They also get toys, furniture, and yes, you guessed it, books.

When we lived in Texas, I had an agreement with one of these companies in which I purchased all of their books and media items for $0.12/pound. Every two weeks I got about four pallets of stuff. At first, I drove to their warehouse to pick it all up with my trailer, but then they agreed to deliver the pallets since their trucks were out anyway picking up the items in their donation bins. I would always find good stuff, but getting rid of the 'rest' was always my problem. I never wanted to just throw things away so I would try to find places for everything. I would put ads on Craigslist for free board games and for boxes of free books. I was always able to get rid of the stuff, but the entire effort of taking pictures of the boxes of books, uploading to Craigslist, taking phone calls, and meeting the people who came to pickup the items was not that hard, but it was taking up time that I would rather spend on something profitable instead of just getting rid of junk.

After we moved to Massachusetts, I contacted one of the clothing and shoe donation places up here. I told them that we had just moved and that I purchased books and media for $0.12/pound from similar places in Texas. They agreed to sell me five pallets of books but also wanted me to take thirteen pallets of VHS tapes. There was no way that I was paying $0.12/pound for VHS tapes, not to mention I had no place to put the extra thirteen pallets (I didn't really know where I was going to put the five pallets of books). They threatened to cancel the whole deal if I didn't buy the VHS pallets as well. I told them that was OK, but no way I am buying that many VHS tapes. They could tell that I was not budging so they asked if I would at least take the VHS tapes off of their hands. I shouldn't have, but I agreed and then I had eighteen pallets of merchandise to deal with. I rented a storage unit and arranged to have all of the pallets delivered.

When you are able to get your hands on so much stuff for so little, it can be easy to become overwhelmed and forget that there are only twenty-four hours in a day. Time is limited and time is valuable. With family, running FBAPower, and all the other things that I wanted to do, sorting pallets of VHS tapes was pretty low on the list, even if I did get them for free. You can now see that getting tons of inventory is not hard if you know where to look. I was not going to be able to sort so many VHS tapes any time soon so I just gave them away. I knew I could find more if I wanted more so I posted a message in the FBAForum Yahoo Group and gave them away for free very easily. Whoever has time to go through inventory like this will make a profit but they need to be set up to manage this kind of quantity.

## Donation Drop Boxes

We just talked about how there are clothing and shoe donation boxes around town and how they get books donated to them. Well, what is stopping you from having your own book donation boxes? The answer is nothing. I've already seen some that say Books For Charity as well as Book Donations. They make specially designed donation boxes just for books.

http://www.recyclingbin.com/product.aspx?id=51

You can market your boxes as keeping books out of landfills. You can also sort and group books that you can then donate back to public and private schools. There are many places that would happily take book donations such as senior centers, daycares, etc. Just be sure to group and sort the leftover books so that the donation is not just seen as discards.

You could also partner with a non-profit organization in order to advertise your book donation drop boxes. You could have an agreement that you donate a fixed amount per book that is donated or you donate a percentage of all sales from the donated books.

If you are partnering with a non-profit, you may be able to give out paperwork for tax donations. Discuss this with the non-profit as they should be familiar with the process. Also be sure to get permission to use the name of the non-profit on any paperwork, flyer, or donation box signage pertaining to the book donation program.

Setting up donation boxes is a commitment. You'll be committing to keeping the boxes in good condition, cleaning up all donations left around the boxes, as well as picking up all of the donated items in a timely manner. People may leave boxes of books by the side of your box and then they get rained on prior to you being able to pick them up. Guess what? Now you have to figure out what to do with these boxes of wet books. If you are able to put out enough boxes, you'll need a box truck to pick everything up. You'll need a schedule that allows for routine pickup of all boxes. You'll need a place to unload and process the items and a way to get rid of unwanted stuff. Profitable? Yes. Difficult? No. Is this the business model for everyone? Probably not.

### Fundraisers

As discussed in Bonus #8, running a book fundraiser is not very complex and can yield a ton of inventory. Just be sure that you make it a win-win for both sides.

### Recyclers

Recyclers recycle all kinds of things including paper and BOOKS. Some places need to get rid of books and they have no idea what to do with them. They may never even consider the fact that someone might pay them for their old books. This could be a business, a library or even a university. They simply call the recycler and they're done. Some recyclers will even pay for paper or books for recycling. Most cities or counties will have a local or regional recycling business. All you have to do is contact them, find the right person, and offer to buy books by the pallet. Once you sort them, you may even be able to sell them back to the recycler, or at least donate them back to get them out of your way.

If you find one that is working out, then you can start to think big. Call the next town over. You are only limited by your imagination and motivation!

**Library Sale Leftovers**

We talked earlier about how there are always good books at library sales if you are patient and not lazy. When a library has a book sale, there is no way that they will be able to sell every single book. They will have leftovers. Some library sales will have a bid sheet where people can bid on the leftovers. They can bid on certain categories of books or bid on everything. When the library sale is over, many libraries simply need the books GONE. They NEED to find someone to purchase them all and you are doing them a huge favor by doing so. For this reason, you should get the leftovers for a very good price. We have paid $1-2 per box and had to rent a big truck to move all the boxes.

Before making deals on library sale leftovers, make sure you have the capacity to move the books in the time-frame required by the library. Some library sales are in rented spaces that have to be vacant by a certain day or time. You also need a place to put the leftovers. Do you have the room? Do you need to rent a storage unit? What are you going to do with the books that are not good to sell online? Large, bulk purchases like this can be very profitable, but you have to be prepared for the logistics.

**Bulk Buys From Thrift Stores**

Thrift stores get lots of books and most of them have many more books in the back compared to what you see for sale in the store. Some thrift stores have a central distribution center. Goodwill in Dallas Texas is this way. All store donations come to one place and are then sorted and sent back out to the individual stores.

They have two kinds of bulk books. Bulk books that have not been sent to the stores yet, and bulk books that have been pulled from the stores and returned to the distribution center. They have people in charge of both of these types of book inventories. All you have to do is talk to the right person and present them with a win-win scenario that makes sense. You could offer to buy unsorted, bulk books by the pound or by the pallet. This would be at a higher price than the returned bulk books (in Dallas, they sold these pallets of pulled books for $0.05/pound and they sold them by the 18-wheeler load!). You can make contact with thrift store managers at every store and inquire about doing bulk purchases. You have nothing to lose. All you have to do if find the right person and present an offer that makes sense for both sides. If they can get a Fast Nickel for their books, they may just take it. If they prefer the Slow Dime, that's OK too.

If you do make a deal, you'll have to be prepared to honor it, especially if it includes regularly scheduled pickups. You'll also have to be able to find a place to get rid of all the leftover items that are not good to sell online.

## Craigslist Advertisements

It is free to post ads on http://www.craigslist.org/ and you can post ads that you buy books. You can offer to buy books in bulk or for people to send you ISBN lists for you to evaluate and then make offers on. You can offer to pickup these books or request that people deliver books to your location. It's free to list, so you set the rules and see what happens. You can just post an ad that says that you buy books, any quantity, and any condition and then take each lead and evaluate them individually. Revise your ads as you learn what you want to focus on and also to find ways to avoid any deals that are not worthwhile.

## Summary

The recurring theme here is that getting tons of unsorted books is not hard, but this type of business does present its own set of challenges. Processing this kind of inventory takes space and time. It also takes commitment if you are buying inventory on any kind of regular schedule. Consider these details before pursuing these types of leads so that you are prepared and able to follow through. The last thing that you want to do is go to the efforts of setting something up and then having to back out because you are not able to keep up your end of the deal.

# Bonus #11 – Why Seasonal Products Sell Year Round on Amazon.com

Seasonal products are products that sell better during one season of the year than they do during other seasons. The easiest type of item to understand is Christmas items. They sell better at Christmas time. This should be no surprise, but it may surprise you to know that Christmas items sell all year long. Sure, they don't sell in the same quantity, but there is demand for Christmas items throughout the year. I don't always know why someone wants to buy Christmas items in July, but maybe they are having a Christmas-in-July party. The population is big enough that it would not surprise me to find out that some people simply celebrate Christmas during an entirely different time of year than December 25th.

Seasonal products also include items such as heaters and air conditioners. Not many retailers in Massachusetts are stocking and selling air conditioners in the wintertime or snow blowers in the spring. But while it may be cold in Massachusetts, it's warm in other parts of the country. I ran into this when I was looking to buy a small fan for a room that had a lot of computer equipment. The room got warm so I wanted a fan. Just try to find a store in Texas selling fans in the wintertime.

Even something as simple as differing climates can represent opportunities. As seasonal items get clearanced out in Texas, there is still a demand for those products in Massachusetts. Think about portable heaters. By the time it is warming up in Texas and all the heaters are on clearance, it's still snowing in Massachusetts. The supply and demand are not matched up due to the physical limitations of the real world. But through online sales channels, you are able to funnel this supply to the demand and keep the profit along the way.

Here is a story about a seasonal product that we purchased at retail and sold through FBA.

The product was an 8-foot long Thomas the Train holiday inflatable decoration. This product was a Home Depot exclusive item. This meant that you could either buy it from Home Depot or you could buy it on the secondary market from someone who bought it from Home Depot. Many people did not know that this was available at Home Depot and many people also did not live near a Home Depot. This was a destination type of item meaning that it was not entirely price-sensitive. People either want an 8-foot long Thomas the Train holiday inflatable decoration, or they don't. At a fair price, they will buy online. We bought these same items the previous year when we were still selling them as merchant fulfilled. This year, we anticipated good sales on the item so we had Home Depot order us 75 of them directly at $79 each. They gave us a bulk purchase discount and of course it was tax-free. We sent them all to FBA and they sold out prior to Christmas.

This was when we were traveling back and forth between Texas and Massachusetts. We were still in Massachusetts when my contact at Home Depot called and asked if I wanted to buy any more Thomas the Train decorations. It was after Christmas so at first I said no, but then I caught myself and asked how much. They had been marked down to $17! Sweet, but how many did they have? Just a few, right? Wrong. They had 81 of them sitting on their shelves. Why on earth did they have so many? Turns out, the Home Depot computer system had automatically ordered more, anticipating strong sales after I ordered 75 of them for our direct purchase. Of course there was no way that this store would ever sell that many. This spike in demand that my order put in the computer system was artificial demand, not real customer demand based on actual sales of the product to end users.

I told him that of course I wanted them all but that I was still in Massachusetts for another two months. He didn't care; he said as long as they were paid for, he would put them up in the overhead and I could pick them up in March. So that's what we did. I paid for them over the phone and picked them up in March. Now we were only in Texas for a few months before planning to come back to Massachusetts for the rest of the year. And now I had 81 holiday products sitting at my house. If I had the option, I would not have sent this seasonal, holiday item to FBA in April. But the FBA storage fees were so low that I decided it would be easiest to send them all to FBA now, even though it was nowhere near Christmas time. If I didn't, I wouldn't be back in time to send them in at all and I would miss Christmas altogether! Super bonus was that they were considered oversize and they went to the Texas oversize warehouse (all gone now) that was less than five miles from our house.

I fully expected them to sit in inventory all year while I paid FBA storage fees and waited on the surge of orders at Christmas time. I was surprised when month after month I sold some of these things. Some months I only sold one, and some months up to three, but every month I sold at least one. I did not expect this but it goes to show you that while demand may be reduced for seasonal items that are out of season, it does not go away completely. Someone, somewhere will still want them. Of course by Christmas time the rest of them sold out very quickly for a nice, handsome profit. Not the way I would have predicted the deal to have gone, but it was a profitable item to be sure.

## Bonus #12 – FBAScout vs. Local Database Scouting Services

So you're ready to start scouting for products to sell on Amazon. You've seen people with scanners, phones, and PDAs. You've seen the laser beams and heard the beeping. Which one is right for you? Are they all the same? What are the differences? I'm glad you asked!

FBAScout for iPhone and Android devices is what is called a LIVE scouting service. There are other types of scouting services that are called local database services. They were mentioned earlier in this book in Chapter 7 - The History of Scouting. They were the best option when wireless data connection speeds were simply not fast enough to support a live scouting service. With the widespread availability of Wi-Fi as well as 3G and 4G data networks, the advantages that the local database services enjoyed are becoming obsolete.

### Live Data vs. Local Database – How They Work

Live scouting services send and retrieve pricing data as you request it. You scan a barcode, the program sends the request, and the pricing data is returned and displayed on your iPhone or Android device.

Local database services run on Windows Mobile PDAs and download a database of pricing data to a memory card. These services primarily cater to the book and media market. As an FBA seller, you need pricing data for much more than just books and media.

The advantages of having live data are simply unmatched. Pricing data is always available, always accurate, and always in sync with the latest market changes. Local database services will have old, stale data the moment that the data is done downloading. Prices and Sales Ranks change constantly.

## Limitations of a 2-Gigabyte (GB) Memory Card

There is a reason that local database services only use up to a maximum 2 GB memory card. This is because Windows Mobile PDAs (with a few, expensive exceptions) cannot read a memory card greater than 2 GB. A local database service will have a hard limit of how much pricing that they can provide of 2 GB. This means that they have to choose what pricing data to INCLUDE as well as what pricing data to EXCLUDE. When you sell using FBA, why would you want ANY pricing data excluded? What items are you going to exclude yourself from selling?

## New Products Added to Amazon.com All the Time

Thousands of new products launch daily on Amazon.com. If a local database has not been updated in three days, then you have three days of new products that you would not even know exist! Some of the newest products are the hottest, most popular products that represent easy arbitrage opportunities.

## Maintenance

FBAScout requires no maintenance. There is never anything to download or maintain. Local databases have to be constantly kept up to date.

## Speed vs. Accuracy

One advantage that a local database service would enjoy over a live service would be speed. Since the pricing data is stored locally, the pricing data returns very quickly. With a live service, there can be several factors that will affect the time that it takes to return product information. Most items will return almost instantly, with speeds matching those of local databases. If your network speeds are slow, then data transfer can take longer. Pricing data can also take longer if an item has an abnormally high number of offers (most common when scanning books) as FBAScout has to sort hundreds, sometimes thousands of offers in order to correctly display the useful pricing information.

Speed is more important when you are scouting in highly competitive environments like day one of a library sale. In retail environments, things are much more relaxed.

**FBAScout Exclusive Features**

Being a live service allows FBAScout to do some pretty fancy things that are simply not possible with local database services.

Features like:

Displaying New, Used, Amazon, and FBA Offers for every item in every category on Amazon.com

FBA Net prices displayed (price + shipping)

Product image

Multiple item match search results

Show each sellers' on-hand inventory levels

You can also always touch the product image displayed in FBAScout to go directly to the Amazon product page in your mobile browser. Complete and accurate data is always at your fingertips.

The importance of these features is discussed in more depth in Chapter 8 – FBAScout - Mobile Scouting App for iPhone and Android.

**Summary**

The advantages that FBAScout users enjoy in terms of complete, live, accurate data is simply unparalleled. It allows users to make the best buying decisions. Every item purchased for resale includes an inherent risk. Those risks are minimized when you have the best data. If you have anything less than the best data, then your risk for buying items that are not actually good for resale will increase. The best data also helps you to not pass over opportunities that you would miss if you were using inferior data.

The number of places that have no Wi-Fi service and absolutely no data service from any cellular provider do exist, but they are few and far between. They dwarf in comparison to 'everywhere else' where there are ample arbitrage opportunities. The last useful feature of the local database, working without a data connection, is slowly becoming irrelevant.

## Bonus #13 – Children's Books

The children's books category as a whole is often overlooked by most book scanners. This occurs at book sales as well as at thrift stores. This is because they believe that there are no valuable children's books, or at least not enough valuable children's books to make it worth their time. There is easy money to be made in this category if you learn what to look for and discipline yourself to not be a Lazy Scanner (see Bonus #7).

Here are two easy examples of valuable children's books that you'll come across often when you are out scouting.

Remember, these aren't good books to buy for resale because I say so, but because you can find them for the artificially low price of $1 at book sales or thrift stores and because of the strong price on the secondary market that is set by supply and demand. These two books are easy to spot because they are fairly large books. Keep your eyes open and you'll be able to buy these without the need of FBAScout.

These two books are great examples of understanding the business and the customer. Look at the conditions of the lowest Used prices on the Thomas the Train book. They are all in Acceptable condition. Are you going to buy an Acceptable condition book (lowest possible grade on Amazon) to read to your child? Or to give as a gift? Me neither.

These examples also show the PREMIUM that you can charge by being an FBA seller on a popular item. Look at the great Sales Ranks of both of these books. More buyers means more chance of finding an FBA buyer that is willing to pay a premium price to get the item fast. Your job is to make your books available to these buyers. The FBA sellers on both of these books understand this and have properly priced themselves way above their merchant fulfilled competition.

Because this category is so often overlooked by your competition, it means that you can almost always find good stuff! Just like we talked about earlier in the book, you have to do what your competition either doesn't do or simply won't do. Where they see nothing, you see opportunity!

You will find that many items in this category of books simply do not have any value. It will help you to scan different types of books in this category and learn what books and what types of books have no resale value so that you can pass over them quickly and efficiently.

**$500 books???**

Here's one more bonus piece of information: you see that $500 FBA price on the Winnie the Pooh book? You may be wondering what that seller is thinking. Here's the explanation; it's one of these scenarios.

1.  They list all of their inbound FBA items at artificially high prices in order to list as fast as possible (listing faster by removing the step of pricing). Once their items arrive at FBA warehouses, they set their prices, either manually or with a repricing service. Sometimes items are made available for sale prior to the proper price being set so they end up with items with prices that are non-competitive (most likely explanation).
2.  They are using FBA for Multi-Channel Fulfillment and they have raised their prices on Amazon to artificially high levels to prevent sales on the Amazon website.
3.  They actually think that they will get a sale at $500.

If they get a sale at $500, I say 'good for them'. I believe this to be unlikely, and they may soon be looking at a return.

## Recommended Reading

These books will change the way you see Amazon, FBA, and selling online. They are invaluable to learning how to sell smart and not just work hard. Learning the WHY behind why things work the way that they do is pivotal to long-term success.

Book #1 – The Long Tail

By Chris Anderson

This book will open your mind about how Amazon is able to profit by selling fewer quantities of a larger selection of products. FBA + The Long Tail is a powerful combination.

There is more money in the tail, than in the bestsellers. Amazon figured this out years ago and the rest is history.

Book #2 – How to Sell at Margins Higher Than Your Competitors

By Lawrence L. Steinmetz & William T. Brooks

This book will blow your mind in terms of pricing and how to price your items. It will also show you that competing only on price is simply not necessary. Remember, this is a margins game, not a volume game. This book will prove it to you.

Book #3 – The Four Hour Work Week, Expanded and Updated

By Timothy Ferriss

I like this book because it points out simple things that you can do to make your entire life more efficient. Things that you are doing now that you don't realize are slowing you down and making you less productive. Identifying these things, and consolidating them (or eliminating them altogether) is well worth the price of this book.

## FREE Online Information

Did you know that you could get an Amazon FBA Specialist to walk you through your first FBA shipment right over the phone? Getting started with FBA couldn't be easier! Here's how:

http://www.amazonservices.com/content/sellers-contact-amazon.htm/

Fill out the form and choose that you are interested in Fulfillment by Amazon, already sell on Amazon, and want help with starting FBA. It will go straight to the FBA Launch Specialist Team.

www.ScanPower.com

The all-in-one suite of tools for successful FBA sellers.

www.facebook.com/groups/scanpower

Popular Facebook group for discussing Amazon and FBA.

Made in the USA
San Bernardino, CA
12 February 2019